Songs from North-East Scotla

Songs from North-East Scotland

A Selection for Performers from
THE GREIG–DUNCAN FOLK SONG COLLECTION

Edited by
KATHERINE CAMPBELL

JOHN DONALD

First published in Great Britain in 2009 by
John Donald, an imprint of Birlinn Ltd
West Newington House
10 Newington Road
Edinburgh
EH9 1QS

www.birlinn.co.uk

ISBN: 978 1 906566 01 2

The publishers gratefully acknowledge the support of the
Scotland Inheritance Fund towards the publication of this book.

British Library Cataloguing-in-Publication Data
A catalogue record for this book is available on request from the British Library

Typeset by Antony Gray
Printed and bound in Britain by CPI Antony Rowe, Chippenham, Wiltshire

Contents

Illustrations

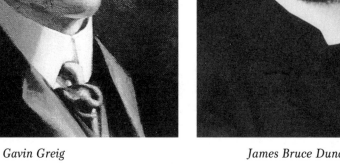

Gavin Greig   *James Bruce Duncan*

Preface

This edition draws on the marvellous work done by a number of people in the twentieth century and into the twenty-first. Between 1902 and 1917, Gavin Greig, a schoolmaster at Whitehill near New Deer, and the Reverend James Bruce Duncan, a Free Church minister at Lynturk near Alford, made their fine collection of songs from the living singing tradition of Aberdeenshire and beyond. Their collection has now been published in its entirety in the eight volumes of *The Greig–Duncan Folk Song Collection* (1981–2002), which contain a total of 1,933 songs, many in multiple variants. The General Editor throughout has been Dr Emily Lyle, and these eight scholarly volumes represent a tremendous contribution to folk-song and ballad research in Scotland. The songs have been grouped thematically and notes have been given with each song which indicate its sources as well as comparative versions. Volume 1 of the collection includes an introduction to the collection by Patrick Shuldham-Shaw, volume 3 includes a study of farm life and the farm songs by Peter A. Hall, and volume 8 includes articles on the formation of the collection, on the music of the collection, on Gavin Greig and James Bruce Duncan and on a number of the contributors. It is from these eight volumes that the songs in the present edition have been drawn.

A good deal is known about how the Greig–Duncan collection was initially made. Greig's fieldwork notebooks (called Argo and Watt) show how Greig noted down tunes in sol-fa and also words (often just the first verse) in longhand. The music was later transferred in most cases into staff notation in books abbreviated as Gm, standing for four volumes that Greig called *Folk-Music*. The words appear in sixty-four volumes of *Folk-Songs (Words)* (known as Gw). Duncan had individual collecting books for some of his major contributors including Robert Alexander, John Bain, Margaret Gillespie, George Garioch and William Wallace, and these and an entire run of fieldwork notebooks (Dsf) show how he noted the texts in shorthand and the music in sol-fa. The music was transferred in staff notation into a single volume of *Folk-Song Airs of the North East* (Dm) and the words appear in six volumes of *Folk Song Words of the North East* (Dw), again in shorthand. Although Greig and Duncan did take down many sets of words from their contributors, they actually relied quite heavily on people writing out words themselves or having relatives or other helpers note them down. There were also some people who helped by writing out music for the collection, e.g. Mrs Margaret Harper who supplied tunes from her mother, Elizabeth Greig, but this group was less numerous than those who contributed words. Another way in which Greig gleaned material was through his column in the *Buchan Observer* between 1907 and 1911 (see list of articles in this edition). Readers were often prompted to send in material as a result of the request of Greig or of one of his informants.

In collections of Scottish folk-song dating from the eighteenth and nineteenth centuries, it is often the case that little context is available on the sources of the material. This is not the case in the Greig–Duncan collection where notes were written by the collectors themselves or their informants, and where others such as Mary Ann Crichton, an assistant of Greig's at Whitehill School, supplied information on singers. A total of four hundred and eighty named people contributed songs: three hundred and eighty-seven to Greig and one hundred and seven to Duncan (including fourteen who were in touch with both collectors). Some individuals contributed only one or two songs, but others such as Duncan's sister, Margaret Gillespie, and Alexander Robb, a janitor at New Deer School, were far more prolific. How would Greig and Duncan have reacted to this edition for performers, emerging over a hundred years after Greig was approached by the New Spalding Club to undertake a feasibility study of making a song collection in the North East in 1902? Greig's retiring presidential address given in 1905 to the Buchan Field Club and published in its *Transactions* (vol. IX, p. 76) is illuminating in this regard:

> A crisis has come. . . . Folk-song is dying out before the march of education and the advance of musical culture. . . . The collector's note-book and the engraver's plates are indeed lethal instruments; but when folk-song is seen to be *in extremis* it has been judged better to have it die in our hands so that we may at least keep and embalm the poor remains, than to let it flutter off into the wild or crawl into the thicket, there to die unseen, and perish quite from off the face of the earth. – Such aim has the folk-song collector; and such is his justification.

Greig and Duncan did succeed in preserving the folk-song of their region, and their collection has helped to reinforce a tradition that, far from dying as they feared, has remained vigorous up to the present day. This selection gives singers and their audiences the opportunity to enjoy a range of these fine songs.

KATHERINE CAMPBELL

Acknowledgements

This edition would not have come about without the aid of a Larger Research Grant from the British Academy. I am very grateful to the British Academy for supporting my Research Fellowship at the Elphinstone Institute, University of Aberdeen, and to Dr Ian Russell, Director of the Elphinstone Institute, for supervising the project and for hosting the Fellowship. I would also like to thank the Carnegie Trust for the Universities of Scotland for their assistance with the fieldwork costs, and the Scotland Inheritance Fund for a grant to Birlinn towards publication of this volume.

The edition draws substantially on the work of the editors of volumes 1–8 of *The Greig–Duncan Folk Song Collection*. I should like to express my appreciation of the work of all these editors and especially of Dr Emily Lyle, Honorary Fellow at the department of Celtic and Scottish Studies, University of Edinburgh, who has been the General Editor throughout. In addition, I am indebted to Dr Lyle for the kind assistance she has offered in connection with the present volume.

Thanks are also due to: Dr Julia Bishop, Sheena Blackhall, Dr Tom McKean, Dr Colin Milton, Stanley Robertson and Alison Sharman at the Elphinstone Institute, University of Aberdeen; Ian MacKenzie, Cathie Scott and Stewart Smith at the department of Celtic and Scottish Studies, University of Edinburgh; Michael Taft at the American Folklife Center, Library of Congress, Washington; the staff of Special Libraries and Archives in Historic Collections at the University of Aberdeen, especially Dr Iain Beavan, Siobhan Convery and Michelle Gait; Mike Craig, Reprographics and Binding Manager, University of Aberdeen; Nick Evans at the Research Institute of Irish and Scottish Studies, University of Aberdeen; and Dr David Bertie, Aberdeenshire Heritage, Aberdeenshire Council. I am indebted to Mairi Sutherland and the team at Birlinn for bringing this edition to publication, to Jackie Henrie for copy-editing it, and to Anona Lyons for the cartography contained therein. Special thanks are due to James Hunter, ARC Recording Studio, Mintlaw, to James Alexander, to Gavin Sutherland, and to Dr Chris Robinson in connection with the CD that accompanies this book. I would also like to thank Alison McMorland, Adam McNaughtan, Dr Ian Olson, Dr Sigrid Rieuwerts and Steve Roud for their kind assistance.

A number of individuals kindly helped with material relating to the singers' biographies. Here I would like to thank Mr A. Angus, Peterhead; Mr F. C. Birch, Ayr; Mrs E. Brown, Huntly; Mr Fred Cruickshank, Peterhead; Mr G. Garioch, Perth; Mrs M. Hay, Turriff; Jeannie Angus Jensen; Mr James Archibald Knowles, Toronto; Elizabeth Knowles, Letham, Fife; Mrs N. Jackson, Keith; Mr Norman Masson, Daviot; Vi and Sandy May; Mr G. F. Milne, Methlick; Mrs N. Murray, Longside; Miss E. M. Ord, Banff; Mrs Marion Peter, Rothienorman; Mrs Dorothy Reid, Aberdeen; Mrs Daphne Robertson, Aberdeen; Mr and Mrs J. Shirer, Aberdeen;

Mrs D. G. Siddall, Manchester; Mrs Rosemary Slack, Dumfries; Mrs Jean Skinner; Martha Stewart, Ellon; Mrs N. Strachan, New Deer; and Mr A. Watson, Drumoak.

Special thanks are due to Dr Margaret Mackay, Director of the School of Scottish Studies Archives, department of Celtic and Scottish Studies, University of Edinburgh, for all her help and encouragement. Lastly, I would like to thank my husband, Mike Sutherland, for his assistance with the photography for this edition and for his support throughout.

All proceeds from this book will be donated to the University of Aberdeen Development Trust and will be divided equally between the Elphinstone Institute and Historic Collections (Special Libraries and Archives) at the University of Aberdeen.

Editorial Method

In volumes 1–8 of *The Greig–Duncan Folk Song Collection*, each song was assigned a number (e.g. 1015), and given a letter to identify the version (e.g. 1015A, 1015E), but in the present selection of 150 songs only one version of each song is given. Unlike volumes 1–8 which were arranged thematically (e.g. volume 1 included Nautical Songs, Military Songs and Songs in which Characters adopt the Dress of the Opposite Sex), this edition takes the singers as its starting point. Twenty-eight singers who contributed seven songs or more – containing both the words and tunes – have been included here. All of them were living in North-East Scotland (apart from Margaret Gillespie and George F. Duncan, Duncan's sister and brother, who both lived in Glasgow), and all were in direct contact with Greig or Duncan with the exception of Elizabeth Greig. The selection of songs in this edition recognises the special contribution of the North East, while at the same time illustrating material from further afield, since the flow of songs occurred both to and from the region. While the collection as a whole contains many songs that employ the same tune, I have chosen to provide a range of musical material in light of the fact that the present selection is aimed at performers.

The edition is organised according to the locations where singers lived, moving from the port of Peterhead, inland to the main area of Greig's collecting, then south to the main area of Duncan's collecting, then emerging again on the coast at Aberdeen (see map). The pages on each singer begin with biographical information and this is followed by a selection of their songs. The music has been reset using a computer program to facilitate sight-reading and also to allow the alteration of keys of songs where necessary (see below). All 150 tunes from the present volume are available online at website www.celtscot.ed.ac.uk/greig-duncan as electronic music files. This will enable readers to hear the tunes, albeit in an electronic format. A selection of songs is also available on the CD that accompanies this edition.

Each song presented here normally uses the title attached to the specific version (by either the singer or collector) rather than the general title that appears in volumes 1–8. In the notes that follow, the number of the song as it appears in the main collection is given, e.g. GD 1516A. In the case of ballads, the Child number and title are also included. Details, where available, concerning the dates of collection of the words and tune as well as information on the song itself, e.g. relating to a particular historical event, follow this.

The final piece of information given is the mode in abbreviated form. The abbreviations used for the modes are as follows: I – Ionian; Dor – Dorian; Ph – Phrygian; Ly – Lydian; M – Mixolydian; and Æ – Aeolian. It should be noted that there are many tunes in which not all the notes of the scale are present and, as a result, we sometimes cannot assign a single mode. Such tunes can fall into a dual category, e.g. I/M. The assignation of mode is also subjective in that it is dependent on where an individual feels the centre of the tonality in a tune falls. In the case of tunes that fall into one modal category but have a note of the scale missing, I have included a minus sign for the absent degree (e.g. I, –2), and in the case of tunes that have an inflected note (either sharpened or flattened), I have mentioned the degree of the scale that is inflected (e.g. I, inflected seventh). Tunes using a five-note scale are marked as pentatonic (abbreviated 'Pent').

The Performance Notes are editorial unless explicitly stated otherwise. It should be noted that a repeated last line or lines at the end of verse 1 indicates that this pattern should be followed throughout. Another common feature not listed in the Performance Note but found in a number of songs is the use of 'èd' (as in 'arrivèd)': this is pronounced as a separate syllable sounding like the 'ed' in 'bed'.

Of course, only so much can be conveyed through the written word and through music notation. The accompanying CD gives my interpretation of some of the songs from the collection, and many other recordings of North East singers and songs are available on labels such as Foot Stompin', Greentrax, The Living Tradition, Ross Records, Rounder Records, Sleepytown and Springthyme. In addition, archives in Scotland which hold sizeable collections include the School of Scottish Studies Archives, University of Edinburgh; the Elphinstone Institute, University of Aberdeen; and the North East Folklore Archive, Mintlaw. A commercial recording which has the collection as its focus is *Folk Songs of North-East Scotland: Songs from the Greig–Duncan Collection* (Greentrax, CDTRAX 5003), and it includes songs such as 'Drumdelgie' and 'Johnnie o Braidisleys' as performed by a variety of singers at the Edinburgh International Festival in 1995. A number of the songs from the singers from whom Greig and Duncan collected are being made available as a result of the 'Save Our Sounds' digitisation project conducted by the custodians of the James Madison Carpenter Collection, the American Folklife Center of the Library of Congress in the United States (see http://www.loc.gov/folklife/sos/index.html and http://www.loc.gov/folklife/guides/carpenter.html).

The Editorial Notes list any changes that have been made by the editor. Changes concerning the tune are given first. Many of the keys have been lowered in order to better accommodate the voices of folksingers, as women often find it difficult to sing comfortably above d' and men an octave below this. Such changes are expressed in terms of the key note (e.g. tonic lowered from E to C).

Grace notes in the original edition that are considered to be more a mark of a singer's individual style than something that is central to the performance are not given in the staff notation here. Any grace notes not included on the stave are listed in the Editorial Note according to the following principles, e.g. 'grace notes 1:2d; 3:1c; 5:d3'. The first digit refers to the bar, the second to the note in the bar and the last to the grace note itself. Thus 1:2d would mean that in bar one, the second note is followed by the grace note 'd'. If the grace note comes before the note, the following occurs, e.g. 5:d3. This would mean that in bar five the note 'd' comes just before the third note of the bar. As is standard practice, c', d', f' etc. refer to the notes in the octave above middle C and c,, e,, f,, etc. refer to notes in the octave below middle C.

Similar principles apply to alternative notes. There are notes that varied as the singer performed different verses of a song or the song itself on separate occasions. Thus, an alternative note of 11:1f would mean that in bar 11, the alternative note of 'f' for the first note was given.

Any changes that have been made regarding the text are then listed. 1.8 in this context would mean verse 1, line 8; 2.4, verse 2, line 4, and so on. Occasionally, gaps have been filled in with text from elsewhere, with the source of this material being identified.

Since Greig and Duncan quite frequently received the music and words of individual songs on separate occasions, there are sometimes differences in the words of the verse (usually the first but occasionally a later one) that accompany the music (known as 'tune lyric'), and the words of the equivalent verse that do not accompany the music (known as 'text lyric'). In this edition the tune lyric is normally used, any exceptions being noted. Any major differences that occur in the wording of the two lyrics are described in the editorial note.

A Glossary of Recurrent Scots Words is given on pages XXIII–XXIV. Non-recurrent words requiring explanation have been glossed at the end of each song.

List of Abbreviations

The following list of abbreviations has been drawn from *The Greig–Duncan Folk Song Collection*, vol. 8, pp. xxvii–viii. Reference numbers indicate locations in Special Libraries and Archives, Historic Collections, University of Aberdeen.

Argo 1–25	A collection of notebooks, etc., formerly owned by Arthur Argo, and now available as originals and copies in Aberdeen University Library (3088/26/1–25) and in the department of Celtic and Scottish Studies, University of Edinburgh.
Crichton	Materials relating to Mary Ann Crichton including her correspondence with Duncan (998/14/1–49), and her notes on contributors (2732/30/1–2).
Dm	Duncan's *Folk-Song Airs of the North-East*. 786.
Dsf	A collection of twenty-two notebooks in which Duncan recorded tunes in sol-fa notation. 998/5/1–11 (1–11); 998/2/13 (12); 998/5/12–21 (13–22).
Duncan, *Letters to Greig*	A collection of letters sent by James Bruce Duncan. 2732/26/1–45.
Dw	Duncan's *Folk-Song Words of the North-East*. 998/1/3–8.
Gm	Grieg's *Folk-Music*. 705-8.
Greig, *Letters to Duncan*	A collection of letters sent by Gavin Greig. 998/13/1–151.
Gw	Greig's *Folk-Songs. (Words)*. 711–74.
Watt	Notebook of Gavin Greig's containing sol-fa transcriptions formerly owned by Mrs Elizabeth Watt. 3173/13.

Map of Locations of Singers

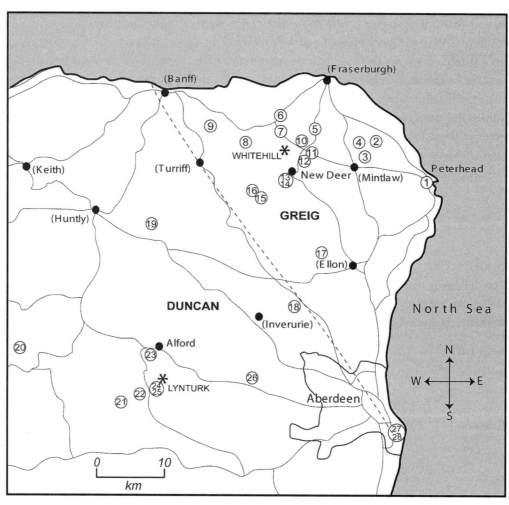

1 James Angus (G)
4 Ann Sangster (G)
7 Miss Henderson (G)
10 Alexander Robb (G)
13 Mary Cruickshank (G)
16 James W. Spence (G)
19 Isaac Troup (D)
22 George Garioch (D)
25 Margaret Gillespie (D)
28 Archibald Knowles (D)

2 Mary Dunbar (G)
5 James Mackie (G)
8 William Watson (G)
11 Eliza Clark (G)
14 Georgina Reid (G)
17 Sam Davidson (G)
20 Robert Chree (D)
23 Alexander Mackay (D)
26 Ann Lyall (D)

3 Kirsty Morrice (G)
6 John Mowat (G)
9 John Quirrie (G)
12 John McAllan (G)
15 Helen Rettie (G)
18 Robert Alexander (D)
21 William Wallace (D)
24 George F. Duncan (D)
27 Elizabeth Greig (D & G)

G = Greig   D = Duncan

Glossary of Recurrent Scots Words

a', a	all
a'body	everybody
abeen, **aboon**	above
ae	one, only
afore	before
aft	often
ain	own
aince	once
ane, een	one
aneath	beneath
anew	enough
auld	old
ava	at all
aye	always
bairn, bairnie	child
ben,	*see* but and ben
bide	live, stay, wait
birken	birch
bodie, body	person
bonnie	pretty, handsome
brae	hill, slope
braw, bra'	fine, handsome, well or grandly dressed
bree	brew, broth
breeks	trousers
brig	bridge
busk	adorn
but and ben	(to the) outer part of a house and (to the) inner part of a house
ca'	call, drive, search, travel
cankert, cankered	ill-natured
cannie, canny	careful, safe, clever, favourable
cannily	skilfully, carefully, kindly, cautiously
cantie, canty	cheerful, lively, pleasant, happy, content
carle	man, old man
cauld	cold
chiel	man, young man, lad
claes	clothes
cogie	bowl
coo	cow
crack	talk, gossip, conversation
craw	crow
croose	cheerful, comfortable, confident
daurna	dare not
daut, dawt	pet
dee; deen	do; done
deid	dead
dinna	do not
dram	drink (generally of whisky), glass of whisky
drap, drappie	glass (of whisky)
draw	pull, pull off
dung	struck, hit
dyke	wall
een	eyes
ere	before
fa, fa'	who
fae	from
faen, faun	fallen
fain	glad, gladly
fan	when
fat	what
faur, far	where
fee	wages, engagement as a servant
files	sometimes
flee	fly
frae	from
fu', fou	so, how, full, drunk
gaed, gied	went
gane, gaen	gone
gang, gyan, gae	go, walk

gar, garr	cause, make	**owre**	over
gaun	going	**owsen**	oxen
gear	property, goods, equipment	**plaidie**	length of woollen cloth worn as outer garment
gie	give		
gig	light two-wheeled, one-horse carriage	**pleuch, pleuchie**	plough
gin	if	**purling**	whirling, babbling
goon	gown	**row**	roll, wrap
guid, gweed	good	**sae**	so
ha'	hall	**sark**	shirt, undergarment
hae	have	**saut**	salt
hale	whole	**shearin'**	cutting, reaping
haud	hold, keep	**sheen**	shoes
heir	inherit (from)	**sic, sick**	such
hizzie, hizzy	hussy	**siller**	money, silver
ilk, ilka	every, each	**sin**	since
ken	know	**sinseen**	since then
kirk	church	**spier**	ask
kist	chest	**spree**	celebration, disturbance, fight
kye	cattle, cows		
lassie	young woman	**spue**	vomit
lat	let	**sta', sta**	stall
lave	rest	**taen**	taken
leal	loyal, true, faithful, honest	**tak**	take
		thegither	together
mair	more	**toon**	farmstead, town
marrow	spouse, comrade, partner	**trig**	neat, nimbly
maun	must	**twa**	two
may	maid	**unco**	very, too, strange
meat	food	**wa'**	wall
mind, min	remember, remind, keep in mind	**wad**	would
		wae	sad
morn	next day, tomorrow	**wan**	reached, gathered, got
muckle	big, great, much	**want**	lack, do without
nae	not, no	**waur**	worse
nane, neen	none	**wee, we**	small, little
neist	next	**weel-faur'd, weel-faurt**	good-looking
neuk	corner		
no	not	**wifie, wife**	woman
noo	now	**wile, wyle**	beguile, entice
ootowre, oot owre		**win, won**	get
	over, above	**winna, wanno**	will not
or	before	**yon**	that, those

The Singers and Their Songs

James Angus

1852–1929

James Angus with his wife Isabella (née Cordiner)

James Murison Angus was born on 20 February 1852 to William Angus, a labourer, and Ann Angus (née Murison). On 4 July 1873 he married Isabella Cordiner.[1] At the time of the 1891 census they were living at 3 Crooked Lane, Peterhead, along with seven children and James's occupation is given as cooper.[2] One of the sons, John Cordiner Angus, who was born on 9 June 1881, contributed two songs to the collection.[3] By 1901 the family was living at 22 Chapel Street. John was working as a butcher's apprentice, and two other sons, William and Murdoch, were following their father's trade as coopers.[4]

Mary Ann Crichton who worked as a teacher with Greig at Whitehill School writes: 'Of all the Peterhead lot mentioned James Angus, a cooper to trade and a very old man is the only one practically whose name stands out clearly in my memory. As a singer he was of little use, but he had a good memory for words. He used to get a child to write them out and then send them on. Once a year, however, he paid a visit to the schoolhouse.'[5] Crichton's assessment of his age was not accurate, however, as he was only fifty-eight on the first of the visits. He apparently made four visits to the schoolhouse in all, three of these taking place around Christmas time in the years 1909, 1910 and 1913. Mrs Annie Sinclair (née Barron), who was a

3

close friend of Greig's daughter, Florence, and spent a lot of time at the schoolhouse in her youth, remembered that Angus used to come and sing to Greig, writing beforehand to say he was coming and was looking forward to enjoying Mrs Greig's fine scones. She also recalled that he was 'not a very big man'.[6]

Part of James Angus's working life was spent on the whaling ships. Greig wrote on 21 December 1909: 'Some ten days ago I had the pleasure of a visit from my enthusiastic correspondent, Mr James Angus, Peterhead. We had a capital song-sederunt, during which we had through hand between thirty and forty different pieces. I noted most of my friend's tunes, many of them being fine specimens of traditional melody. I was particularly interested to hear "Once more for Greenland we are bound" sung by one who had himself gone through the experiences detailed in the song.'[7] Only one verse of Angus's version of the song (10J) is given in the collection, however. Greig also attached the note 'Heard in Greenland' to Angus's version of 'When Shall We Meet Again' (1250B). Angus's obituary in the *Buchan Observer* stated:

> Mr Angus was a direct link with the port's whaling days. After serving his time as a cooper he subsequently took up what is known as iron-bound coopering and in the capacity of iron-bound cooper he made two voyages to the Arctic in the whaler *Perseverance*. One of the last of the whalers, he was almost if not altogether the last survivor of the band who made the great iron-bound casks in which the whale oil was stored.[8]

Angus was a major contributor to the Greig–Duncan collection and eighty-eight items appear from him in total. He was 'a performer at social gatherings such as Freemasons' meetings'.[9] Greig commented that Angus sang his sea songs 'with the true spirit and complete understanding of one who had himself been many a day on the deep in calm and storm'.[10] Two sea songs have been included in this selection: 'The Loss of the London' and 'The Bold Princess Royal'. According to the tunes notated by Greig, particularly in the case of the latter song, Angus's singing seems to have contained a good deal of ornamentation.

Greig's field notebooks along with his comments in the *Buchan Observer* often reveal what was collected in an individual session. For example, Greig wrote in the newspaper on 20 December 1910: 'On a recent Saturday I had a visit from my friend Mr James Angus, Peterhead, and of course the old minstrelsy was much in evidence. Mr Angus, who is a worthy type of the true traditional singer, gave me a hearing of a number of songs and ballads which we had not previously had through hands. These included "Young Emma," "Covent's Garden," "My guid Kilmarnock bonnet," "Irish Molly," "The Banks of Inverness," "Jamie Foyers," "To row her in my plaidie," "Erin-go-bragh," "Davie's Wooin'," "The Carse o' Pommaize," "The Highland Soldier," etc. Words as well as tunes were forthcoming in most cases.' The records of this session appear in Argo 21.

Angus died on 27 November 1929 at the age of seventy-seven. His obituary stated:

> The passing of Mr James Angus, cooper, 83 Queen Street, Peterhead . . . removes a most interesting personality. . . .
>
> Mr Angus was a many-sided man, and possessed a unique acquaintance with Scottish

4

folk-song. He gave most valuable assistance to the late Gavin Greig in the latter's monumental and successful efforts to preserve the folk-songs and ancient tunes of the north-east. . . . Mr Angus was in every sense Mr Greig's collaborator and as such deserves to be held in affectionate remembrance by all who value our heritage of national song and music.

NOTES

1 Death record 1929/232/1/174 and marriage record 1873/232/44. Isabella's father was a cooper. I am most grateful to Jeannie Angus Jensen for the photograph of her grandparents.
2 Census record 1891/232/1/004/016.
3 Birth record 1881/232/1/204.
4 Census record 1901/232/1/014/019.
5 *Greig–Duncan*, vol. 8, p. 504.
6 Interview with Emily Lyle, SA 1982.128, School of Scottish Studies Archives, University of Edinburgh.
7 *Buchan Observer*, 21 December 1909.
8 *Buchan Observer*, 3 December 1929, p. 5, col. 4. The obituary is headed: 'Collaborated with Gavin Greig: Peterhead Cooper Who Was Authority on Folk-Songs'.
9 See article on James Angus by Peter Cooke in *Greig–Duncan*, vol. 8, p. 550.
10 *Buchan Observer*, 3 May 1910.

1. The Emigrant's Farewell to Donside

JAMES ANGUS

Come, friends and ac - quain - tan - ces, once more let us join, And raise our sweet voi - ces in cho - rus wi' mine; Let us drink and be mer - ry, from sor - row re - frain, For we may and may ne - ver meet all here a - gain. For we may and may ne - ver meet all here a - gain.

1 Come, friends and acquaintances, once more let us join,
   And raise our sweet voices in chorus wi' mine;
   Let us drink and be merry, from sorrow refrain,
   For we may and may never meet all here again.
   For we may and may never meet all here again.

2 I ance had a lassie, I liket her weel,
   For modesty and beauty none could her excel;
   When she looked in my face as she sat on my knee,
   There were none in the world more happy than we.

3 The time is fast approaching when I must away;
   Farewell to my comrades wherever you be;
   And wherever I wander by land and by sea,
   I'll never forget all your kindness to me.

4 Ye hills and low valleys of Donside, farewell,
   For if ever I return there is none here can tell;
   Farewell to your lasses of every degree,
   Long in vain will I wish for your sweet company.

5 Farewell to the jewel, to you I love best,
   For you and your beauty excel all the rest;
   But if you prove constant, as constant can be,
   Wherever I go, love, my heart is with thee.

6 Long may you be merry, while I'm very sad,
   When I think of the pleasures that you and I've had;
   When I mind on the times that you've sat on my knee,
   There were none in this world more happy than we.

7   The time has now arrivèd that I must away,
     Cold winter is over, sweet summer draws nigh,
     There is an old proverb, I believe it is true,
     That 'true love is more precious than the wealth of Peru.'

8   Farewell to your sorrows, drink it round with a glass,
     Drink a health to each lad, and his sweet smiling lass;
     Drink a health to each lover whose loved one is true,
     Here's good health, peace and plenty, so farewell and adieu.

GD 1516A. The tune of this song was collected from James Angus when he visited Whitehill School-house on the first of four visits, and Greig acknowledged his contribution in the *Buchan Observer* on 21 December 1909. Greig noted in the newspaper (19 January 1909): 'The song appears to belong to Donside, and strong efforts have been made to identify the author; but as we have had occasion to remark before, such quests rarely establish anything. Quite likely the song is an adaptation and a localisation.' Greig noted that there are some similarities between this song and 'The American Stranger'. Fifteen versions of 'The Emigrant's Farewell to Donside' appear in the collection. [Dor/M].

Performance Note It can be difficult to fit all the words into the tune of the song. Suggestion: miss out 'fast' (3.1) and 'now' (7.1).

Editorial Note Tonic lowered from E to C; grace notes 1:2d; 3:1c; 5:d'3; alternative notes 5:2c'; 11:1f.

2. The Bold Princess Royal

JAMES ANGUS

1   On the seventeenth of February we sailed from the land,
     With the bold Princess Royal bound for Newfoundland.
     We had forty brave seamen for our ship's company,
     To the eastward, to the westward so boldly steered we.

2   We had scarcely been sailed but days two or three
    When a man from our mast head strange sails I do see
    When a man from our mast head strange sails I do see
    And under his mizzen black colours wore he.

3   Good, good cries our captain, what will we do now,
    There comes a bold pirate to rob us I know.
    Oh no, cried our ship mate it will never be so
    We will shake out our reef boys and from him we'll go.

4   Being the hour of twelve when he hove alongside
    With a large speaking trumpet where comest thou from
    Our captain being aft and he answered him so
    We are from fair London and bound for Peru.

5   Ye will haul up your courses and you will leaf your ship to
    I have got a long letter to send home with you
    I will haul up my courses and I will lay my ship to
    But it will be in some harbour not alongside of you.

6   He chased us to the eastward for all that long day
    He chased us to the westward but could not keep away.
    He then fired shot after us but none could prevail
    The bold Princess Royal soon showed her till.

7   Go down to your grog, boys, go down every one
    And drink up your grog boys, And be of good cheer
    And drink up your grog, boys and be of good cheer
    For as long's we've got sea room, my boys, never fear.

GD 47A. This pirate song was probably collected in 1909. [I].
Editorial Note Tonic lowered from Eb to C; grace notes 3:e1; 3:1c; 5:e3; 6:3c; 11:1g; 14:f4; 15:1e;
    alternative notes 8:1a (with question mark beside it), 10:3c; Greig adds an extra crotchet 'g' (bar 7,
    following note 1) which is not taken to be part of the first verse and is not included here; text lyric
    has 'west' in place of 'westward' (1.4).

leaf – heave;   *till* – tail

3. The Loss of the London

JAMES ANGUS

Ye landsmen and seamen, come listen to me, To a fearful gale on the raging sea; Our good ship London for Australia's shore, With emigrants which are now no more.

1 Ye landsmen and seamen, come listen to me,
   To a fearful gale on the raging sea;
   Our good ship London for Australia's shore,
   With emigrants which are now no more.

2 We had good weather as the coast we sailed round
   And we took more on board at Plymouth Sound;
   As we set sail our ship did roll,
   With two hundred and thirty-nine poor souls.

3 Day after day the gale increased;
   Each prayed to Heaven to be released;
   Till the 19th of January, that fearful day,
   When our masts and sails were all blown away,

4 Our captain cried, 'Put about the ship,
   And return to Plymouth to refit;'
   But the sea being raging mountains high,
   From the Bay of Biscay we could not fly.

5 Good Mr. Drapier, a minister,
   On board our ship a passenger,
   He prayed aloud our souls to save,
   Soon down to sink in the briny wave.

6 We lowers a boat from the vessel's side,
   With nineteen men to battle with the tide;
   We called our captain, but all in vain,–
   'With those on board I will remain.'

7 He bade us God-speed to the land,–
   'With those on board I'll die like a man.'
   Brave guester broke, and our hope was o'er,
   And the ship went down to rise no more.

8   Nineteen escaped in the boat that night
     For twenty long hours there was no ship in sight
     At last our boat by a ship was spied,
     We were took on board, and with joy we cried.

9   At Falmouth we were put ashore;
     We thank our Maker o'er and o'er;
     Such a fearful loss you will seldom hear
     And for those on board pray shed a tear.

GD 31A. The words of this song were sent to Greig by Angus and appeared in the *Buchan Observer* on 2 February 1909. The music was collected on one of Angus's visits to the schoolhouse at Whitehill and was acknowledged on 21 December in the same year. The song relates to an actual event in which the steamship, the *London*, carrying 239 on board, set off from Gravesend on 30 December 1865 bound for Melbourne, stopping at Plymouth on the way. Following a storm, the ship started taking in water at the Bay of Biscay and, although the captain tried to return to Plymouth, only 19 men survived after being rescued by a passing boat the next day. Mr Daniel James Drapier was the minister on board (*Greig-Duncan*, vol. 8, p. 505). Greig noted in the *Buchan Observer* (2 February 1909): 'Mr J. Angus, Peterhead, sends me the following song which he had when he was young.' Here, his version has been supplemented in places by text from other singers (see below). [I].

Editorial Note   Tonic lowered from E to D; time-signature changed from 4/4 to 2/4 throughout – this change is suggested by the bar line separating the triplets in bars 6 and 7 of the original (bars 11 and 12 here); an extra quaver has been added at the end of bar 10 to accommodate the words of verse 1; a question mark under bar 14 has been omitted. In line 7.3, 'Brave guester broke' is obscure, and so is the equivalent half-line in version B 10.3, which runs 'That brave gusty broke'; however, version C 9.3 has 'I hope you will all get safe to the shore' at the equivalent point in the verse. Line 8.1 originally 'For fourteen days we battled with the tide'; replaced with text from 31C (James M. Allan), 10.1. Line 8.2 missing; replaced with text from 31B (Annabella Bissett), 11.2. Line 9.3 'Such a fearful gale on the raging main' in original and line 9.4 missing; replaced with text from 31B, 12.3-4.

4. Davie's Wooin'

JAMES ANGUS

O mi-ther, I am gaun to tell you That I'm gaun a-wa' to woo; For twen-ty years we've lived to-ge-ther, But a wife I maun hae noo. Whirn a-ra a-roo a-rad-die, Whirn a-ra a-roo a-ree.

1   O mither, I am gaun to tell you
    That I'm gaun awa' to woo;
    For twenty years we've lived together,
    But a wife I maun hae noo.
    Whirn ara aroo araddie,
    Whirn ara aroo aree.

2   O dinna be like Geordie Lowrie,
    Courtin' for the sake o' brass,
    For tho' they get the name o' siller,
    They are a' as peer as craws.

3   Sae canty's I gaed owre yon hill,
    Till I came to my lassie's hoose;
    Sae canty's we sat doon thegither
    Kissed and crackit unco croose.

4   First when me and Maggie was merriet,
    Sic a dandy girl was she;
    But we hadna been a month thegither,
    When Meg kicked up an awfu' spree.

5   Meg ran but, and Meg ran ben,
    And in the hurry broke the pan,
    Meg took up the iron poker,
    And knappit Davie on the croon.

6   Davie rinnin fae the hurry,
    Met the parson in the door;
    Says he to Davie, You're in a hurry,
    See that a' your breeks are tore.

7   Man, minister, I'm gaun to tell ye,
    But gie me time to dry my cheeks,
    For sic a hoose I never saw,
    And wi' a most confunit reek.

8   The parson he gaed to the door,
    Little thinkin' on the rig,
    And Meg just thinkin' it was Davie
    Knappit aff the parson's wig.

9   The parson he ran after Davie,
    After Davie ran wi' speed,
    Says, Davie I hae gotten a rattle,
    Yon's an awfu' reek indeed.

10 Some folk thinks that they are happy,
    When they are made twa and twa,
    But faith, gin this be matrimony,
    Nae mair o' it I'll hae ava.

GD 1281A. The words and tune of this song about a disastrous marriage were acknowledged by Greig in the *Buchan Observer* on 20 December 1910 after one of Angus's visits to Whitehill Schoolhouse. Greig earlier wrote in the newspaper: 'This ditty would appear to belong to the eighteenth century when wigs were worn by the better classes. It is very popular. This may be due partly to the moral; but we think that "Davie and his Kye" has been more helped by the tune than by anything else. It is a very lively melody, modal in character, with suggestions of the strathspey.' (8 February 1910) [Dor/M].

Editorial Note Tonic lowered from D to B. The text lyric gives the refrain as: 'Whirriné raw rue a ruddy, Whirriné raw rue a ree'.

brass – money;   *rig* – trick;   *merriet* – married;   *knappit* – struck;   *man* – expression of surprise; *confunit* – confounded;   *reek* – smoke, and also a source of annoyance comparable to a smoking chimney, especially a nagging wife

11

5. To Row Her in My Plaidie

JAMES ANGUS

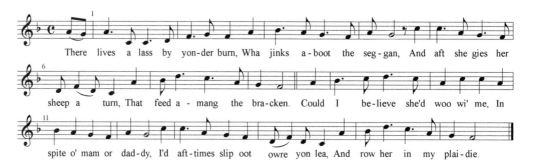

There lives a lass by yon-der burn, Wha jinks a-boot the seg-gan, And aft she gies her sheep a turn, That feed a-mang the bra-cken. Could I be-lieve she'd woo wi' me, In spite o' mam or dad-dy, I'd aft-times slip oot owre yon lea, And row her in my plai-die.

1   There lives a lass by yonder burn,
        Wha jinks aboot the seggan,
        And aft she gies her sheep a turn,
        That feed amang the bracken.
        Could I believe she'd woo wi' me,
        In spite o' mam or daddy,
        I'd afttimes slip oot owre yon lea,
        And row her in my plaidie.

2   Her breast to busk I'd violets pu',
        Frae yonder glen sae foggy,
        And bluebells hingin' wat wi' dew,
        Frae yonder den sae boggy.

3   I'll ben the spence and dress a wee,
        Wi' knots and bots fu' gaudy,
        For I canna rest until I see
        Gin she'll gang in my plaidie.

GD 799Aa. The words and tune were obtained on a visit by Angus to the Schoolhouse at Whitehill, which was mentioned in the *Buchan Observer* on 20 December 1910. Two similar versions of the tune for this song were collected by Greig from Angus. [I/M].

Editorial Note Tonic lowered from G to F; the quaver rest in bar 4 is editorial; the second crotchet in bar 10 is editorial and has been inserted to accommodate the text. The text lyric has been used here. Tune lyric has 1.2 'What jouks aboot the seggin' '; 1.5 'woo me' in place of 'woo wi' me'. The word 'loe' is offered in brackets in place of 'woo' at 1.5 in the tune lyric.

jinks – darts;   *seggan* – wild irises;   *foggy* – mossy;   *spence* – inner apartment;   *bots* – folds

Mary Dunbar
1855–1932

Mrs Mary Dunbar is described in some detail in a letter to Alexander Keith from the Rev. Robert T. Monteith, Manse of Crimond, Lonmay, dated 10 September 1925:

> I have now had an opportunity of interviewing Mrs John Dunbar, Longhill, St. Fergus (Longhill, Crimond, Lonmay is the postal address), re ballads. Her maiden name was Mary Angus and she was born at Rora, Longside on 3rd October 1855, so that she is almost seventy years of age. Her husband, John Dunbar, is a shepherd and crofter.[1] Mrs Dunbar learned the ballads and airs in her youth by hearing them sung in farm kitchens during harvest time or in the winter evenings. She cannot indicate more definitely what was their source or origin, nor can she tell anything about the authors. She sang over the ballads to Mr Gavin Greig when he called to see her in connection with the matter fourteen or fifteen years ago. I may add that Mrs Dunbar was engaged at farms in the Buchan district in such parishes as Lonmay, Rathen, Byth, etc.[2]

Mary's parents were Andrew Angus, a farmservant, born in Longside, and Mary Angus (née Simpson). The pair had married in 1850 at Peterhead and Mary was their third child.[3] In 1878 Mary married John Dunbar in Kininmonth. John was a tailor journeyman at the time, and became a master tailor between 1880 and 1882. He later worked as a shepherd and crofter.[4] The 1901 census lists Mary Dunbar at Mains of Ballearn in Kininmonth aged forty-five with four sons and one daughter: Charles aged fifteen (a general labourer), George aged nine, James aged seven, Robert aged five and Christina aged three.[5] Mary had twelve or thirteen children altogether.[6]

Greig was fortunate to have a number of local contacts who recognised the importance of his project and introduced him to further singers. One of these was Annie Shirer (1873–1915) who lived in the same area as Mary Dunbar.[7] Shirer had been sending Greig the words of Mrs Dunbar's songs, and we can gather that the relationship between the two women went back some time, since Shirer notes that she got the words of 'The Road to Dundee' from her 'years ago'. Greig refers to Shirer as 'A Kininmonth Lassie' in the *Buchan Observer*, and we might regard this as an expression of fondness or good humour since she would have been a middle-aged woman at the time. Greig seems to have cycled as far as Shirer's home and then walked with her the rest of the way to Mary Dunbar's home in the visit he reported in the *Buchan Observer*, 19 July 1910.

> On a recent Saturday I had an exceedingly pleasant outing on cycle followed by a delightful tramp through the heather – and not unaccompanied either – all in search of old tunes. Our destination was Longhill of Crimond, where from Mrs Dunbar I got records of the tunes of a number of the fine old ballads and folk-songs – 'The Laird o'

Aboyne,' 'Sweet Willie and Fair Annie,' 'Lord Brechin', 'Lord Douglas', 'Fair Rosie Ann,' 'The Laird o' Drum', 'Hynd Horn,' 'The Hanky,' 'The Road to Dundee,' 'The Isles o' Daniel,' 'Forglen's plantin's,' 'The beggar man,' 'I'll get my good ship in order,' 'Bold Johnston', 'Captain Glen,' 'The Spanish lady,' and 'The lumbering boys'. Also from Mr A. [Andrew] Dunbar, Crimongorth – for singing runs in the line – I got a record of the tune of 'Bogie's bonnie Bell'. I hope to see my good helpers again some time, as I feel pretty sure that their stores are not by any means exhausted. My warm thanks are also due to my untiring friend 'A Kininmonth Lassie,' for her very kind and quite indispensable services in connection with my visit.

Greig visited the Kininmonth and Crimond districts later that same year and again reported on this in the newspaper. He received 'The Lea-boy's Lassie' from Mrs Dunbar – including a verse which was new to him – along with songs such as 'Charlie Mackie', 'Young Emma', 'Oh, no, no', 'The Lions' Den', 'Ramble away', 'The Cowdenknowes', 'Hey bonnie laddie', 'Binorie', and 'Annie dear, good-bye'. He also received a single item from 'Girl Dunbar', noting: 'Very acceptable was the rendering, by a young member of the family, of "The Maid of the Don".'[8]

50 'Green Leaves So Green' A

The thirty-seven songs collected from Mary Dunbar included five 'A' versions: 50 'Green Leaves So Green', 746 'The Spanish Lady', 1040 'The Hanky', 1317 'Bonnie Lassie, Braw Lassie, Faur Are Ye Gaun?', and 1485 'Ramble Away'. Not one of Mary Dunbar's songs is found in volume 3 of the collection on the themes of songs of the countryside and songs of home and social life. This is rather surprising in view of the statement by the Rev. Robert Monteith above regarding her learning material in farm kitchens – one would expect at least some farm songs to be amongst her repertoire. In addition, the statements from Annie Shirer regarding specific songs all refer to Mary Dunbar's learning of them from close relatives rather than from farm workers. 212 'Sweet Willie and Fair Annie' B was learned from her grandmother, and 227 'Pretty Caledonia' C and 275 'The Beggar Man' F were both her mother's songs. It may well be that the details of her sources had simply faded from her memory by 1925. One source for her material, however, may well have been her cousin, Ann Sangster (née Angus), who is included in this book. The pair have nine songs in common in their repertoires and it is interesting that Greig made his first visit to Ann Sangster shortly before 20 September 1910, around two weeks after his visit to Mary Dunbar of *c.*6 September. Their tunes for 'Lescraigie' (GD 1490) exhibit considerable similarities.

Mary Dunbar died on 11 September 1932 at Longhill Croft, Crimond, aged seventy-six, and was survived by her husband, who died in 1941.[9] Mrs Nan Jackson, her great-granddaughter, did not know of her as having been a singer but said that she herself sang, as did her grandmother, Ann Park.[10]

NOTES

1 The 1891 census lists John Dunbar, aged forty-five, as a shepherd at Mill Farm in the parish of Rathen (1891/235/1/001/001).
2 *Greig–Duncan*, vol. 8, pp. 507–8.
3 Birth record 1855/218/73.
4 Information from Mrs Nan Jackson, Keith, a great-granddaughter of Mary Dunbar.
5 Census record 1901/210/B/002/001.
6 Information from Mrs Nan Jackson who has found records for twelve children.
7 See entry by Anne Neilson on Shirer in *Greig–Duncan*, vol. 8, pp. 586–7.
8 *Buchan Observer*, 6 September 1910.
9 Death record 1932/184/6, and information from Mrs Nan Jackson.
10 Letter to Katherine Campbell, 1 December 2003. I am most grateful to Mrs Jackson for her kind help.

6. The Hanky

MARY DUNBAR

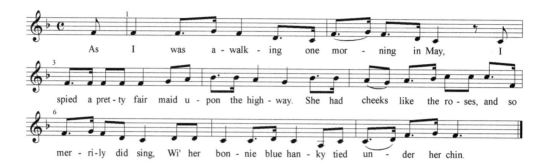

As I was a-walk-ing one mor-ning in May, I spied a pret-ty fair maid u-pon the high-way. She had cheeks like the ro-ses, and so mer-ri-ly did sing, Wi' her bon-nie blue han-ky tied un-der her chin.

1   As I was a-walking one morning in May,
    I spied a pretty fair maid upon the highway.
    She had cheeks like the roses, and so merrily did sing,
    Wi' her bonnie blue hanky tied under her chin.

2   Where are you going to my pretty maid?
    I'm going to yon factory kind sir she said
    I'm going to yon factory where cotton they spin
    With my bonnie blue hanky tied under my chin.

3   Why wear you that handkerchief that's tied around your head?
    It's my country fashion kind sir, she said
    And it's the fashion I like to be in
    With my bonny blue hanky tied under my chin.

4   That is the colour that grows in yon dell
    It is the true blue and it will never fail
    Like the sailor's blue jacket that fights for his king
    And my bonny blue hanky tied under my chin.

5   That is the handkerchief my lovie gave to me
    He told me the colour would never false be
    And I'll be as true as the colour to him
    With my bonnie blue hanky tied under her chin.

6   He found her so loyal he could not forbear
    He took her in his arms and called her his dear
    And to kiss her sweet lips he was then to begin
    With her bonny blue hanky tied under her chin.

7   Stop stop a minute kind sir, she said
    Show me the crooked sixpence before you kiss me
    Beside the crooked sixpence he pulled out a ring
    With her bonnie blue hanky tied under her chin.

8   Now they got married, got married in speed
    And they live happy, live happy indeed
    When their day's toil is over they both sit down and sing
    And my bonny blue hanky tied under her chin.

GD 1040A. The words of the song were sent to Greig by Annie Shirer and the tune was collected by
    Greig *c*.19 July 1910. [I/M].
Editorial Note Tonic lowered from A to F; text lyric has 'met' for 'spied' (1.2), and 'full' for 'and so'
    (1.3). The word 'her' (5.4) is editorial and replaces 'his'.

7. Green Leaves So Green

MARY DUNBAR

1   An auld wifie lived at the back o' yon hill,
    Green leaves so green O;
    If she hadna been deid she'd been aye livin' still,
    And you know very well what I mean O.

2   She keepit a cask o' braw guid ale,
    Green leaves so green O;
    And a bonnie wee daughter to draw in the trade,
    And you know very well what I mean O.

3   Ae day as a sailor cam' ridin' by,
    Green leaves so green O;
    He asked for a pint o' very guid ale,
    And you know very well what I mean O.

GD 50A. The song was collected by Greig *c*.6 September 1910. [Æ, inflected 2nd].
Performance Note   A final verse could be taken from James Angus's version (50B): 'The cat she went
    up to the high butter shelf, / If you want any more you can sing it yourself.'
Editorial Note Tonic lowered from D to B; verses 2 and 3 are taken from Miss Annie Shirer (50C)
    who got the song from Andrew Dunbar, Crimongorth. Alternative notes 1:4e, 1.5e, 1.6e, 2:1d,
    2.2d, 2.3c#, 2.4b, 4.4a.

8. Bonnie Lassie, Braw Lassie

MARY DUNBAR

1. O bonnie lassie, braw lassie, faur are ye gaun?
   Whar lies your dwelling, or whar lies your hame?
   My hame and my dwelling are yonder doonbye,
   And I'm gaun to the greenwoods for to milk kye.

2. My bonnie braw lassie, fain wad I lay ye doon,
   If it werena for spoilin' your bonnie new goon.
   The grass is all wet, but the sun will soon dry,
   And I'm gaun to the greenwoods for to milk kye.

3. He laid her doon where the grass grew so green,
   And what was done there and there's nobody seen,
   And what was done there and there's no one shall hear,
   But there's milk in the lassie's breast all the long year.

GD 1317A. The words of the song were sent to Greig by Annie Shirer and the tune was collected by Greig *c*.6 September 1910. Only one other version of this song appears in the collection; it was collected by Greig from John Johnstone and has the title 'Bonnie May'. But cf. the similar song 'The Brannit Coo' (1318) also from Mrs Dunbar. [I/Ly].

Performance Note It is suggested that in verse 2 singers use crotchet rhythms only in bar 1 and make the last note of bar 2 into 2 quavers for the words 'fain wad'. In verse 3, omit the anacrusis and make the first note of bar 1 into a crotchet.

Editorial Note Tonic lowered from F to C; a quaver was added in bar 1 and two crotchet notes (g) were made into a minim in bar 5 to accommodate the words. Verse 4 is fragmentary and runs: 'When six weeks were over and three months were gone/This bonnie young lassie . . .'.

doonbye – down there

Kirsty Morrice

c.1879–1913

Catherine Elizabeth Morrice, referred to as both Kirsty and Kate Morrice in the collection, was born in Lonmay c.1879. Her parents were John Park Morrice, a farmer, and Catherine Morrice, née Baigrie.[1] The 1891 census shows the couple living at East Mains, Kininmonth, Lonmay, along with a son, William, aged twelve, a daughter, Mary, aged five, and two servants and a boarder.[2] In 1901, Kirsty Morrice's occupation is listed as domestic servant, and another sister, Joan, aged five, is mentioned.[3]

Greig first collected from Morrice, who was then living at Loch, Kininmonth, around 6 September 1910, noting in the *Buchan Observer*:

> A second visit to the Kininmonth and Crimond districts, under the same kind guidance as before, was exceedingly pleasant as an outing, and highly satisfactory as regards results. From Miss K. Morice I got records of 'The Handsome Shepherdess,' 'Bervie's Bowers,' 'The Beggar's Dawtie,' 'The Broom-Cutter,' 'I wonder all ye young men,' 'Haud awa',' etc.

On this occasion, he received ten tunes from her as well as material from Mary Dunbar.[4] The 'kind guidance' Greig referred to was from Annie Shirer (see entry on Mary Dunbar) who had been sending him words from Morrice prior to this, the first mention being made in the *Buchan Observer* on 8 March 1910. Greig's collecting notebook Argo 14 probably reflects the results of a later collecting visit undertaken in the summer of 1911 or 1912. One song that appeared there was 1142 'Mormond Braes' B.

Forty-four songs from Kirsty Morrice appear in the collection including thirteen 'A' versions and five songs for which she is the only contributor. In three cases we have specific information on when or from whom she learned her material. 258 'Brannon on the Moor' A was learned in her youth and 825 'A Pennyworth o' Preens' D was 'got from an old lady'. 1055 'The Hireman Chiel' L was learned 'mostly from her father, [with] two or three verses from an old lady who said she sang it twice over more than fifty years ago at a meal-and-ale'. The double performance of this song, which is as much as fifty-eight verses in version H, must have been quite a challenge! Kirsty almost certainly learned material from her aunt Miss Annie Morrice too, since Annie contributed four songs to the collection. Mary Ann Crichton described Kirsty Morrice as 'a most valued contributor'.[5]

Kirsty seems to have worked as a domestic servant throughout her life and did not marry. She died on 6 March 1913 at Cortiecram, Kininmonth, aged only thirty-four.[6]

NOTES

1 Death record 1913/210/B/5.
2 Census record for Kininmonth, 1891/210/B/002/003.
3 Census record for Kininmonth, 1901/210/B/002/009.
4 *Greig–Duncan*, vol. 8, p. 508.
5 *Greig–Duncan*, vol. 8, p. 508.
6 Death record 1913/210/B/5.

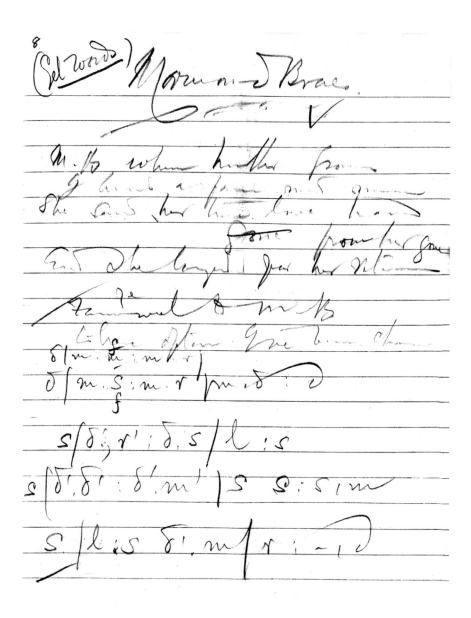

'Mormond Braes' from Argo 14, p. 8

9. Bervie's Bowers

KIRSTY MORRICE

Ber - vie's bowers are bon - nie, they're a' built roon a - boot, Ber - vie's seas are mo - ny, as they roll in and oot; As they roll in and oot, so do they up and doon; My lo-vie is a boy more hand - so-mer, he's the flower o' Ber - vie's toon.

1   Bervie's bowers are bonnie, they're a' built roon aboot,
     Bervie's seas are mony, as they roll in and oot;
     As they roll in and oot, so do they up and doon;
     My lovie is a boy more handsomer, he's the flower o' Bervie's toon.

2   Cauld and frosty is the nicht, and cauld, cauld blaws the win',
     Open the door to me, he said, oh, rise and lat me in.
     Cauld and frosty is the nicht, and the leaves fa's frae the tree;
     And if I wis in and ye wis oot, I wid open the door to thee.

3   Altho' the nicht wis never sae cauld, and the frost wis never sae snell,
     My father locks the door at nicht, and he keeps the keys himsel';
     The keys they lie aneath his heid, until the break o' day;
     Ye canna win in, young man, she said, so ye may bound on your way.

4   Cauld and frosty is the nicht, and cauld, cauld blaws the win',
     Open the door to me, he said, oh, rise and lat me in.
     Slowly, slowly she rose up, and so shyly drew by the bar;
     And she's ta'en him into her airms, for fear he'd been the waur.

5   He lay doon where she rose up, to haud the cauld away,
     And there they lay thegither until the break o' day.
     When nine long months were past and gone, this lassie she grew pale and wan,
     She was sick and very sick, and her stays they widna lace on.

6   And aye the lassie sighed and sighed, and aye mair did she say,
     What tarries my yellow-haired laddie that went oot by the break o' day?
     That went oot by the break o' day, she said, I'm afraid he'll never return,
     For he has left me in sorrow my folly for to mourn.

7   All the fish that's in the sea they may take wings and fly,
     And all the birds that's in the air may build their nests on high;
     And all the leaves on the rotten trees may flourish and grow green,
     Before that I prove false to you, you're the fairest of womenkind.

8   If all the hills were paper white, and all the seas were ink,
And all the woods in Norway prepared for pens to write,
I would sit doon and write, my dear, and praise your high renown;
Ye are my love and ye shall be my wife, and the Lady o' Bervie's toon.

GD 789A. Greig acknowledged the words on 5 July 1910 in the *Buchan Observer* where he noted: 'It is a genuine folk-song. Some bits of it are particularly fine.' The music was acknowledged in the newspaper on 6 September 1910. [Pent.].

Editorial Note Tonic lowered from E to D. The tune has been adapted to fit the lyric of verse 1: in the original the rest in bar 4 was given as a quaver (a), the dotted crotchet in bar 10 was a crotchet and a quaver, and the two semiquavers in bar 13 were originally one quaver. The incomplete text of verse 7 in the original running 'Neat is the shape of my lovie's leg, and neater the shape of his han',/His body is still more handsome than any silver wan' has been omitted.

snell – cold

10. Milguy

KIRSTY MORRICE

1   A friend and I struck frae Milguy,
To Glasgow Fair we took our way;
And all the roads along were strung
Wi' lads and bonnie lasses gay.

2   And drawing nigh, one I did spy,
And she was walking by hersel',
For fear the rain her clothes would stain,
She did display an umberell.

3   Faur are ye gaun, my bonnie lass,
How far are ye bound this way?
To Glasgow Fair, sir, I am bound,
For this you know's the feeing day.

4   Says I, The day looks to be rather wet,
Altho' the morning did look fine;
When smiling she said, I am afraid
I'll no be in by feeing time.

5   Cheer up your hert, my bonnie lass,
We'll hae guid weather by-and-by;
Don't be sad when with a lad,
A roving baker frae Millguy.

6   If ye will accept a gill
Of whisky, brandy, rum, or wine,
A gill we'll hae, and then we'll be
In Glasgow Fair by feeing time.

7   She did consent, and in we went,
To an alehouse by the way;
Glass after glass, and the time did pass,
And we baith forgot 'twas feeing day.

8   The clock struck three, she smiled on me,
She said, Young man, the fault is thine;
I'm far from home and night is on
Besides I've lost my feeing day.

9   Cheer up your hert, my bonnie lass,
     I do not mean to harm you;
     Marriage I will surely try,
     For baker lads they aye prove true.

10 It's I'm owre young to wed a man,
     Besides, my mither has nane but me;
     But I'll comply, and I'll ne'er deny
     And wed before I take a fee.

11 We spent that night in merriment,
     And we got wed the very next day;
     And aye sinseen my love does say,
     I'm glad I lost my feeing day.

12 My love and I we do agree,
     I do not think that she'll repine,
     For every day she smiles and says,
     I'm glad I lost my feeing day.

GD 883A. The words for this song came in to Greig via Annie Shirer, and he collected the music from Kirsty Morrice in 1911 or 1912. He wrote in the *Buchan Observer*, 26 May 1908, that: 'Though this song hails originally from the west it is quite popular in the north. It has been printed as a ballad leaflet, and appears in Ford's *Vagabond Songs and Ballads*, but with modifications which appear to us unwarrantable. The tune [is] brisk and breezy.' There are seventeen versions of the song in the collection. 'Milngavie' (pronounced 'Milguy') is an area of Glasgow. [Pent].

Editorial Note   Tonic lowered from G to F. 'Milguy' (1.1) is from the tune title; the text lyric has 'Millguy'. 'And night is on' (8.3) is editorial and has been taken from version C from Mrs Walker.

feeing – hiring

11. There Was a Squire

KIRSTY MORRICE

It's I hae haughs and I hae bowers,
And I hae castle and I hae towers,
And I swear my wedded wife ye'll be,
For I canna live and want ye.

GD 837. Greig collected this fragment on one of his last visits to Kirsty Morrice. [M, -4].

Editorial Note   Tonic raised from Ab to A; alternative notes 4.1–4.2f#, 4.3e; the word 'And' in line 2 is editorial.

haughs – river-meadow lands

12. Saxpence Lace

KIRSTY MORRICE

Saxpence lace the dress is grand,
Dadle eedle diddle dowdle dandy O,
She aye gaed to the castle lookin' for a man,
Dadle eedle diddle dowdle dandy O.

GD 1418A. Greig probably collected this song in the summer of 1911 or 1912. [Dor, -7].
Editorial Note Tonic lowered from G to E; a crotchet 'b' is given as an anacrusis. One line is given for
verse 2 in Argo 14.4: 'She's pitten on the apron afore' and Greig gives additional words at the foot
of that page which seem also to belong to this song: '. . . knee when I couldna get you'.

13. Mormond Braes

KIRSTY MORRICE

1   Mormond Braes where heather grows,
    I heard a fair maid mournin',
    She said her true love had from her gone,
    And she longed for his returnin'.
    Mormond Braes whar heather grows
    Where aft times I've been cheery
    It's Mormond Braes whar heather grows
    It was there I lost my dearie.

2 Young men they're o' a fickle race
   And maids they will believe them
   And however true a maid may be
   Young men they will deceive them.

3 I asked him when he'd marry me
   And how long we would tarry
   When heather cowes grows ousen boughs
   It's that's the day we'll mairry.

4 It's mony a horse may stumble and fall
   And rise again fu brawly
   It's mony a lass has lost her lad
   But I hae lost mine fairly.

5 But I'll put on the robes o' green
   As a forsaken token
   And that will let the young men know
   That our engagement's broken.

6 It's I'll gang doon to Strichen toon
   The place where I was born
   And there I'll get anither sweetheart
   That will mairry me the morn.

7 There's as good fish into the sea
   As ever yet's been taken
   I'll cast my net and fish again
   For I've been but once forsaken.

GD 1142B. The words for this song came in to Greig via Annie Shirer and he collected the music from Morrice probably in the summer of 1911 or 1912. He wrote in the *Buchan Observer*, 3 December 1907, that the song was 'the most popular folk-ditty circulating in our north-eastern angle' and that it was known in Perthshire under the name 'Farewell to Blairgowrie'. There are thirty-two versions of the song in the collection. [I/M].

Editorial Note Tonic lowered from C to Bb; anacrusis quaver Bb; alternative note 1.2f. The tune of the chorus was not included in the original. Text lyric 'had gane frae her' in place of 'had from her gone' (1.3).

cowes – stems;   *ousen boughs* – ox-collars;   *rise again fu brawly* – make a good recovery from a fall

Ann Sangster
1843–1920

Ann Sangster　　　　　　　*Ann Sangster (second left) at Cortiecram Farm*

Ann Jane Angus was born at Pitscow in the parish of Lonmay and was baptised on 12 January 1843.[1] Her parents were Alexander Angus, a shoemaker, and Eleanora Angus (née Cheyne). The 1861 census places her at North Cortiecram, Kininmonth, Lonmay, aged eighteen, and close by at East Cortiecram was her cousin, Mary Angus, aged five. Ann and Mary's fathers were brothers, and Mary is another of Greig's contributors who is treated here, her married name being Dunbar.[2] On 13 December 1863, Ann married James Sangster, a farmer. The couple lived at Cortiecram, a farm of 127 acres which would have been rented; there had been Sangsters at Cortiecram from as far back as the late 1700s or early 1800s.[3] It is thought that the couple had twelve children: James, Robert, Ann Nora, William, Andrew (or Fraser), John, Laurence, Margaret, Helen (or Nell), Peter, Alexander, and Angus.[4] The Sangster family was known as being a musical one: James played the fiddle and sang and Mrs Murray, a great-great-granddaughter of Mrs Sangster, remembered her father, who is descended from William, singing songs like 'Mormond Braes' and the 'Barnyards of Delgaty'.

Mrs Sangster corresponded with Greig via his columns in the *Buchan Observer*, being known latterly as 'M. S., Mintlaw'. Greig's first visit to notate her tunes was described in the newspaper on 20 September 1910:

> Holiday leisure has enabled me to give some extra attention to tune hunting, with the result that I have managed to add considerably to my store of records. Visiting an old correspondent who has helped me off and on with words from the beginning of my series of articles I was delighted to find that her strong point after all was tunes, of which she

has an amazing lot. I managed to secure about the half of her treasures, and hope erelong through her continued kindness to get the other half recorded.

A second visit described in the *Buchan Observer* less than a month later on 11 October 1910 was also very fruitful:

As the result of a second very pleasant visit to 'An Old Correspondent' I have got another big instalment of tunes, of which I may mention a few by way of specimen:– 'Bervie's Bowers,' 'The Begging,' 'Bonnie Udny,' 'The Coortin','' 'When I am on the sea sailing,' 'Hame to my Nancy,' 'Mary Ann,' 'The sinnerin' o' me and my love,' 'Dumb, dumb,' 'Speculation,' 'Ythanside,' etc. I may mention that some of them were contributed by a younger member of the household.

Greig recorded sixty-five tunes from Ann Sangster on these visits, as well as four from her granddaughter, Miss Sangster. According to Mary Ann Crichton, Mrs Sangster: 'Made up songs herself but picked up others from people in district.'[5]

Mrs Sangster died at Cortiecram on 17 November 1920 aged seventy-seven.[6] Her obituary in the *Buchan Observer*, 30 November, signed J.R.I. (i.e. John Ross Imray, a local poet and teacher of music), gives some indication of her interests and character:

Mrs Sangster inherited a love for all descriptions of Scottish literary and poetical work. During her long life she composed a large number of exquisite verses on diverse subjects, written principally in the broad Aberdeenshire Doric, of which as an exponent she had few equals, 'here aboot or far awa'.' Several of these have from time to time appeared in the local and northern press, and been most favourably received by the reading public. . . . During her long lifetime she collected a large number of poetical effusions from the press, many of which are of outstanding merit; these forming one of her choicest treasures.

Well versed in the old ballad and song-lore of Scotland, and singularly gifted with a deep and most retentive memory, Mrs Sangster was of great assistance to the late Mr Gavin Greig, New Deer. . . .

In every sense of the word the deceased was one of the best types of old-time Scottish womanhood now regrettably passing rapidly away. Free from all ostentatious display, Mrs Sangster possessed great versatility; and her homely hospitality was shared and appreciated by rich and poor alike.[7]

A poignant example of her poetry written in remembrance of her son, Donel, or Angus C. Sangster, who died on 16 August 1908 aged twenty-one, has survived. Verses 1–3 of fifteen are quoted below:

> Oh! the cruel hand of Death
> To take away my boy,
> He was the youngest of the fold,
> So full of life and joy.

But oh! alas! poor Donel's gone,
And never will return,
Left all his loving friends behind,
And all do sadly mourn.

Oh! when I think upon my boy
Who never grieved my heart,
It makes me all more sad to-day
That I must with him part.[8]

NOTES

1 OPR 1843/219/3.
2 I am very grateful to Mrs Nora Murray, Longside, Peterhead, for this information (interview 9 October 2003, EI2003.131).
3 Information from Mrs Murray.
4 Information from Mrs Murray.
5 *Greig–Duncan*, vol. 8, p. 486.
6 Death record 1920/210/B7.
7 The obituary on p. 5, col. 3, of the newspaper carried the subtitle 'An Appreciation by One who Knew Her'. I am grateful to Mrs Murray for identifying J. R. I. who died in 1921.
8 I am grateful to Mrs Murray for a copy of the poem.

14. I Will Set My Ship in Order

ANN SANGSTER

I will put my good ship in or-der And I will sail out owre the main I've sailed in-to some for-eign coun-try To see what tid-ings I can bring home.

1   I will put my good ship in order
    And I will sail out owre the main
    I've sailed into some foreign country
    To see what tidings I can bring home.

2   I've sailed east and I've sailed west
    I've sailed far far seeking land
    Till I came unto my true love's window
    And rapped loudly and would be in.

3   Who's that, who's that raps at my window
    It's raps so loudly and would be in
    It's I, I your true love Johnnie
    I pray arise love and let me in.

4   Few few lovers have I out,
    And as few lovers have I in,
    Unless it be my true love Johnnie
    And I'm well sure it's nae him.

5   Oh then go and ask your mother
And see if she will let you my bride be
If she deny you come back and tell me
It may be the last time I'll visit thee.

6   My mother's in her chamber sleeping
You knock so loudly an' she winna hear
She bids you love and court another
And whisper slowly into her ear.

7   Oh then, oh then go and ask your father
See if he'll let you my bride be
If he deny you come back and tell me
It may be the last time I'll visit thee.

8   My father's in his chamber writing
And setting down at his merchandise
In his hand he holds a letter
That speaks much unto your dispraise.

9   To my dispraise my bonnie lovey
To my dispraise, how can that be
For I've neither wronged nor yet denied thee
And thrice this night you've denied me.

10 Up she rose, put on her clothes
It was to let her true lovie in
Before she got herself araiked
The ship was sailing out owre the main.

11 Come back my bonnie lovey come back my bonnie lovey
Come back come back speak now wi' me
How could I come back and speak wi' you
And our ship sailing out owre the seas.

12 The fish may fly, love the sea go dry
The rocks may moulder and sweep the sand
The husbandmen may forget their labour
So keep your love till I return.

GD 792B. Greig acknowledged collecting this song from Mrs Sangster in the *Buchan Observer*, 11 October 1910. [Pent].

Editorial Note Tonic lowered from E to C. The tune lyric for verse 1 is incomplete but runs as follows: 'I will set my good ship in order, And I will set her to the sea; And I will sail . . .'. The title is that given with the text lyric; the tune lyric is headed more briefly 'I Will Set'. The expression 'moulder and sweep' (12.2) is obscure; version Q has 'may melt down wi' the sun'.

araiked – arrayed, ready

15. The Old Maid's Lament

ANN SANGSTER

I've fer-lied sin' I kent my-sel' Fat ails the men folk a' at me, I'm jist as braw's my cou-sin Bell, And she wad get her wile o' three.

1 I've ferlied sin' I kent mysel'
   Fat ails the men folk a' at me,
   I'm jist as braw's my cousin Bell,
   And she wad get her wile o' three.

2 I had some thocht o' Donal' ance,
   An' Donal' was my only ane;
   I thocht I thocht o' Donald lang,
   But the thocht o' Donal's a' o'ergane.

3 He socht a kiss, I gied him three,
   On the craft heid amang the hay;
   Next when we met he gazed and
                  glowered,
   And turned his heid the other way.

4 My braw pink sash my uncle sent
   Frae Lunon to wear aboot my waist,
   I ware't I ware't for mony a year,
   But never an eye on it did cast.

5 A braw new cloak I neist was sure
   Wad catch a lad in Charles' Fair;
   But fareyeweel aye cloak and sash,
   I'll never never wear ye mair.

6 I've aften heard my granny say,
   And she's a wife that widna lee'd –
   Th'll never may can get a man
   Unless there's ane for her decreed.

7 But I'll gang hame, and I'll spin my wheel,
   Never lat the saut tear blin' my e'e;
   I've aften thocht but noo I'm sure
   There's never ane decreed for me.

8 Noo I am aul' and by mysel'
   I'll drink the bitter without the sweet,
   The simmer day may pleasure gain
   And winter wearies me wi' lang nichts.

9 But oh an I were young again,
   And I in my bloomin' twenty-ane,
   With hints and smiles and cunnin' wiles,
   I wid try to get a haud o' ane.

GD 1375B. The words were sent to Greig in January 1908 and the tune was collected on his first visit to
    Mrs Sangster in September 1910. The text lyric is from C, attributed to an anonymous person about
    Mintlaw, who has been identified as Ann Sangster. [Pent].
Editorial Note Tonic lowered from G to F. Text lyric has 'I ferlie' for 'I've ferlied' (1.1), 'What' for 'Fat'
    (1.2), and 'wiles' for 'wile' (1.4).

ferlied – wondered;   *wile* – wale, choice;   *craft heid* – upper part of the croft

16. When Ye Are on the Sea

ANN SANGSTER

When ye are on the sea sai - ling And far from a - ny shore, Ye will ne - ver think on me, Nor mind me a - ny more, Nor mind me a - ny more.

1 When ye are on the sea sailing
   And far from any shore,
   Ye will never think on me,
   Nor mind me any more,
     Nor mind me any more.

2 When I am on the sea sailing,
   And far from any shore,
   My prayers will be to the High Power above
   To guard you evermore.

3 You mind me on yon milkwhite dove
   Sits mourning on yon tree,
   Lamenting over her marrow so sweet,
   And so will I for you.

4 The fish may fly, the sea go dry,
   And the rocks melt wi' the sun;
   Before that I prove false to you,
   My heart's blood shall be run.

5 Now winter's gone and past,
   And summer's come at last,
   And I am free from all harm,
   And you and I into one bed shall lie,
   And I'll guard you in my arms.

GD 1541Aa. Two tunes for this song were collected from Ann Sangster on different occasions, and they exhibit considerable differences. The music for 1541Aa was collected by Greig in September 1910. [Dor].

Performance Note It is suggested that 'you' be changed to 'ye' or 'thee' (3.4) in order to rhyme with line 2. Since verse 5 already has five lines, there is no repeat at the end.

Editorial Note Tonic lowered from A to G.

17. The Auld Wife and Her Cattie

ANN SANGSTER

There was an auld wifie she clippet her cattie,
For takin' a moose upon Christmas Day,
And oh fat befell the silly auld bodie
The half o' her cattie was clippet away.

GD 690A. The song was collected by Greig in September 1910. [I/M].
Editorial Note Tonic lowered from Bb to A. Greig included an extra two bars of tune without words at the end of the song which probably represent a variant for bars 7 and 8. They run (first bar) E D′ D′ C#′ C#′ B and (second bar) C#′ A A A. The rhythm is the same except for the first E being a crotchet and the following two notes being semiquavers.

18. Cam' Ye by the Salmon Fishin'

Cam' ye by the salmon-fishin',
Cam' ye by the roperie?
Saw ye my love Jack the sailor,
Sailin' on the ragin' sea?

GD 1607A. The song was collected by Greig in September 1910. This is a children's song, but William Walker notes that it was sung by mill girls 'as they marched home in groups after the day's work (about 1850)' (see GD 1607 note to 'B', and GD 56 note to 'B'). The response to the question in this verse is given in Iona and Peter Opie's *The Singing Game* (Oxford: Oxford University Press, 1988, p. 333): 'I cam' by the salmon fishers, / I cam' by the roperie, / I saw your dear sailor laddie, / Sailin' on the deep blue sea.' [M].
Editorial Note Tonic lowered from D to C.

roperie – rope-walk

James Mackie

1830–1920

James Mackie's birth is listed on 9 May 1830 in the Old Parish Records for Strichen.[1] His parents were George Mackie and Isabella Mackie (née Milne).[2] The 1891 census places him in Strichen, aged sixty, working as a joiner (the same trade as his father). His other family members were his wife, Margaret, aged fifty-seven, b. Rothiemay, and three daughters: Bathia Ann, aged twenty, b. Strichen, an unmarried domestic servant; Jemima Laing, a pupil teacher, aged nineteen; and Margaret Laing, aged fourteen.[3] Mackie would have been one of Greig's oldest contributors when he corresponded with him from 56 High Street, Strichen, in 1908.

When Greig published a version of 'Pitcaithly's Wells' in the *Buchan Observer*, 14 April 1908, he received a fuller version from Mackie which he acknowledged in his column in the following week. In the meantime Greig had written a letter to Mackie to which he responded on 20 April (see illustration), sending Greig a copy of the 'Diamond Ship', with the comment that it had been many years since he had sung it himself or had heard it sung.

Letter 3088/27 from Mackie to Greig

Mackie continued to send Greig contributions, and when Greig became aware that he could also give him tunes he began to plan a visit. On 12 May he commented:

> From Mr James Mackie, Strichen, I have another consignment of songs, some of them very old, – 'The Gardener Lad,' [840 'The Gardener' A], 'The Waukin' o' the Kiln,' [1476 'The Caul's Takin' Me, Gudeman' B],[4] 'I'm gaen to the Wud,' [811A] and 'The Rovin' Sailor' [1477A]. Mr Mackie's accompanying remarks are most enjoyable and prove him to be a born humorist. He admits that he can sough the tunes, and some evening soon I mean to 'gang doon to Strichen toon' and have a sederunt with my friend.

Greig described his meeting with Mackie in the newspaper on 2 June:

> On a subsequent evening [i.e. after his evening visit to New Pitsligo to record John Mowat] I went down to Strichen and looked up my correspondent, Mr Jas. Mackie, who proved to be, as I had expected, a man of strong intelligence, alert mind, and abounding humour. We had a most enjoyable sederunt over the old songs, my friend's memory carrying him far back into last century and fishing up some fine specimens of the old minstrelsy. I kept him mostly singing and made a number of records. For these I feel very grateful; and my gratitude, like that of the constitutional beggar, will send me back for more.

He obtained thirteen tunes from this visit. Greig acknowledged receiving another batch of songs from Mackie on 23 June:

> Mr Jas. Mackie, Strichen, sends me a quantity of genuine traditional minstrelsy – 'The Banks o' Ugie,' 'Under her Apron,' 'Fy upon Fumblers Fy,' 'The Flowers of Edinburgh', 'The Widow Woman's Son,' 'Binnorie.' My friend, who has the gift of language, touches up one of the verses of 'Ugie' – needing it, I may say – in a very successful manner. He also adds characteristic comments from time to time, and in particular contributes an important and valuable note on the authorship of 'Mormond Braes' and 'Ugie' – for all which I thank Mr Mackie very much.

None of this material was entered into Greig's notebooks, so this statement gives some additional information about Mackie's repertoire including the points that he knew the words of 1314 'The Banks of Ugie' (he had already given Greig the tune) and that he had versions of 213 'Binorie', 830 'The Flowers of Edinburgh' and 1493 'Under her Apron'.

Sixteen songs from Mackie appear in the collection. According to Arthur Barron, his oral sources included an elder brother who was a millwright and Alexander Robb's mother.[5] The connection with Ann Robb seems highly probable since she was living at 82 Bridge Street, Strichen up until her death in 1909.[6] Mackie also drew, directly or indirectly, on printed sources. In the case of 1789 'The Hermit of St. Kilda', Greig noted: 'words of ballad from *Chambers' Miscellany*', and for 310 'The Shepherd's Son' A he noted: 'from Herd'.

James Mackie died on 16 January 1920 at 56 High Street, Strichen, aged eighty-nine.[7]

NOTES

1 OPR Strichen 1830/241/3.
2 Death record 1920/241/3.
3 Census record 1891/241/003/003. The 1881 census lists the family at West Street in Strichen and includes two additional daughters: Helen, aged twenty-five, b. Pitsligo, a domestic servant; Isabella, aged fifteen, b. Strichen, a mill worker; and a son, William, aged twelve, b. Strichen. James Mackie is listed as a house carpenter in 1881 (census record 1881/241/002/012).
4 This was identified as Mackie's in the Supplementary Notes to *Greig–Duncan*, vol. 8, p. 444.
5 *Greig–Duncan*, vol. 8, p. 491.
6 Death record of Ann Robb, 1909/241/18.
7 Death record 1920/241/3.

19. I'm Gaun to the Wud

JAMES MACKIE

1   I'm gaun to the wud,
    Quo' Nansie, quo Nansie;
    I'm gaun to the wud,
    Quo' kind-hearted Nansie.

2   What if I come after ye?
    Quo' Wilsie, quo' Wilsie;
    What if I come after ye?
    Quo' slae cowardly Wilsie.

3   And what the deil's to hinder you
    Quo Nancy, quo Nancy
    And what the deil's to hinder you
    Quo kind hearted Nancy.

4   And fat gin I sud lay ye doon
    Quo Wilsie, quo Wilsie
    And fat gin I sud lay ye doon
    Quo Wilsie, quo Wilsie.

5   Faut maitter, I can rise again
    Quo Nancy, quo Nancy
    Fat maitter, I can rise again
    Quo kind hearted Nancy.

6   But faur'l I'll tie my beastie tee
    Quo Willsie, quo Willsie
    But faur'l I'll tie my beastie tee
    Quo slae cowardly Willsie.

7   Tie him to my muckle tae
    Quo Nancy, quo Nancy
    Tie him to my muckle tae
    Quo kind hearted Nancy.

8   But fat gin he sid rin awa
    Quo Willsie, quo Willsie
    But fat gin he sid rin awa
    Quo slae cowardly Willsie.

9   The Deil gae wi' ye steed and a'
    Quo Nancy, quo Nancy
    The Deil gae wi' ye steed an a'
    Quo kind hearted Nancy.

GD 811A. The words were acknowledged in the *Buchan Observer*, 12 May 1908, and the tune collected by Greig in May 1908. [I/Ly].
Editorial Note Tonic lowered from D to A.

faut maitter – what matter

20. The Shepherd's Son

JAMES MACKIE

1　There was a shepherd's son
　　Kept sheep upon a hill.
　　He laid his pipe and crook aside,
　　And there he slept his fill.
　　Sing fal de reedle adie,
　　Fal de reedle adie,
　　Fal de rit to my fal de reedle ee
　　Fal de reedle adie.

2　He looked east and he looked west
　　Then gave an under look
　　And there he spied a lady fair
　　Swimming in a brook.

3　He raised his head from his green bed
　　And thus approached the maid
　　Put on your claes, my dear, he says
　　And be you not afraid.

4　'Tis fitter for a lady fair
　　To sew her silken seam
　　Than to rise up on a May morning
　　And strive against the stream.

5　If you'll not handle my mantle, she said
　　If you do not touch my gown
　　Then I'll give you as much money
　　As you can carry home.

6　It's I'll not handle your mantle
　　And I'll lat your claes alane
　　And I'll tak you out o' the clear water
　　My dear to be my ain.

7　He set her on a milk-white steed
　　Himsel upon anither
　　And all along the way they rode
　　Like sister and like brother.

8　When she came to her father's yett
　　She tirled at the pin
　　And ready stood the porter there
　　To let this fair maid in.

9　And when the gate was opened
　　Sae nimbly she swept in
　　Pough, you're a fool without she said
　　And I'm a maid within.

36

10 Now farewell my modest boy
I thank you for your care
But had you done, as you should done
I had not left you there.

11 Oh, I'll cast aff my hose and sheen
And lat my feet gang bare
And gin I meet a bonny lass
Hang me gin her I spare.

12 In that do as you please she says
But you shall nevermore
Have the same opportunity
With that she shut the door.

13 There is a guid auld proverb
I've often heard it told
That he that winna when he may
He sanna when he would.

GD 301A. Child 112 *The Baffled Knight*. The words were acknowledged in the *Buchan Observer*, 26 May
1908, and the music was collected by Greig just afterwards. [I/M].
Editorial Note   Tonic lowered from F to D; text lyric has 'Fal de reedle do my fal-de-reedle ee' (1.7).

sanna – shall not

21. Pitcaithly's Wells

JAMES MACKIE

It fell a-bout a Lam-mas time, And a fine time o' the year, When
youth-ful girls a-spor-ting went To drink the wa-ters clear When
youth-ful girls a-spor-ting went To drink the wa-ters clear.

1   It fell about a Lammas time,
    And a fine time o' the year,
    When youthful girls a-sporting went
To drink the waters clear
    When youthful girls a-sporting went
To drink the waters clear.

2   There was a girl among the rest
Whose beauty did excel
And the bonniest lassie that ere I saw
She lives near Pitcaithley's Wells.

3   The first time that I saw my love
I thocht nae shame to say
Will ye be my physician
But she blushed and said me nay.

4   I asked if she would take a walk
She said we would be seen
At length we went and took a walk
Down by Pitcaithly green.

5   We walked up, so did we down
To breathe the caller air
We walked down by woods and groves
I and my Jeannie fair.

6 We walked east, so did we west
   Till nature did its part
   We walked by yon pleasant stream
   Till I gained Jeannie's heart.

7 Altho' the down beds be so scant
   I'd choose a place unseen
   While other swains do oftimes choose
   Their loves upon the green.

8 How could you choose a place unseen
   When you have stole my heart
   For walking by Pitcaithly's stream
   I'm afraid I'll pay the smart.

9 He turned him right and round about
   And this to her did say
   Come to my arms my dearest dear
   I will not you betray.

10 Oh, if I were some shepherd swain
   I'd skip the heather bells
   And dawt the lassie in my airms
   That lives near Pitcaithly's Wells.

11 Oh, happy, happy would I be
   If I could call her mine
   I would treat her in my father's house,
   To the country cheer so fine.

12 Lang [may] Pitcaithly's Wells run fine
   And lang may they run there
   And mony a ane frequent the place
   Where I gainèd Jeannie fair.

GD 925A. The words were acknowledged in the *Buchan Observer*, 21 April 1908 and the music was collected in May of that year. Greig wrote in the newspaper on 14 April 1908: 'Pitcaithly, celebrated for its mineral wells, is situated near Bridge of Earn in Perthshire. . . . The tune to which [the song] is sung is a very pleasing bit of melody, with a smoothness of flow that is almost modern.'

Editorial Note 7.1 is given as corrected by Mackie from the line in the text he supplied first which ran: 'Oh if I were some shepherd swain'. [I].

caller – fresh

22. The Auld Mare's Lament

JAMES MACKIE

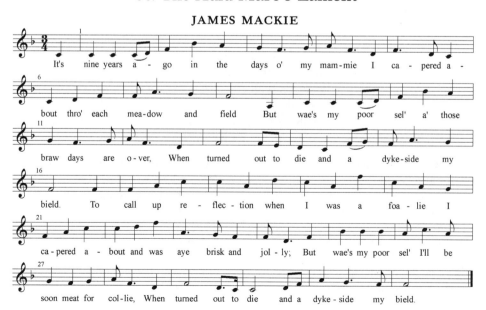

It's nine years a - go in the days o' my mam - mie I ca - pered a -
bout thro' each mea - dow and field But wae's my poor sel' a' those
braw days are o - ver, When turned out to die and a dyke - side my
bield. To call up re - flec - tion when I was a foa - lie I
ca - pered a - bout and was aye brisk and jol - ly; But wae's my poor sel' I'll be
soon meat for col - lie, When turned out to die and a dyke - side my bield.

1 It's nine years ago in the days o' my mammie
     I capered about thro' each meadow and field
     But wae's my poor sel' a' those braw days are over,
     When turned out to die and a dykeside my bield.
     To call up reflection when I was a foalie
     I capered about and was aye brisk and jolly;
     But wae's my poor sel' I'll be soon meat for collie,
     When turned out to die and a dykeside my bield.

2 When young Mr Galloper bought me to ride on
     And he like mysel' was a rambling chiel,
     With spurs my poor sides, there was scarce a bit hide on
     My back wi' the saddle was blistered and beeled.
     For pleasure he rode in and out at the gallop
     And ilka noo and than he o'ertook me a wallop
     But I flang him fae me ae nicht in the shallop
     And bade him lie there till his humours were queeled.

3 For this the neist day I was saul to a cadger
     Braw niffer thocht I, but I was beguiled
     For he wrought me hard ilka day like a navvy
     Till ye may believe me, my rumple was peeled.
     Hard toiled all the day, scanty fare was my supper
     My drink was the dregs o' some foul stinkin gutter
     And noo when my life's worn oot to a twither
     I'm turned out to die and a dykeside my bield.

4 Ye mortals take warning from this my sad story
     Scarce able to shift for mysel' in the field
     What though my poor neighbours they a' should be sorry
     Their pity affords me ne'er shelter nor bield.
     Lay something in store when ye hae strength and vigour
     Lest old age comes on you the thin chafted beggar
     And then like mysel' ye'll but cut a poor figure
     When turned out to die and a dykeside your bield.

GD 492A. The words were acknowledged in the *Buchan Observer*, 26 May 1908, and the music collected by Greig in May of the same year. [I].

Performance Note The high F could be sung as a D in bar 19 and as a Bb in bar 22.

Editorial Note Text lyric does not include 'It's' (1.1), and has 'these' in place of 'those' (1.3). The word 'nigger' has been replaced editorially by 'navvy' and 'beggar' (3.3 and 4.6 respectively).

bield – shelter; *beeled* – sore; *queeled* – cooled; *cadger* – itinerant dealer;
  niffer – exchange; *rumple* – rump; *twither* – thread; *thin chafted* – thin-jawed

23. The Rovin' Sailor

JAMES MACKIE

1   I am a sailor stout and bold, oft-times I've ploughed the ocean;
    I've ventured my body thro' heat and cold for honour and promotion.
    Many's the battle I've been in, some I've lost and some I've won,
    And it's a' for the honour o' George our King that I've been a rovin' sailor.

2   Gentlemen I tell you plain my body's deeply wounded
    I've been in the wars and I've lost a limb and death has me surrounded
    Messmates I'll bid you adieu, I'll sail the salt seas no more with you
    But I range the country through and through and I'll aye be a rovin sailor.

3   I will rove the country through and through until I please my fancy
    I will drink with Kate and Nelly too, and likewise lovely Nancy;
    When I get drunk then I will go swigg for swagger to and fro
    Down to the place where the girlies flow and I'll aye be a rovin sailor.

4   When I will go further down where sporting girls are plenty
    Till I meet with one of a modest mien and I'll court wi' her fu dainty
    Hat in hand to her I'll swear I'll be true to you my dear
    Away to her house for the night we'll steer and I'll aye be a rovin sailor.

5   In the morning when I wake I'll court with her an hour
    And then I'll rise and bid her wait till I come from the door
    But if she wait until I come that will be at the day of doom
    And another girlie will be in her room and I'll aye be a rovin sailor.

6   If you want to know my name I'm called Jack the Rover
    A title that I got from Venus the Queen for turning girlies over.
    With my fause heart and flattering tongue I've cheated the girlies both old and young
    So now to conclude and put an end to my song here's a health to the rovin sailor.

GD 1477A. The music was collected by Greig in May 1908.

Editorial Note Tonic lowered from A to G. Missing lines at 3.1–2 have been supplied from a broadside published by James Kendrew in York (British Library 1870.c.2; no. 86). Mackie also had lines 3–4 of another stanza before the final verse: 'Now since of me she has seen the last, what she's got she may hold fast / For she's nae the first and she winna be the last that's been cheated by a rovin' sailor.' It has not been possible to complete this stanza from the broadside. In singing, the lines could either be omitted or could be added to verse 5 and sung as a repeat of the second half of the tune.

swigg for swagger – staggering about

John Mowat
1841–1916

John Mowat

Craigmaud, New Pitsligo

John Mowat was born in 1841 at the Moss of Carno, not far from Fraserburgh, to John Mowat, a crofter, and June Mowat (née Morice). He was fee'd at several farms in the neighbourhood after leaving school, and at the age of nineteen became foreman at Tyrie Mains.[1] John Mowat married Isabella Fraser in January 1860 at Gamrie. Following Isabella's death, he married Ann McKessar, a farmer's daughter, at Percyhorner, Fraserburgh.[2] Among their children was a son, John, who was a singer also, and was recorded by James Madison Carpenter.[3]

A tribute to Mowat entitled 'Esteemed by All: Lifetime Spent on the Soil', tells us of his character and interests:

> Of a quiet, retiring disposition and 'honest to the core,' there are few men in the Buchan district who have completely gained the whole-hearted respect of his fellows . . . [more] than Mr. John Mowat, Craigmaud. . . .
>
> Mr. Mowat started farming on his own account in the early seventies, his first occupancy being his father's croft of twelve acres at Moss of Carno. . . . Mr. Mowat is, however, best known as the tenant of Craigmaud, on the estate of Lord Clinton, New Pitsligo. Since taking over this farm Mr. Mowat has greatly improved the holding, which is now recognized as a model in the district. He is an authority on trenching and draining and improving the soil. . . . His speciality has been the breeding of Clydesdales. With regard to cattle, while he did not particularise in any special breed, the Craigmaud stock has often found first places for excellence at the local cattle shows.
>
> Mr. Mowat has been President of the Craigmaud Ploughing Association since its inauguration. . . . In his younger days Mr. Mowat was a champion ploughman, having had an honourable record in possessing four Highland Society medals.

He can tell a good story in his 'ain' quiet way, raise a hearty laugh by a witty remark, and he brims over with that happy kind of humour that is always infectious.

Possessed of a good voice, John is one of our best exponents of the ballads of Buchan. The late Mr. Gavin Greig, Whitehill, found in him a valuable assistant helping to secure many old folk-songs for his collection, remarking that Mr. Mowat had done incalculable good work in preserving in a pure form the native Doric and minstrelsy of the district. . . . It is worthy of note that Mr. Mowat has been a generous supporter of the war relief fund. Not long ago the steam mill had a half-day's thresh at Craigmaud, and to show his sympathy with the poor Belgians, Mr. Mowat very handsomely paid over all that he received above £1 a quarter to the fund being raised on their behalf. Still more recently, when requested to sing after the dinner at the Tyrie ploughing match, John agreed, but only after he had passed the hat, and made a collection which amounted to 32s 6d, this being also given to the Belgian Relief Fund.[4]

Greig entered a batch of six tunes and two batches of eleven tunes into his *Folk-Music* volumes in September 1907.[5] In the *Buchan Observer* on 24 March 1908 he mentions having spent several evenings in Mowat's company:

My best thanks are due to my friend, Mr John Mowat, Craigmaud, for copies of a number of the old songs and ballads which he has kindly got written out for me. Mr Mowat is widely known as a first-rate singer of these, and I have already had the great pleasure of two or three evenings with him over the good old minstrelsy, and I look forward to more, for one can see that his stock of song and ballad is not likely to be exhausted in a hurry.

He later mentions (2 June 2008) having had a musical evening with Mowat at the home of James Will, a schoolteacher in New Pitsligo. Following this, he received a letter from Mowat which he writes of on 23 June:

From my friend Mr Mowat, Craigmaud, I have a fine hearty letter from which I must extract a sentence – 'I cannot keep from congratulating you on the old songs. They are most charming, and make me mind on youth when we met in the winter evenings and tried to amuse one another with our songs.' He refers to the position which Aberdeen-shire and Fyvie in particular hold in the realm of song, and is glad to see that New Pitsligo is also likely to have a place.

On 11 August 1908, Greig discusses the evening gathering at Craigmaud where John McAllan was present (see entry on him in this edition). A further session at James Will's home where Mowat was present is recorded on 13 April 1909, and another visit to Craigmaud is mentioned on 5 October 1909.

Seventy-five songs from Mowat appear in the collection, and Greig commented on him in a letter to Duncan: 'Elderly man. Fine specimen of the old folk-singer. Extensive repertoire but mostly songs [rather than ballads].'[6] The largest number of his songs (eighteen) to be found in a single volume is in volume 3 on Songs of the Countryside and Songs of Home and Social

Life, and this is not surprising given his occupation as a farmer. Little is known about the sources for his songs, but 59 'Jacky Tar' C was sung by an old salt on the streets of Rosehearty *c.*1859, and 10 'Greenland' C was sung in the Fraserburgh district *c.*1849–59 (*Buchan Observer*, 16 March 1909).

John Mowat died on 15 April 1916 at Craigmaud, aged seventy-four, and his wife, Ann, died in June of the same year.[7] His great-granddaughter, Mrs Jean Skinner, knew that her grandfather Mowat had been a singer, and said that she and her siblings are all interested in the music of the North East. Although they are not public singers, they like to sing together at family events.

NOTES

1 Information from 'Esteemed by All: Lifetime Spent on the Soil', see note 4.

2 Information on the first marriage from Mrs Jean Skinner (interview 14 October 2003, EI2003.130); information on the second from New Register House, 1876/196/31.

3 See further *The James Madison Carpenter Collection Online Catalogue* http://www.hrionline.ac.uk/carpenter. He was also recorded by Kenneth Goldstein (School of Scottish Studies Archives, University of Edinburgh, SA1960/154–5).

4 The typing errors in the document have been corrected here. This document is in the possession of his great-granddaughter, Mrs Jean Skinner, whose mother was a Mowat. I am most grateful to Mrs Skinner for her kind help.

5 *Greig–Duncan*, vol. 8, p. 483.

6 Letter from Greig to Duncan, 28 January 1914, see *Greig–Duncan*, vol. 8, p. 483.

7 Information from Mrs Jean Skinner. Ann died on 10 June 1916 at Tyrie (death record 1916/248/1).

24. Barnyards o' Delgaty

JOHN MOWAT

In New Deer par-ish I was born, A child of youth to Meth-lick came; And
if you do mis-doot me, The ses-sion-clerk will tell the same.
Lil-tin a-die tu-rin a-die, Lil-tin a-die tu-rin ae.

1 In New Deer parish I was born,
   A child of youth to Methlick came;
   And if you do misdoot me,
   The session-clerk will tell the same,
   Liltin adie turin adie,
   Liltin adie turin ae.

2 Good education I did get,
   And I did learn to read and write,
   My parents they did me admire,
   My mother I was her whole delight.

3 But as the years they did roll on,
   My dad and me could not agree,
   I loved the lasses double weel,
   And aye the drap o' barley bree.

4 Fae Methlick parish I cam' fae
   To Turra market for to fee,
   When I met in wi' drucken Scott
   Fae the Barnyards o' Delgaty.

5 When I arrived at the Barnyards,
   The sicht o' things near upset me,
   We had nae tools to work oor wark,
   Oor beddin' it was unco wee.

6 Oor cairts they were all in a wrack,
   Oor harrows scarce a teeth ava;
   Oor ploos they were a lump o' roost,
   And handles they had nane ava.

7 Oor horses they were unco thin,
   The auld gray meer she widna ca;
   The auld Jock horse lay in the theets,
   And clawed his legs in spite o' a'.

8 But when the turnips we got in,
   Oor horse a' parkit ane and a',
   And we to Turriff on Saturday went,
   And jolly we got ane and a'.

9 When I went to the church on Sunday,
   Mony's the bonnie lass I see,
   Sit shyly by her daddie's side,
   And winkin' owre the pews to me.

10 I can drink and nae be drunk,
   I can fight and nae be slain,
   I can coort my neebor's lass,
   And aye be welcome to my ain.

GD 347B. The music was collected by Greig in September 1907. John Mowat had heard his mother
singing it when he was a boy. Delgaty is near Turriff in Aberdeenshire. [Pent].

Editorial Note Text lyric has 'in' for 'of' (1.2), 'you doubt me to believe' for 'you do misdoot me' (1.3), and
'Lintin' for 'Liltin' (1.5 and 1.6). Greig inserted square brackets both above and below bar 8 with a
star noting that the cadence was also given by William Forsyth, aged eighty-five, Durie, Mintlaw,
in June 1908.

misdoot – doubt; *barley bree* – whisky; *drucken* – drunken; *theets* – traces, ropes

45

25. Jonnie Moir

JOHN MOWAT

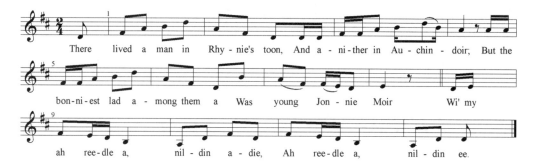

There lived a man in Rhy-nie's toon, And a-ni-ther in Au-chin-doir; But the bon-ni-est lad a-mong them a Was young Jon-nie Moir Wi' my ah ree-dle a, nil-din a-die, Ah ree-dle a, nil-din ee.

1 There lived a man in Rhynie's toon,
And anither in Auchindoir;
But the bonniest lad among them a
Was young Jonnie Moir
Wi' my ah reedle a, nildin adie,
Ah reedle a, nildin ee.

2 Jonnie was a sturdy blade
Both sturdy stout and tall
And the sword that hung by Jonnie's side
Was fully six feet long.

3 The press gang came quickly round
For soldiers to our king
And they enlisted Jonnie Moir
He suited them right well.

4 He had not been in London town
Years but barely three
When he'es fa'en in love wi the king's
daughter
And for her he could die.

5 Word's gane up and word's gane down
And word's gane to the king
That this Scottish laddie's faen in love
Wi his daughter Lady Jean.

6 When the king got word o this
An angry man was he
He swore before he ate or drank
And hanged he should be.

7 When Jonnie heard his sentence passed
A loud loud laugh gave he

Says As long as I can wield my blade
And ye daurna a hang me.

8 But the English rouges are cunning dog[s]
Around him they did creep
And they gave him drams wi lodumy
And caused him to sleep.

9 Jonnie wakened out of sleep
An angry man was he
He was lying bound in iron bands
And his feet in fetters three.

10 Where would I get a little we boy
Fit to won meat and fee
That would rin on to my uncle
At the fit o Benachie.

11 Here am I a little we boy
That wid won meat an fee
That would rin on to your uncle
At the fit o Benachie.

12 When you come where brig's broken
You'le bend your back and swim
And when you come where the
grass grows lang
You'le slack your shoes and run.

13 And when you come to my uncle
Bide neither to chap nor ca
So weel's you'le ken auld Jonnie More
Three feet above them a.

14 You'll bid him tak this broad letter
Sealed wi my faith an trueth
And you'll bid him bring alang wi him
That bodie Jock o Noth.

15 Benachie lies very low
And the tap o Noth lies high
And for all the distance that was between
They heard auld Jonnie cry.

16 As they went down thro London town
The cokneys all did stare
To see t[w]o Scots with shoulders broad
And their heids set in the air.

17 O what's the matter says Jonnie Moir
What's the matter within
That the drums do beat and the
                  fifes do play
And they make a dumbful din.

18 There's nothing the matter the proud
                  kepper replied
There's nothing the matter within
But a wighty Scotch man lying bound
And tomorrow he must die.

19 Open your gates says Jonnie Moir
Open them unto me
Out spake the proud kepper
Says I have not got the key.

20 Open your gates says Jonnie Moir
Open them unto me
Or there is a bodie at my back
From Scotland's brought the key.

21 Open your gates says Jock o Noth
Open them at my call
And with his fit he'es driven
Three yards of their high wall.

22 Oh is't for murder, is't for theift
Or is it for robberie
If it be for any of these crimes
And hanged ye shall be.

23 It's not for murder not for thieft
It's not for robberie
For the loveing o a lady fair
That their gaun to gar me die.

24 When the king got word o this
An angry man was he
I will hang this little we boy
That brought tidings unto thee.

25 If you do hang this little we boy
Brought tidings unto me
I will attend the funeral
And rewarded ye shall be.

26 Have you any masons in this place
Or any within your call
That you might employ a few of them
To build up your broken wall.

27 We have masons in this place
And masons at our call
But gang ye back the way you came
Neer mind our broken wall.

28 Auld Jonnie Moir and young Jonnie Moir
And Jock o' Noth a three
The king's daughter and the little wee boy
And their a at Benachie.

GD 246B. Child 251 *Lang Johnny More*. The ballad was collected by Greig in September 1907. In the *Buchan Observer*, 2 June 1908, Greig refers to it as 'the raciest perhaps of our old ballads', and notes '[it] has long been popular in the north but seems to have escaped the notice of the collector till it was printed by Peter Buchan in his *Ancient Ballads* (1828). For the sake of those who may never have heard an old ballad sung it may be pointed out that frequently at the end of a line, and sometimes elsewhere, there occurs a word of two syllables which should, properly, have the accent on the first syllable, – "London," "Johnny," "uncle," "standard." In such cases the accent is frankly shifted on to the final syllable to suit the rhythm of the tune; and in reading, to get the right effect, the same thing has to be done. In metrical terms, the trochee becomes an iambus. The tune to which "Lang Johnny More" is sung is brisk and breezy in character, accommodating itself admirably to the style and sentiment of the ballad.' [Pent].

Performance Note 'Die' (4.4) should be pronounced 'dee' to rhyme with 'three' (4.2).

Editorial Note Tonic lowered from F to D; text lyric has 'land' for 'toon' (1.1), and 'And sing' for 'Wi' my' (1.5). Lines 1.3–4 are absent in the tune lyric and have been drawn from the text lyric. The word 'And' is superfluous (6.4); 'And hanged' in this context simply means hanged. 'Wee' misspelled as 'we' in original (10.1, 11.1, 24.3, 25.1).

loodumy – laudanum;   *slack* – slacken;   *chap* – knock;   *dumbful* – doleful;   *wighty* – powerful

26. The Soldier Maid

JOHN MOWAT

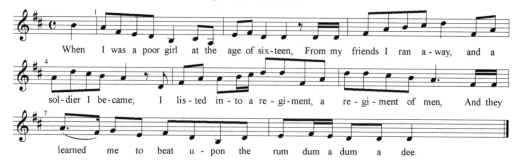

When I was a poor girl at the age of six-teen, From my friends I ran a-way, and a sol-dier I be-came; I lis-ted in-to a re-gi-ment, a re-gi-ment of men, And they learned me to beat u-pon the rum dum a dum a dee.

1   When I was a poor girl at the age of sixteen,
    From my friends I ran away, and a soldier I became;
    I listed into a regiment, a regiment of men,
    And they learned me to beat upon the rum dum a dum a dee.

2   With my coat, hat and feather if you had but seen
    You would have said and sworn a man I had been
    The soldiers all admired me with fingers long and thin
    That I beat up the row dow the best o' them a'.

3   Many a prank have I seen in the field
    And many a poor French boy for me's been forced to yield
    Many a prank have I seen among the French
    And so boldy as I fought tho' I was but a wench.

4   But now the wars are over and I am come home
    And lying in our barracks I often did think shame
    When pulling off my breeches and with a sly smile
    To lie with a man and a maid all the while.

5   That might not be known until this very hour
    But they sent me up to London to keep sentry o'er the tower
    When a girlie fell in love wi' me, I told her I was a maid
    And to my officer my secret she betrayed.

48

6   My officer he sent for me, to see could that be true
    For such a thing could never been believed of you
    And now I must return to my parents at home
    And with my old comrades no more I will roam.

GD 182B. John Mowat wrote out the words for Greig who collected his tune. This is an example of the type of song quite frequently found in Scots tradition in which a character adopts the dress of the opposite sex. There are eight versions of it in the collection. [I].

Editorial Note Tonic lowered from F to D. The text lyric has 'about' for 'at' (1.1). The word 'she' (5.4) is editorial (cf. version A, 4.4). The third note in bar 5 is editorial, and notes 5.4–5 were originally quavers – the changes were made to accommodate the words.

listed – enlisted;   *beat up the row dow* – beat the drum

27. The Ewe Buchts

JOHN MOWAT

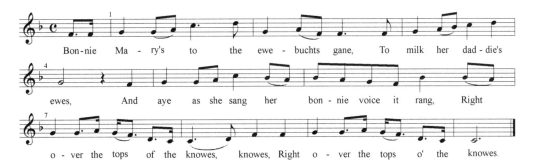

Bon-nie   Ma - ry's   to   the   ewe - buchts   gane,   To   milk   her   dad - die's

ewes,   And   aye   as   she   sang   her   bon - nie   voice   it   rang,   Right

o - ver the tops   of   the   knowes,   knowes,   Right   o - ver the tops   o'   the   knowes.

1   Bonnie Mary's to the ewebuchts gane,
    To milk her daddie's ewes,
    And aye as she sang her bonnie voice it rang,
    Right over the tops of the knowes, knowes,
    Right over the tops o' the knowes.

2   There came a troop o' merry gentlemen
    All merrily riding by
    And ane o' them to the ewe buchts did gang
    To see Mary milkin her ewes.

3   Milk on, milk on, my bonnie, bonnie lass
    Milk on milk on said he
    Ride on, ride on young man, she said
    And do not tarry wi' me.

4   He's taen her by the milk white hand
    And by the waist gown sleeve
    And he's kissed her owre and owre again
    And asked no one's leave.

5   He mounted on his milk white steed
    And he's ridden after his men
    And all that his men ever said unto him
    Oh master you've tarried long.

6   I've ridden east, I've travelled west
    I've ridden amongst the knowes
    But the bonniest lassie that ever I saw
    Was milkin her daddie's ewes.

7   She's taen the milk pail on her heid
    And she's gaen singin hame
    And all that her father ever said unto her
    Oh daughter you've tarried long.

8 But it fell on a day, on a bonnie simmer's
                                            day
   She was ca'in out her father's kye
   And who did she spy but the same
   All merrily riding by.   [gentlemen

9 One of them did say unto her
   Oh maid have you got a man
   And the answer that she gave unto him
   O I have got one at home.

10 You lie, you lie, you weel-faur'd maid
   And so loud as I hear you lie
   Don't you mind on the dewy dewy night
   You was in the ewe buchts wi' me.

11 He has ordered one of his men to go down
   And set her on behind
   Says Your father can ca' in his kye
                                      when he likes
   For they'll never be ca'ed in by mine.

12 I am the laird o' Logan Braes
   I've got fifty ploughs and three
   And I'm sure that I've met wi' the ae bonniest lass
   That's in all the north countrie.

GD 838C. The music was collected by Greig in September 1907. [Dor/Æ].
Performance Note 'Ewes' should be pronounced 'yowes' to rhyme with 'knowes'.
Editorial Note Tonic lowered from A to G; text lyric has 'Bonnie Mary to the ewe buchts did gang' (1.1)
    and the word 'and' is inserted between 'sang' and 'her' (1.3). The title is given from the text lyric;
    the tune lyric is headed 'Bonnie Mary is to the ewe-buchts gane'. 'By' is a correction from
    manuscript of 'my' (11.4). It is likely that the introduction of cattle instead of sheep into the song –
    see 'kye' (8.2 and 11.3) – is a later addition. The rhyme with 'by' (2.4) suggests the word 'kye' (as
    found in the 'A' version from Alexander Robb).

ewebuchts – small pens used for milking ewes;   knowes – hillocks;   ploughs – ploughlands

28. The Laird o' Windywa's

JOHN MOWAT

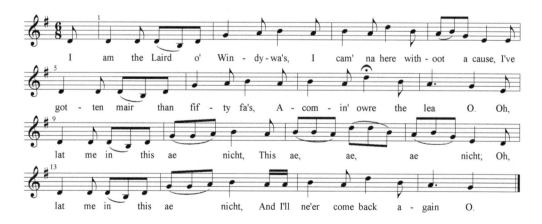

I am the Laird o' Win-dy-wa's, I cam' na here with-oot a cause, I've
got-ten mair than fif-ty fa's, A-com-in' owre the lea O. Oh,
lat me in this ae nicht, This ae, ae, ae nicht; Oh,
lat me in this ae nicht, And I'll ne'er come back a-gain O.

1   I am the Laird o' Windywa's,
   I cam' na here withoot a cause,
   I've gotten mair than fifty fa's,
   A-comin' owre the lea O.
   Oh lat me in this ae nicht,
   This ae, ae, ae nicht;
   Oh lat me in this ae nicht
   And I'll ne'er come back again O.

2 Thro' the moss and owre the muir
  I've come this dark and rainy hour,
  And now I stand and rap at your door,
  Oh, rise, lovie, lat me in O.
  Oh, lat me in this ae nicht,
  This ae, ae, ae nicht;
  Oh, lat me in this ae nicht,
  And I'll ne'er come back again O.

3 My feet they are baith cauld and weet,
  My sheen is frozen to my feet,
  Into your bosom I would creep,
  Gin ye wad lat me in O.
  Oh, lat me in this ae nicht,
  This ae, ae, ae nicht;
  Oh, lat me in this ae nicht,
  And I'll ne'er come back again O.

4 Your feet they are baith cauld and weet,
  Your sheen are frozen to your feet,
  Into my bosom ye wad creep,
  If I wad lat ye in O.
  Wear awa' this ae nicht,
  This ae, ae, ae nicht;
  Wear awa' this ae nicht,
  And come nae back again O.

5 The lassie rose, put on her clothes,
  Unto the chamber door she goes,
  And cannily slipt aff the bar,
  She oiled the hinges I suppose,
  For fear o' makin' din O.
  Says, Venture in this ae nicht
  This ae, ae, ae nicht;
  Says, Venture in this ae nicht,
  But come nae back again O.

6 When he wan in he was sae gled,
  He dang the boddom fae the bed,
  The lassie tint her maidenhead,
  The mither heard the din O.
  Sae weel's she liket that ae nicht,
  That ae, ae, ae nicht
  Sae weel's she liket that ae nicht
  Bade him come back again O.

7 When he was oot he was sae gled,
  He shook the bunnet frae his head,
  Says, Ye may be sick, and ye may be sad,
  Ere I come back again O.
  Sae fare ye weel this ae nicht
  This ae, ae, ae nicht;
  Sae fare ye weel this ae nicht
  And I'll ne'er come back again O.

GD 778A. The song was collected by Greig in April 1909. [Pent].

Editorial Note Tonic lowered from Ab to G; alternative note 'e' in anacrusis and at 12.5, and 'b' at 14.5 and 14.6; the first chorus is drawn from the text lyric rather than the tune lyric; note 8.2 was originally a dotted crotchet (and the following quaver was given in a separate bar); the semiquavers in bar 14 replace a quaver, the change being made to accommodate the words; Greig has written 'aye' in brackets below each 'ae' in the tune lyric perhaps suggesting that this was the pronunciation, but the norm is 'ae' (meaning one) rhyming with 'day'. 'Bunnet' is editorial (7.2); only the letter 'b' followed by a space was given in the original. This word has been drawn from Lizzie Higgins's version given in Ailie Munro's *The Democratic Muse*, p. 108.

moss – boggy ground; *muir* – heather moorland; *boddom* – bottom; *tint* – lost;
   wear awa' – make off quietly

29. The Souters' Feast

JOHN MOWAT

There wis a sou-ter and a soo, Tan-ti-ee-rie o-rum, And for her birse he kissed her mou, Sing how-dle il-ti o-rum.

1 There wis a souter and a soo,
Tantieerie orum,
And for her birse he kissed her mou,
Sing howdle ilti orum.

2 The souters they had a feast,
And wasna that a merry jeest?

3 Souters cam' fae far and near,
And some o' them ayon New Deer.

4 Some o' them cam' oot o' Turra,
And some as far's the laigh o' Moray.

5 Ane o' them cam' oot o' Fife,
Ridin' on a rusty knife.

6 The souters they got a' fou,
And ane o' them began to spue.

7 He spued some leather and some lasts,
And sharpit knivies five or sax.

8 Ballies o' roset and broken gless,
Cam' rattlin' fae the souter's arse.

9 And when they thocht the breet was clean,
He spued a muckle beatin' stane.

GD 629A. The music was collected by Greig in March 1908. The 'laigh o' Moray' (4.2) refers to the fertile plain south of the Moray Firth. [Pent].

Performance Note Greig inserted a slur mark between notes 2.2 and 2.3 which possibly indicates a sung slide between these notes. He has given verse 10 as 'And when they thocht, etc.' probably indicating that Mowat only partly remembered a final verse which, on analogy with version B from James Brebner, would have been something like: 'And when they thocht the breet was clear, / Up cam' the steel and a' the gear.'

Editorial Note Tonic lowered from G to E; alternative note 'd' in anacrusis; text lyric has 'Tanteerie' for 'Tantieerie' (1.2); the final word in verse 8 was omitted in the original but is strongly suggested by the rhyme.

birse – bristle; *mou* – mouth; *ayon* – beyond; *ballies o' roset* – balls of resin; *breet* – brute

Miss Henderson

Travellers (Stewarts and Reids) at a campsite in Ballinluig, 1932[1]

In October 1906 Greig received seven songs 'from a girl Henderson, New Pitsligo', whom he describes as 'a wandering damsel who sang for coppers'.[2] These songs were 20 'Scarborough Banks' B, 783 'I Must Away' A, 'The Road to Dundee' A, 1012 'The Lass o' Benachie' D, 1038 'The Single Sailor' F, 1129 'The Old Soldier' and 1195 'Bruce's Lines' B.

Greig's comments suggest that Miss Henderson belonged to the group known as Travellers who moved from place to place, often earning a living from seasonal activities. New Pitsligo is famed amongst Travellers for peat cutting and for the gathering of sphagnum moss which was used as a base for flower displays and was bought by florists.[3] The only Traveller singer from whom we know Duncan collected also came from New Pitsligo. She was Miss Lizzie Stewart, a hawker girl who sang at the door of his Manse at Lynturk on 3 July 1908,[4] and Duncan collected only one song from her – 1038 'The Single Sailor' G. He writes: 'The singer was a girl of thirteen years, singing at the door for money. She stated that she came from New Pitsligo, and that she was travelling with her father, who was a hawker. The 9/8 time was very

53

distinctly sung.'[5] Miss Henderson also sang this song in 9/8 time and it is interesting that out of the fifteen tunes for it given in the collection, there are only three notated in this time signature (the other being from Miss H. Rae). The 'Single Sailor' texts from Lizzie Stewart and Miss Henderson are also very similar. Given their social circumstances, their connection with New Pitsligo and their ages, it is very possible that the singers were acquainted.

Although Greig collected 1528 'The Bonnie Banks o' Loch Lomond' from an anonymous 'wandering wife' and Traveller material also came into the collection through secondary sources, e.g. George Innes's version of 42 'Box Them Off, My Jolly Tars' from his father who 'had it from two gypsy girls living in a cave near Portgordon', it was not until the 1950s that collecting began on a serious scale from the Travellers in Scotland. This was as a result of the efforts of collectors such as Hamish Henderson of the School of Scottish Studies at the University of Edinburgh, who were prepared to learn from Traveller society.

NOTES

1 Left to right: Donald Reid jnr, Jean Reid (née McKenzie), Mary Stewart (small child), Agnes Foxton McKenzie (Jean Reid's sister), Martha Stewart, a baby from the Stewart family, and David Stewart. I am grateful to Martha Stewart, Ellon, for identifying the people in the photograph (Martha and David Stewart are her maternal grandparents and Jean Reid is her great-grandmother).

2 *Greig–Duncan*, vol. 8, p. 478.

3 Information from Stanley Robertson, Aberdeen, April and November 2003. I am grateful to Stanley for his help.

4 *Greig–Duncan*, vol. 8, p. 521.

5 *Greig–Duncan*, vol. 5, p. 627.

30. Scarborough Banks

MISS HENDERSON

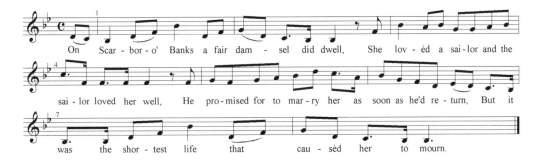

On Scar-bor-o' Banks a fair dam-sel did dwell, She lov-èd a sai-lor and the
sai-lor loved her well, He pro-mised for to mar-ry her as soon as he'd re-turn, But it
was the shor-test life that cau-sèd her to mourn.

1 On Scarboro' Banks a fair damsel did dwell,
   She lovèd a sailor and the sailor loved her well,
   He promised for to marry her as soon as he'd return,
   But it was the shortest life that causèd her to mourn.

2 One day as they were sailing a storm did arise,
   Which causèd the poor sailor to swim for his life,
   As thus he was a-swimming he happened to go down
   Instead of being married he got a watery tomb.

3 As soon as this news entered Scarboro's shore
   She fell a-wringing of her hands and a-tearing of her hair,
   It's Oh you cruel billows wash my true love ashore,
   That I might enjoy his cauld features once more.

4 One day as she was walking down by yon Ruby sands
   To her amazement she spied the drownded man,
   And hasting up unto him it's amazed she did stand,
   For she knew it was her Bill by the marks upon his hands.

5 It's now since I have found you your death I will employ
   For sure I have loved you since you were a boy,
   And kneeling down beside him she bade her people farewell
   She kissed his cold lips, broken-hearted she died.

6 In Scarboro' churchyard this couple they were laid,
   And bright on a tombstone these words were thus engraved
   Come all ye pretty fair maids a warning take by me
   Never let your true love sail on the raging sea.

GD 20B. This song was collected by Greig in October 1906. He wrote in the *Buchan Observer*, 13 July 1909: 'This ballad is widely known and sung. The tune is bold and sweeping in its melodic curves.' Twelve versions of it appear in the collection. The song is also found in *Bothy Songs and Ballads* (1930:332) by John Ord who noted: 'This is an English folk-song which has found its way to the North-east of Scotland, where it has been a great favourite for the past sixty years.' [I].

Editorial Note Tonic lowered from C to Bb; grace note 4:1a; alternative notes 2:2eb, 4:4e natural, and 8:2eb.

31. A Fair Maid

MISS HENDERSON

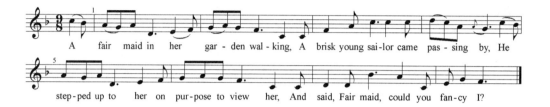

A fair maid in her gar-den wal-king, A brisk young sai-lor came pas-sing by, He step-ped up to her on pur-pose to view her, And said, Fair maid, could you fan-cy I?

1   A fair maid in her garden walking,
    A brisk young sailor came passing by,
    He stepped up to her on purpose to view her,
    And said, Fair maid, could you fancy I?

2 It's no kind sir, I'm not to marry,
   A servant girlie o' low degree,
   It's I have a true love and he is a sailor
   He sails upon the dark blue sea.

3 I wonder how you could love a poor sailor
   I wonder how you could love him so,
   He might be married, he might be
                    drownded,
   And the wide wide ocean become his
                    grave.

4 It's if he's married I wish him pleasure,
   And if he's drownded I wish him rest,
   And if in yon ship he's sailing
   He might come back and marry me.

5 Don't you see yon high high castle
   All decorated by lilies white? –
   I'll give you gold, love, I'll give you silver,
   If you'd only say you'll be mine to-night.

6 What care I for your high high castle,
   And what care I for your lilies white,
   What care I for your gold or your silver,
   If my true love was here to-night?

7 He put his hand into his pocket,
   His fingers they being long and small,
   He pulled out the ring which they
                broke between them
   When she saw it she droppèd down.

8 He raised her up into his arms,
   And gave to her a loving kiss,
   Saying, I am your true love and
                your Johnnie,
   And I've come back to marry you.

9 This couple now they have got married
   And lived a splendid and happy life
   And she was a poor servant girlie
   And now she is a bold captain's wife.

GD 1038F. Greig collected this song in October 1906. He wrote in the *Buchan Observer*, 5 May 1908, that the hero is the sailor who has 'been so long away that his sweetheart fails to recognise him, and he manages to try the old ruse to test her fidelity – with of course the usual satisfactory result.' There are twenty-eight versions of this song, known as 'The Single Sailor', in the collection. [I].

Editorial Note Tonic lowered from G to F; text lyric has 'A lady' in place of 'A fair maid' (1.1), and 'would' in place of 'could' (1.4).

32. Open and Let Me In

MISS HENDERSON

I must a - way I can stay no lon - ger, This mor - ning's tem - pest I have to cross So o - ver the high hills I'll roll with plea - sure Till my arms I love my dear.

1 I must away I can stay no longer,
   This morning's tempest I have to cross
   So over the high hills I'll roll with
                           pleasure
   Till [in] my arms I love my dear.

2 When he came to his true love's window
   He kneeled low down upon a stane
   And through the window he whispered
                           slowly
   Is my true love now within?

3 She lifted her head off the soft
                           down pillow
   And slowly rose there her lily white breast
   And thro' the window she whispered
                           slowly
   Who's disturbing me thro' my night's rest?

4 Arise arise it's your own true lover
   Arise and open and let me in,
   For I am wet love, besides I'm weary
   I'm wet, love, unto the very skin.

5 It's up she has got with the greatest
                           of pleasure,
   She opened the door and she let him in
   And there they clasped in each
                           other's arms
   Till this long night was at an end.

6 When this long night was past and over
   And all the small cocks began to crow
   They both shook hands love and
                           kissed and parted
   Sounded his trumpet and away did go.

GD 783A. Greig collected this night visiting song in October 1906. He wrote in the *Buchan Observer*, 16 May 1911, about two records of the song he had collected: 'One of my records was got a year or two ago from a wandering damsel [Miss Henderson] who sang for coppers – and was worth them. Her tune for this song was a fine bit of melody, albeit the rhythm was somewhat irregular. I may say that while our English friends seem to encounter a good lot of irregularity in the rhythms of the folk-tunes which they collect, the experience both of Mr Duncan and myself is that anomalies of this kind are by no means frequent in northern folk-tune.' This song is a favourite with Scottish Travellers and is sung by Stanley Robertson from Aberdeen. [I].

Performance Note It would be effective to keep the rhythm flowing in bar 6 rather than to rigidly count each 5/4 beat. The note 'd' is given as a crotchet in brackets by Greig in bar 6 after the rest; it seems to be needed only when the last line in a verse is a long one.

Editorial Note Greig has written this song out in 4/4 time but seems to have been undecided on this, putting 3/2 at the side and giving indications for barring in that time signature (e.g. dotted bar lines) in the music itself. The 3/2 time-signature has been selected here. Verse 4 is taken from the tune lyric; the text lyric omits 'very' (4.4).

33. I Fell in Love wi' a Bonnie Lass

MISS HENDERSON

1 It's I fell in love wi' a bonnie lass
   At the keepin' o' her cattle
   Her father he has me beguiled
   And sent me off to battle.

2 It's over hills and it's over dales
   And over dykes and valleys,
   He tried to take my true love from me
   'Twas all thro' spite and malice.

3 The peace it came and I came home
   And spierin' for my dearie
   They told me not such a one was there
   It put my heart to fury.

4 I went up to her uncle's house
   Asking for my dearie
   They told me not such a one was there
   It put my heart to fury.

5 My bonnie lovie she heard my voice
   She cried oot thro' her high window
   Here I am but I daurna come
   Till the locks and keys be sindered.

6 I stood awhile to amuse mysel'
   Bein' in an angry passion
   Till my passion flew and my sword I drew
   And so boldly I stepped over.

7 I made open doors o' double deals
   I made locks and keys to sinder
   For I've taen my true lovie by the hand
   And my broadsword in the other.

8 Her uncle and her uncle's men
   They all did follow after
   I told them all to return again
   Or try it in a battle.

9 For it's I have been where the bullets flew
   And cannons loudly rattle,
   They who cannot fight for their heart's
                                          delight
   They could never fight in the battle.

10 It was at the back o' Benachie
   Where the blood lies clean and shallow
   It was at the back o' Benachie
   It was there I met my marrow.

GD 1012D. Greig received this song in October 1906. He noted in the *Buchan Observer*, 21 January 1907, that the lady of the song was said, according to tradition, to be 'a Miss Erskine, heiress of Pittodrie, an estate close to Benachie in the Parish of Chapel of Garioch. She was born about 1747 and married to her soldier lover about 1770.' However, he goes on to outline some discrepancies concerning the dates and other features of the legend. This ballad according to Greig was widely known and very popular, and was 'sung to a variant of the "Dowie Dens of Yarrow" tune, one of our oldest melodies and belonging to a type very common in the north.' [Æ/Dor].

Editorial Note Tonic lowered from Bb to A; text lyric omits 'It's' 1.1, and gives 'had' in place of 'has' (1.3). The title given is from the text lyric; the tune title is 'The Back o' Benachie'. The sense of 10.2 is not clear. Other versions, e.g. 1012 B, 10.2, have 'Where swiftly flies the swallow'.

cried – called; *sinder* – split apart; *deals* – planks

34. The Road to Dundee

MISS HENDERSON

Dark was the night and the wind be - ing how - ling Rol - ling the
waves on the wide rol - ling sea I met a fair las - sie as I
home-ward was wal - king She was as - king the road to bon - nie Dun - dee.

1   Dark was the night and the wind being howling
    Rolling the waves on the wide rolling sea
    I met a fair lassie as I homeward was walking
    She was asking the road to bonnie Dundee.

2   It's well my fair lassie I cannot well tell you
    The road and the distance how far it may be
    But if you permit me I am willing to show you
    The road and the distance to bonnie Dundee.

3   It's arm in arm we onward did wander
    Till I ere did spier where that lassie cam frae
    But she appeared like an angel in form and feature
    That morning we went to bonnie Dundee.

4   We shook hands and parted, and I bade her morning
    That lassie turned round wi' a tear in her e'e
    Look here my laddie I'm going to reward you
    For showing me the road to bonnie Dundee.

5   Here is twenty bright guineas I got o' my father,
    It's bound to support you and let it go free
    Go down to St Andrews and tak' a wee drappie,
    For a body that's travellin' it will help him a wee.

6   Here is luck to that lassie as it will request her
    Be she married or single whate'er she may be
    I'll never be bashful to show a young lassie
    The road and the distance to bonnie Dundee.

GD 971A. Greig collected this version of the popular song in October 1906. [I].

Editorial Note Tonic lowered from G to F; a crotchet anacrusis (note C) has been omitted; an extra
    quaver has been added at 10.3 and 12.3 to accommodate the words. Tune lyric has 'I'm' in place of
    'I am' (2.3). 'I got o' my father' (5.1) is from 971E (John Mowat), 8.1; the original was 'bright guineas
    my father's . . .'.

William Watson

1836–1919

William Watson was born at Burnside of Biffie, Old Deer, on 21 August 1836. His parents were George Watson, a farmer, and Isabel Watson (née Cooper), and William was the youngest of their nine children.[1] The census records list him at Millfieldhill, Monquhitter, in 1871; at Farm Cottage, Craignetherty, Marnoch, in 1881; and at New Byth in 1891.[2] The 1901 census lists William, aged sixty-five, along with his wife, Elspet (née Brebner), aged sixty-four, at Main Street, New Byth.[3] Watson's occupation is usually given in the records as farm servant or agricultural labourer, but he is also recorded as being a carter, a farmer and a farm grieve.[4]

Greig appears to have been introduced to William Watson by the schoolmaster at New Byth, William Cumming, and described his meeting with him in the *Buchan Observer*, 3 November 1908:

> I have . . . to thank Mr Wm. Watson, New Byth, for a large number of records. I had the pleasure lately of meeting Mr Watson at the Schoolhouse, where with old songs and kind hospitality we spent a very happy evening. Concentrating on the tunes I managed to secure a lot from our friend's singing, my professional brother, Mr Cumming, kindly engaging to take down the words for me.

Greig numbered sixteen songs in Roman numerals in his notebook (Argo 12), but actually collected eighteen during the evening. He noted tunes and partial words in the following order: 1269 'Old Adam and Eve' A, 1286 'The Struggle for the Breeches' A, 1492 'The Waukin' o' the Claes' C, 550 'The Present Time Is Oors', 463 'The Masons' B, 1012 'The Lass o' Benachie' A, 224 'The Banks of Sweet Dundee' A, 443 'The Braes o' Broo' A, 170 'The Jolly Ploughboy' F, 317 'The Wee Toon Clerk' S, 1262 'The Auld Gardener's Wife' A, 618 'The Cantie Carlie' B, 1032 'Charlie Mackie' E, 389 'Cameloun' D, 791 'The Soldier Lad' A, 1273 'Charlie' I,[5] 1709 'What Folk Are Made Of' C, and 557 'A Wee Drap o' Whisky' A. No tune is given for 'Charlie' but Greig noted that it was sung to the same tune as 'Cantie Carlie' (618B).

Twenty-four songs, including nine 'A' versions, were collected by Greig from Watson, and these are fairly evenly spread through the volumes of the collection. The direct sources are named for only two of his songs: his father (618 'The Cantie Carlie' B), and Mrs Imlah, Whitebog (1284 'The Scolding Wife' F), with 463 'The Masons' B being heard at Aberdour, 1012 'The Lass o' Benachie' A learned in Methlick, and 1286 'The Struggle for the Breeches' A heard at Ellon Market. The dates at which he learned his songs span the period between *c*.1848 (e.g. 1284 'The Scolding Wife' F), when he was aged twelve, and *c*.1860 (550 'The Present Time Is Oors'), when he was around twenty-four. Greig was particularly impressed with one of Watson's tunes, writing in the newspaper on 26 October 1909: 'The tune which I have for "The waulkin' o' the claes" is one of the finest melodies I have ever recorded. I took it down from the singing of Mr Wm. Watson, New Byth.' Greig's sol-fa notation for this tune from Argo 12 is given below. The note '60 yrs' means that Watson had learned it sixty years previously.

Although Greig wrote in the newspaper on 3 November 1908 that 'Mr Watson's stock of minstrelsy is not exhausted, and we expect to have another meeting erelong when more records can be made', he did not make a return visit. However, on 25 May 1909 and 8 February 1910, he acknowledged receiving some additional texts, noting in the latter: 'Mr Wm. Cumming, M.A., New Byth, forwards copies of the following songs taken down from the singing of Mr Wm. Watson, New Byth:– [1054] "The Rigs o' Rye," [1173] "When I was young," [1219] "The young sailor," [23] "Sally Munro," and [918] "Come all ye men." I am greatly indebted to Mr Cumming and Mr Watson for their kind help.'

William Watson died on 31 May 1919 at Main Street, New Byth, aged eighty-two.[6]

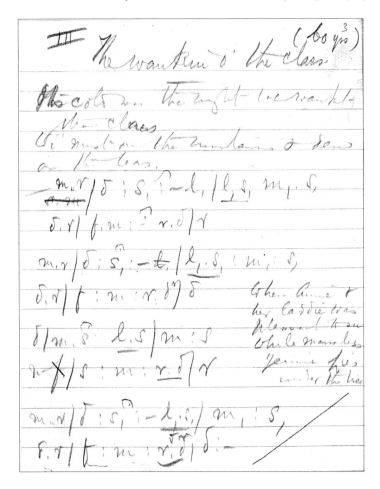

'The Waukin o' the Claes', from Argo 12, p. 3

NOTES

1 Information from G. F. Milne, Methlick, whose great-great-great grandmother Christian was a sister of William Watson's, and from OPR 1836/228/4*. I am most grateful to Mr Milne for his help.

2 Three daughters are listed in the 1891 census: Amelia, aged thirty, a domestic servant b. New Deer; Maggie Ann, aged eighteen, a dressmaker b. Monquhitter, and Willimena, aged fifteen, a domestic servant b. Gamrie in Banffshire (census record 1891/210/A2/005/007), and the couple's other children were Jane b. 1857, Jessie b. 1863, Mary b. 1865, William b. 1868, James b. 1868, and Christian b. 1869 (information from G. F. Milne).

3 Census record 1901/210/A2/005/013.

4 Information from G. F. Milne, from death record 1919/210/A2/12 and from census records 1891 and 1901.

5 This version was mistakenly allocated to the Reverend John Calder in the main edition, and a related note signed W.W. was mistakenly attributed to William Walker (see correction in *Greig–Duncan*, vol. 8, p. 442).

6 Death record 1919/210/A2/12.

35. The Waukin' o' the Claes

WILLIAM WATSON

Oh cold was the night when we wau - kit the claes; Wi' mist on the moun - tains and dew on the leys; When An - nie and her lad - die was plea - sing to see, While mar - row - less Jean - nie lies un - der the tree.

1   Oh cold was the night when we waukit the claes;
     Wi' mist on the mountains and dew on the leys;
     When Annie an' her laddie was pleasing to see,
     While marrowless Jeannie lies under the tree.

2   It's out spake bonnie Annie, says, 'Jeannie aren't ye cauld?
     For I'm in my Johnnie's arms, he does me uphauld.
     I'm in my Johnnie's arms, he keeps a' cauld fae me,
     But I am sorry to see you lying under the tree.'

3   'Oh, hold yer tongue, bonnie Annie, and do not taunt me,
     There's a rose in yonder garden, it's budding for me;
     It's budding and blooming and blowing all three,
     There's a house and a bonnie laddie provided for me.'

4   When all things was ended as they had begun
     Bonnie Annie's fine petticoats they would not tie on,
     They would not tie on, nor meet by a span,
     An' the red rose in Annie's cheek it grew pale and wan.

5   Out speaks bonnie Jeannie, wi' her sunny face,
     Says, 'Ye should have been cannie and ta'en my advice;
     Ye should have been cannie, and lien doon wi' me,
     When ye said I lay marrowless under the tree.'

6   When six weeks was over, an' now at an end,
     Bonnie Jeannie and her laddie was married, ah, then
     They were married and bedded, an' kirket a' three,
     An' she lies nae mair marrowless under the tree.

GD 1492C. The music was collected by Greig *c.*3 November 1908, and he describes it as one of the finest melodies he has ever recorded (see biographical pages on Watson). The song was heard by Watson *c.*1848. The clothes are being watched (wauked) while they are spread out overnight on the grass to be bleached or dried (information from DSL, 2007). [I].

Editorial Note Tonic lowered from Ab to G; text lyric has 'night we' in place of 'night when we' (1.1).

leys – pastures;   *kirket* – churched after the birth of a child

36. The Plooman Laddie

WILLIAM WATSON

Get up, get up, ye la-zy loons, Get up an' waur them a', man, For the Braes o' Broo are ill to ploo, They're roch and ree-sky a', man. But the ploo-man lad-die's my de-light, And the ploo-man lad-die loves me, They say the ploo-man lad's wi' me When I'm sure he is no near me.

1   Get up, get up, ye lazy loons,
     Get up an' waur them a', man,
     For the Braes o' Broo are ill to ploo,
     They're roch and reesky a', man.
     But the plooman laddie's my delight,
     And the plooman laddie loves me,
     They say the plooman lad's wi' me
     When I'm sure he is no near me.

2   Oh, he's ta'en up his owsen gaud,
     An' it sets him weel to ca', man,
     He's laid it o'er the owsen bow,
     Says, Scurry, come awa', man.

3   What think ye o' oor ploomen noo,
     Wi' their high-cuttin' ploos and a', man?
     But it wasna sae ance in a day
     When the wooden pleuchie ploo'd a', man.

4   What think ye o' oor fairmers noo
     Wi' their binders ane and a', man?
     But it wasna sae ance in a day
     When the plooman shure it a', man.

5   What think ye o' oor fairmers noo
     Wi' their thrashin' mulls and a', man?
     But it wasna sae ance on a day
     When the plooman threesh it a', man.

6   What think ye o' oor lasses noo
     Wi' their bicycles sae braw, man?
     But it wasna sae ance on a day,
     That widna dee at a', man.

7   It's I will wash my plooman's hose,
     And brush his dubby sheen, man,
     An' I'll maybe be a plooman's wife
     Or a' thae days be deen, man.

GD 443A. Greig acknowledged this song, known as 'The Braes o' Broo' in the collection, in the *Buchan Observer*, 16 March 1909. He had written of it in the newspaper two weeks earlier (2 March): 'This is a popular song. There is a good deal of difference in the versions which one gets. The original would seem to be fairly old, but later hands have brought it up to date by references to modern inventions. . . . I have heard the ditty sung to different tunes.' [I].

Editorial Note Tonic lowered from F to C; the tune of the chorus (same as the verse) was not present in the original and has been added here with some minor rhythmic adjustments. The text lyric has been used for verse 1; the tune lyric has 'warn' in place of 'waur' (1.2), and 'is' in place of 'lad's' (1.7).

waur – get the better of; *roch* – rough; *reesky* – marshy; *gaud* – a stick with a point on it;
sets – suits; *bow* – yoke; *shure* – reaped; *dubby* – muddy

37. The Present Time Is Oors

WILLIAM WATSON

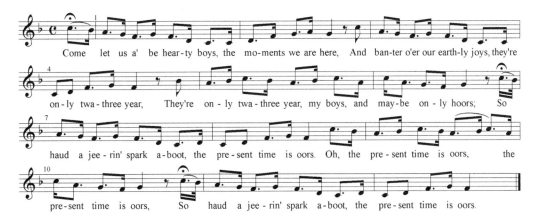

Come let us a' be hear-ty boys, the mo-ments we are here, And ban-ter o'er our earth-ly joys, they're
on-ly twa-three year, They're on-ly twa-three year, my boys, and may-be on-ly hoors; So
haud a jee-rin' spark a-boot, the pre-sent time is oors. Oh, the pre-sent time is oors, the
pre-sent time is oors, So haud a jee-rin' spark a-boot, the pre-sent time is oors.

1   Come let us a' be hearty boys, the moments we are here,
And banter o'er our earthly joys, they're only twa-three year.
They're only twa-three year, my boys, and maybe only hoors;
So haud a jeerin' spark aboot, the present time is oors.
Oh, the present time is oors, the present time is oors,
So haud a jeerin' spark aboot, the present time is oors.

2   Awa wi' a yer gaudy shirts, what signifies a show?
For multitudes o' cares and griefs they only prove a foe.
A raggit coat wi' elbucks oot will bang the winter shoo'rs,
So haud a jeerin' spark aboot, the present time is oors.

3   Let ministers say what they will, they'll tell ye this and that,
Sae blithe are we and sae are they when quietly they meet,
When quietly they do sit roon, secure wi' lockit doors,
So merrily they laugh and sing, The present time is oors.

4   They'll bid ye raise yer hopes abeen, and greet where'er ye dwell,
They'll mak' ye lairds ayont the meen, but grip the gless themsel',
But let us learn tae be wise, and pu' the sweetest floo'rs,
Leave thistle leaves to them that please, the present time is oors.

GD 550. The music was collected by Greig around 3 November 1908 and the words, taken down by William
   Cumming of New Byth, were acknowledged in the *Buchan Observer*, 16 February 1909. [I/M].
Performance Note The words of the refrain should reflect the last line of each verse.
Editorial Note Tonic lowered from G to F; alternative note 3.8d. The tune of the chorus was not
   included in the original, and has been based on the verse. 'Jeerin' may possibly originally have
   been 'cheering' (1.6).

twa-three – two or three, a few;   *spark* – drop, nip of spirits;   *elbucks* – elbows;   *bang* – defeat;
   greet – cry, weep

38. Oh What Is Bachelors Made O' Then?

WILLIAM WATSON

Oh what is ba - che - lors made o' then? Oh what is ba - che - lors made o' then? They're made o' lea - thern tag and they're aye rea - dy wi' the gab And that's what ba - che - lors are made o' then.

1 Oh what is bachelors made o' then?
   Oh what is bachelors made o' then?
   They're made o' leathern tag and they're aye ready wi' the gab
   And that's what bachelors are made o' then.

2 Oh what is auld maidens made o' then?
   Oh what is auld maidens made o' then?
   They're made o' nettle seed and they're a cankert weed
   And that's what the auld maidens are made o' then.

3 And what is the young men made o' then?
   Oh what is the young men made o' then?
   They're made o' skate bree, gin they'd wings they wad flee
   An' that's what the young men are made o' then.

4 Oh what is the young weemen made o' then?
   Oh what is the young weemen made o' then?
   They're made o' sugar saps, an' they taste like honey draps
   An' that's what the young women are made o' then.

GD 1709C. The music was collected by Greig around 3 November 1908 and the words, which were noted down by William Cumming, were acknowledged in the *Buchan Observer*, 25 May 1909. [Pent].

Editorial Note Tonic lowered from G to E. The title is given here as in the first line; the title Greig gave with the music was 'Oh, What Is the Bachelors Made Of?' Greig gives no words with his music and the rhythm in bars 5–8 has been altered in order to accommodate the text; note 'd' (4.5) is editorial.

tag – strap, tab;   *gab* – chat;   *saps* – juices

John Quirrie

1848–1913

John Quirrie was born at New Byth on 21 December 1847. His parents were Alexander and Eleonora (née Gibson).[1] John Quirrie (spelt Quirie in the records) married Jean (or Jane) Gerrie in 1868 at New Byth in King Edward parish. Jean was a domestic servant from New Byth who was born in New Pitsligo. Alexander Quirrie's profession is given as sailor (master) at this time,[2] and this may possibly explain the prevalence of the theme of sailing in John Quirrie's repertoire. In 1881, Quirrie was living in Turriff parish at Knockiemill Agricultural Labourers' Cottage and was working as a cattleman. Five children are listed in the census: Eliza (or Elizabeth), Robert, John, William and Alexander. They were born between 1871 and 1879 in New Deer, New Byth, King Edward and Banffshire respectively.[3] In 1891 the Quirries were at Little Rettie in Boyndie parish in Banffshire where John was working as a farm servant. A further five children are listed: Isabella, Alfred, Jane, Leith, and Eleonora (or Ella). Isabella and Alfred were born in Turriff and the others in Boyndie.[4] The eldest of their eleven children, Mary Anne, was born in 1868.[5]

Quirrie was a crofter at North Mains of Craigston, King Edward, when he was involved with the collection, and Greig referred to him as 'Johnnie Quirrie of Craigston' in a letter to Duncan of 1 October 1911. A substantial notebook (Watt) contains the results of Greig's first collecting from Quirrie in August 1906, as well as songs from James W. Spence, Alex Murison and James Ewen.[6]

The eleven items from Quirrie in Watt are found in the following order (pp. 71–95): 1535 'Jamie Raeburn' I, 743 'The Old Bog Hole' A, 1898 'Bob Ridley', 1897 'Peter Gray', 1891 'Whitehills Harbour', 653 'Jean Pirie', 1904 'The Torry Brig', 54 'The Apprentice Sailor' E, 1022 'Hynd Horn' J, 792 'I Will Set My Ship in Order' I, and 174 'The Merchant's Daughter and Her Sailor' A. In September, he collected twenty-two tunes from John Quirrie and two from Miss E. Quirrie,[7] who could have been either Eliza or Eleonora.

Fifty-nine songs from Quirrie appear in the collection, and these are spread throughout the eight volumes. Eight songs are found in the final volume, including the children's song 1669 'Ki-Ma-Dearie' B. His sources or the locations where he learned his songs are given in a number of cases: 29 'The Middlesex Flora' E was learned c.1886 from James Ironside, Gamrie; 401 'Pitgair' A was learned at Northfield of Gamrie in 1869; the words of 653 'Jean Pirie' came from the *People's Journal* in 1880; and 1193 'Barbara Allan' D was sung by his mother. Two versions of 1198 'The False Bride' were obtained from Quirrie: version K came from another man's singing, and version M from his mother.

1891 'Whitehills Harbour' is an interesting case of a song composed as a fund-raiser for a particular occasion. The tune used was the one that would have been familiar as 'The Lass o' Glenshee'. Greig noted in Watt (p. 79): 'Made up for Mr. Quirrie by Wm Park Blacksmith and sung by J. Quirrie at Concert in aid of Whitehills Harbour.' The community evidently regarded John Quirrie as someone who would give a fine platform performance. Miss E. M. Ord, his great-granddaughter, also knew of him having been a singer, noting: 'Many times we have heard from my late mother of great-grandfather's writing and singing songs.'[8]

John Quirrie died on 10 June 1913 at North Mains of Craigston, aged sixty-five.[9]

NOTES

1 OPR 1848/184/2 and information from Mr F. C. Birch.
2 Marriage record 1868/210/10.
3 Census record 1881/247/004/001.
4 Census record 1891/149/004/003.
5 Information from Mr F. C. Birch, Ayr, Mary Anne's grandson (letter of 11 September 2003).
6 *Greig–Duncan*, vol. 8, p. 477.
7 *Greig–Duncan*, vol. 8, p. 477.
8 Letter from Miss Ord, Banff, 5 September 2003. I am very grateful to Miss Ord, Mr F. C. Birch and Mrs Daphne Robertson for their help in connection with this article.
9 Death record 1913/210/A1/7. For further information on Quirrie, see 'J. W. Spence and John Quirrie' by Tom McKean in *Greig–Duncan*, vol. 8, pp. 590–1.

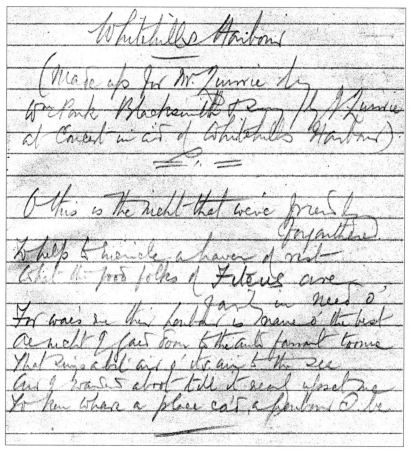

Verses 1 and 2 of 'Whitehills Harbour' from Watt, p. 79

Whitehills Harbour

39. Pitgair

JOHN QUIRRIE

O Char-lie, O Char-lie come owre frae Pit-gair, And I'll gie ye oot a' my or-ders, For I'm gaun a-wa' to yon high high-land hills To leave a' this low Buch-an bor-ders.

1   O Charlie, O Charlie come owre frae Pitgair,
     And I'll gie ye oot a' my orders,
     For I'm gaun awa to yon high Hielan' hills
     To leave a' this low Buchan borders.

2   O Charlie, O Charlie, tak' notice what I say
     And put every man to his station,
     For I'm gaun awa to yon high Hielan' hills
     To view a' the parts of the nation.

69

3   To the lowsin' ye'll pit Shaw, ye'll pit Sandieson to ca'
     To the colin ye'll pit Andrew Kindness,
     And auld Colliehill he'll feed the mill
     And see that he dee't wi' great fineness.

4   Ye'll pit Eppie to the mill and Janet to the cole
     And the ither twa men for to carry,
     And as for George and Jeck ye'll pit them to the rake
     And see that they do not tarry.

5   To the gatherin' o' the hay ye'll pit little Isa Gray,
     And wi' her ye'll pit her cousin Peggy
     And it's in below the bands it's there ye'll pit your hands
     And see that they do it right tidy.

6   It's you Willie Burr ye'll carry on the stir
     And ye'll keep a' the young maids a-hoein'
     And ye'll tak' care o' Jeck or he'll play you a trick
     And will set a your merry maids a-mowin'.

7   And it's you Annie Scott ye'll pit on the muckle pot
     And mak' unto them porridge plenty
     For yon hungry brosiers that's comin' frae Pitgair
     They live both bare and scanty.

8   Ye'll tak' little Annie Mack frae the colin' o' the quack
     To help ye the denner for to carry
     And at the hour o' one ye will mak' them a' to stan'
     At the mull for a moment to tarry.

9   O Charlie, O Charlie, so early's ye'll rise
     And see a' my merry men yokin'
     And you Missy Pope ye'll sit in the parlour neuk
     And keep a' my merry men frae smoking.

GD 401A. Greig collected the music of this song in August 1906. Quirrie had learned the song at Northfield of Gamrie in 1869. Greig wrote in the *Buchan Observer*, 17 November 1908: 'This is [a] Banffshire song, and of comparatively recent date. Pitgair is a farm in the parish of Gamrie, and the characters referred to – the chief ones at least, can be identified. The song, unsurpassed among local pastorals for simplicity and natural truth, is said to have been written by a man named Shaw, who was long beadle at Alvah and had considerable local reputation as a rhymer and as a character. The air to which it is sung is a very common one.' Shaw is also credited with 'Mrs Greig of Sandlaw' (GD 316) and 'Lucky Duff' (GD 373); the Gamrie census for 1881 lists Andrew Kindness as being sixty-six years of age. [Æ or Dor with inflected 6th].

Editorial Note Tonic lowered from A to G; change of time-signature in bar 3 is editorial; alternative note 6.6eb; Greig inserted a question mark below note 7.6 and was unsure whether it was a natural or a flat. The word 'Hielan' from the text lyric has been substituted for 'highland' (1.3); text lyric has 'Charlie' for the opening words 'O Charlie' (1.1), 'Or I' for 'And I'll' (1.2), and 'your' for 'my' (1.2). The manuscript indicates a gap between 'ye' and 'the denner' (8.2) but the sense runs coherently.

lowsin' – unyoking;   *cole* – making of haycocks;   *brosiers* – brose-eaters;   *colin'* – cutting;
   quack – bog

40. The Laird o' Esselmont

JOHN QUIRRIE

There lives a lad in-to this place, Which we think worth re-cor-din', They
ca' him the Laird o' Es-sel-mont, Or Char-lie Na-pier Gor-don.

1   There lives a lad into this place,
      Which we think worth recordin',
      They ca' him the Laird o' Esselmont,
      Or Charlie Napier Gordon.

2 One night he came thro' Foveran
    On some o' his carouse
    He came up to a country girl
    Near by to Fontainbleau.

3 As far as we do recollect
    A visit she had been
    To a friend in the Infirmary
    O' bonnie Aberdeen.

4 Her father bein' wi' her that nicht
    As far as we do hear
    He took them baith in owre the gig
    Nae danger bade them fear.

5 But when he cam to Tipperty
    He to the man did say
    Gang ye oot owre and walk a bit
    Or we win up the brae.

6 He asked the lassie's name
    Likewise where she did bide
    She said she cam frae Rora
    Three miles below Langside.

7 Ye winna gang there the nicht my love
    The road's too lang for you
    But ye'll gang on to Esselmont
    This nicht to lie wi' me.

8 The lassie when she heard o' this
    She then began to cry
    But Charlie, he held on the whip
    And onward fast did fly.

9 The beastie bein' sae terrified
    So clean's did lift its heels
    It hadna run owre mony yards
    Till aff cam baith the wheels.

10 Then Charlie tried to ravish her
    Whereon they both did lie
    A weaver fra Kinharachie
    Just chanced to come by.

11 And seein' the gig turned upsides doon
    Sae fast's it made him rin
    But Charlie clured the weaver's back
    Gude faith it was a sin.

12 In the hurry o' the weaver
    The lassie wan awa
    And doon the road to Tipperty
    She flew jist like a craw.

13 The weaver's work bein' very scarce
    And wages very low
    The weaver wisna at nae loss
    When Charlie let him go.

14 It's gien him five pounds
    Left him to sigh and moan
    Says Keep a'thing quaet unto yersel'
    And tell it unto none.

15 Willie Dalgairn is my name
    I winna seek to hide
    At Auchterlethen I do dwell
    On bonnie Ythanside.

GD 1266A. The music was collected by Greig in September 1906. Charlie Napier Gordon was born in 1811 and lived at Wallhead Esslemont (*Greig–Duncan*, vol. 6, p. 591). Esslemont is not far from the town of Ellon in Aberdeenshire. [I].

Editorial Note Tonic lowered from F to D.

clured – hit, thumped; *quaet* – quiet

41. Ki-ma-dearie

JOHN QUIRRIE

Frog-gie cam' to the mill door Ki-ma-dea-rie, ki-me. Sad-dled and brid-led and shod a-fore Ki-ma-dea-rie, ki-me. Ki-ma-dea-rie, kil-a-gee-rie, Ki-ma-dea-rie ki-me. Wi' my Rum strum bum-a-ree-dle Lul-la-bul-la rig-dum, Rig dum bo-mi-mee-rie ki-me.

1   Froggie cam' to the mill door
    Ki-ma-dearie, ki-me.
    Saddled and bridled and shod afore
    Ki-ma-dearie, ki-me.
    Ki-ma-dearie, kil-a-geerie,
    Ki-ma-dearie ki-me.
    Wi' my Rum strum bumareedle
    Lullabulla rigdum,
    Rig dum bomi-meerie ki-me.

2   When they were all at supper sat
    In cam the kittlin and the cat.

3   It's next cam in the sulky deuk
    And she plucket Froggie out o' the neuk.

4   Wouldna that mak a hale heart sair
    To see sic a company gathered wi' care.

5   And wadna that mak a hale heart crack
    To see sic a company a' gone to wrack.

GD 1669B. The music of this widely known children's song was collected by Greig in September 1906. The celebrations at the wedding of the frog and the mouse end in disaster when some of the guests eat up the others. [I/M].

Performance Note Greig gives the words 'Wi' my' in brackets without associated music, which suggests that these may have been spoken.

Editorial Note Tonic lowered from G to F; the semiquavers in bar 12 are editorial (Greig has a quaver rest); text lyric has 'Bullabulla' for 'Lullabulla' (1.8).

kittlin – kitten;   *deuk* – duck

42. The Plains of America

JOHN QUIRRIE

I'm a stran-ger in this coun-trie, From A-me-ri-ca I came; There is no-bo-dy knows me, nor can tell my name; But in this strange coun-try I'll re-main for a while, Far, a-far from my dar-ling, for mo-ny's the lang mile.

1   I'm a stranger in this countrie, from America I came;
    There is nobody knows me, nor can tell my name;
    But in this strange country I'll remain for a while,
    Far, afar from my darling, for mony's the lang mile.

2   Some says that I am rakish, some says that I am wild
    Some says that I am guilty, fair maids to beguile
    But I will prove them all liars if they'll go along with me
    To the plains of America my darling to see.

3   The sun that's in the firmament may give no more light
    And the stars in the elements may fall in one night
    The rocks may rend and the mountains may move
    Before that I prove false to the girlie I love.

4   The ship that's on the ocean may sail without sails
    And the smallest of fishes may turn to large whales
    In the middle of the ocean there may grow a myrtle tree
    Before that I prove false to the girl that loves me.

5   Give my kind love to Annie she lives on yon shore
    Likewise unto Nancy, she's the girl whom I adore
    Likewise unto Susan, she's my whole heart's delight
    I could roll her in my arms in a cauld winter's night.

6   Now this couple they've got married and away they've set sail
    May a' good maintain them with a fine pleasing gale
    And when they are landed they will dance and they'll sing
    On the plains of America a-serving their queen.

GD 1469A. The music was collected by Greig in September 1906. He noted: 'The hero of this song is a somewhat queer character. He disclaims being rakish, but from the list of flames to which he confesses one would at least take him to be a fairly miscellaneous lover. Then from the versions of the ditty which one now gets it is not easy saying where exactly his true darling is. In the original version no doubt the account which the hero gave of himself had been at least consistent, but subsequent singers have evidently mixed him up a bit. The popularity of the song would seem to be due in considerable measure to its excellent tune, which, as far as records show, varies much less than the words. The song is also well known in the North of England.' (*Buchan Observer*, 19 January 1909) [I/M].

Performance Note The word 'queen' (6.4) could be replaced by the rhyming word 'king', as in version J from Sam Davidson.

Editorial Note Tonic lowered from D to Bb; the change of time-signature in bar 13 is editorial.

43. It Fell Aboot a Lammas Time

JOHN QUIRRIE

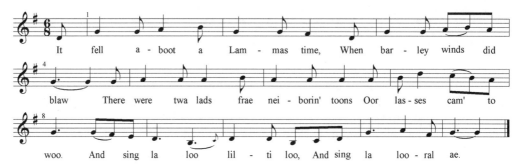

1   It fell aboot a Lammas time,
    When barley winds did blaw
    There were twa lads frae neiborin' toons
    Oor lasses cam' to woo.
    And sing la loo lilti loo,
    And sing la looral ae.

2   The lasses they sat at ae side o' the fire,
   And the lads they sat at the tither;
   And a' their news the hale lang nicht
   Was praisin' their auld mither.

3   One bragged aboot his horses
   And what he could do
   The other aboot smoothin' brass
   And teasin' tarry 'oo.

4   They hadna sitten very lang
   When words began to fail,
   So he craved her for a ribbon
   For to tie up Rosie's tail.

5   When nine o'clock began to strike
   Says he, I must away,
   For I've up yon Mullburn side to gang,
   My coulter for to lay.

6   Fare ye weel, my lassie,
   And I must haste away
   For we're a' gyaun to the dung the morn,
   And I'm afraid to yoke my cairt.

7   Oh gin ever ye come this way again,
   Or at my window reel,
   Be sure and hae your coulter weel laid
   And tempered up wi' steel.

GD 893A. The song was collected by Greig in 1906. There are two versions of it in the collection, the other being from James Greig. [I].

Editorial Note Tonic lowered from Bb to G; alternative note 10.2c; text lyric has 'was' for 'were' (1.3). The title is from the text lyric; the tune lyric has simply 'It Fell Aboot'. The title in the main collection is 'Twa Lads Frae Neiborin' Toons'.

tither – other;   *oo* – wool;   *craved* – asked;   *lay* – re-steel

Alexander Robb

1863–1940

Alexander Robb (left) and with pupils at New Deer School

Alexander, or Sandy, Robb was born on 14 February 1863 at Claystiler in the parish of Rathen to Alexander Robb, an agricultural labourer born in New Aberdour, and Anne Robb (née Davidson), born in Monquhitter.[1] Robb was one of Greig's most important informants, and he contributed two hundred and seventeen items to the collection beginning in March 1905. His mother also contributed songs to the collection, as did his sister, Miss Annie Robb, born *c.*1872. Greig gives an account of a visit to Annie Robb's home in Strichen in the *Buchan Observer*, 18 October 1910:

> Under the guidance of my good friend Mr Robb I lately visited the hospitable abode of Miss Robb, Strichen, where, after seeing the venerable pet seagull which is a curiosity unique of its kind, we had a very pleasant and profitable song-sederunt. From the singing of our hostess I made a number of records of tunes. . . . My store of words was

also much helped, and in particular I secured substantial parts of two old ballads never got elsewhere. I am hopeful that the members of the household may be able to dig from the depths of memory more of those valuable records of the old-time minstrelsy.

A visit that Alexander Robb paid to Greig at the Schoolhouse at Whitehill just after Christmas 1907 was mentioned in a letter that Greig sent to Lucy Broadwood, the English folk-song collector. Greig wrote very enthusiastically about him:

> Yesterday evening in came a folk-singer with whom I had made an assignation for the *previous* night. I am sure you will excuse me devoting the rest of the evening to a sederunt with him when I tell you that I bagged eighteen songs. He has been my best subject, his record running to *considerably* over a hundred songs, and I don't seem to have exhausted him by a long way. Further, he is only some forty-five years of age.[2]

James Madison Carpenter later made cylinder recordings of over one hundred and forty songs from Alexander and his sister Elizabeth or Lizzie Robb, born *c.*1864.[3]

At the time of the 1881 census Robb was working as a stonemason, but he is listed as a farm servant in 1899 when he married Georgina Coutts, a domestic servant, in the parish of Longside. He was working as a janitor at New Deer School when he was in contact with Greig and is still remembered by former pupils.[4] He died on 24 July 1940 in Aberdeen Royal Infirmary.[5]

We are fortunate to know a good deal about Robb's early life thanks to his manuscript, 'Memories of Mormondside'.[6] The manuscript takes the form of a small brown folder containing loose-leaf material along with a series of twenty-two notebooks. It opens with Robb reminiscing on his upbringing at Mormond Croft in Rathen parish and makes many references to the customs found in the countryside at the time.

Robb's father was a crofter with eighteen acres of land, and the manuscript describes how, when they ran short of animal fodder, whin ('fun') or gorse bushes were cut each week and then ground down.

> We cuttit a loadie ilka ook an' dreev't tae Upperton's fun-mull tae get them grun'. The mear hid tae be lowsed [unyoked] oot o' the cairt an' yokit tae the mull. I ca'd her . . . an' my fadder ful't the track an' cuttit aff a' the stowrie shanks [dusty stalks]. Syne we yokit the cairt again an' ful't wir funs, an' though we had a guid thumpin' load tae the mull, we hidna muckle buik [bulk] fan they war grun'.[7]

This activity also provided a context for learning songs, according to *Last Leaves*: 'Some of his memories were family tradition, but he got many songs and tunes while he was a boy in farm service from his employer, who used to sing them while working the whin-mill, turning the whins into cattle fodder'.[8]

Broadsides were another source for his songs, and he describes purchasing one at the market. This followed being hired for his first fee at 'Boggie Neuk':

> Doon the market I gaed tae see the fairlies [curiosities]. A mannie an' a wifie wis singin' an' I gaed in aboot an' bocht 'Sir Jeams the Rose' fae them. Ye see they saul' the broad

sheets yon time. Awa' I gaed haddin' my cheenge in my han' an' winnerin' fat I wad buy
aff o' a stan'. Ae mannie had a barra fu' o' horn speens an' ilka chiel wis buyin' fae him so
I thocht I wad need ane noo I wis fee'd.[9]

Greig noted the first verse and the tune of 'Sir James the Rose' from Robb (235M) but makes
no mention of Robb's source. Besides absorbing and transmitting a great many traditional
songs, Robb made up verses himself and would write to his friends in rhyming lines.[10]

Memories of Mormondside, chapter 1, p. 1

NOTES

1 Birth record 1863/235/18.
2 Letter dated 26–8 December 1907, Broadwood Collection (LEB/7/18), held in the Vaughan Williams Memorial Library, Cecil Sharp House, London.
3 These are located at The Library of Congress in Washington; see *The James Madison Carpenter Collection Online Catalogue* http://www.hrionline.ac.uk/carpenter
4 Census record 1881/225/7/15 and marriage record 1899/218/13. See entry on Robb in *Greig–Duncan*, vol. 8, p. 578 for some recollections from former pupils of the school.
5 Death record 1940/168–1/943.
6 Now held in Special Libraries and Archives in Historic Collections (MS 2129) at the University of Aberdeen.
7 Book 1, p. 5.
8 *Last Leaves*, p. 289.
9 Book 1, p. 20.
10 *Greig–Duncan*, vol. 8, p. 578.

44. There Was a Maid

ALEXANDER ROBB

There was a maid and she was fair,
At kirk or market aye to be seen;
And a' that this young maid langed for
Was a man to come to her bed at e'en.
Was a man to come to her bed at e'en.

GD 1335. The song was probably collected by Greig around October 1909. Robert Burns's song 'There was a lass and she was fair' was written for a traditional tune and it is likely that a version of this song – both words and tune – was his source. [Æ/Dor].
Editorial Note Tonic lowered from G to E.

45. The Laird o' Elfin

ALEXANDER ROBB

The Laird o' El - fin stands on yon hill - Ba ba ba lee - lie ba: And he blows his trum - pet loud and shrill, And the wind blows aye my plaid a - wa.

1   The Laird o' Elfin stands on yon hill –
Ba ba ba leelie ba:
And he blows his trumpet loud and shrill,
And the wind blows aye my plaid awa.

2 O gin I'd that horn in my kist
And then get wedded wi' him next.

3 But afore that I do that to thee
A weel-sewed sark ye maun sew to me.

4 And ye maun sew it needle-thread free
And a weel-sewed sark ye maun sew to me.

5 But afore that I do this to thee
I'll gie ye some wark to do to me.

6 I have a little wee acre o' lan'
That's atween the salt seas and the san'.

7 And ye maun ploo't wi your bugle horn
And ye maun saw't wi' Indian corn.

8 And ye maun cut it wi' your penknife
And bind it up just as your life.

9 And ye maun thrash't in your shee-sole
And ye maun riddle't in yonder moose hole.

10 And ye maun winny't in your nieves
And ye maun seck it in your gloves.

11 And ye maun stook it on the sea
And a dry sheaf ye maun bring to me.

12 Robin Redbreast and the wran
They'll bring me my corn hame.

13 And when ye have done a' this wark
Come ye to me and ye'll get your sark.

GD 329A. Child 2 *The Elfin Knight.* Robb's version of this supernatural ballad was acknowledged by
Greig in the *Buchan Observer,* 13 October 1908. Greig wrote: 'Mr A. Robb, New Deer, from whom
I have got at one time or another a very great number of tunes, is still adding to the list. Quite
lately I took records from his singing of "The Elfin Knight," "The carle cam' owre the craft," and
"Robin's Testament" – words as well as tunes. I have to thank Mr Robb very much.' James
Madison Carpenter also recorded this ballad from Robb (cylinder 134) and notes that Robb
learned it from William Booth, Rathen, '55 years ago'. Since this version was recorded in 1929,
Robb would have learned it *c*.1874. Carpenter's typescript (pp. 04808–9) has thirteen stanzas as
here, although they are in a slightly different order, and Carpenter's music transcription of the
first stanza (p. 08198) is very similar to the above and is in the same key. [Æ/Dor].
Editorial Note Alternative note 'd' for anacrusis.

riddle – sieve; *winny* – winnow; *nieves* – fists; *seck* – sack; *stook it* – set it up in sheaves;
wran – wren

46. The Maskin Rung

ALEXANDER ROBB

There was a fair maid went doon thro' a park, To milk her dad-dy's kye O; And her ain true lov-ie he heard o' that, And he fol-lowed her spee-di-ly O.

1 There was a fair maid went doon thro'
             a park,
To milk her daddy's kye O;
And her ain true lovie he heard o' that,
And he followed her speedily O.

2 Hold off your hands, young man, she said,
For fear that we be seen O;
And gin ye be willin' it's I'm content
That we may meet again O.

3 Oh, where shall we meet, or into
             what place,
Oh, when shall we meet again O?
In yonder green woods by yon willow tree,
And I pray you don't tell it to nane O.

4 She's pitten her milk-pail on her heid,
And she gaed singin' hame O;
And she has min't a' that lang
             simmer nicht,
Foo she wad beguile this young man O.

5 Noo she's gane in to an auld widow wife,
And borrowed a suit o' clothes O,
And she's buckled them on o' the
             maskin' rung,
And awa' to the woodie she goes O.

6 Her hands was made o' the willow wand,
And her fingers o' the apple tree O;
And on every finger she placed a gold ring,
To shine in this young man's e'e O.

7 Her ain true lovie cam' thro' the wood,
He whistled and he sang O,

Says, A wile false maid's been my
             true love,
But she hasna trysted me wrang O.

8 He lifted up her petticoats
And then her smock so sma' O,
But naething was there but the
             maskin' rung,
And his maid she was away O.

9 This nearly pat this young man mad,
To get sick a taunt and a mock O;
And he's embraced the maskin' rung,
And the auld wife's petticoats O.

10 A wile false maid's been my true love,
Sae false as she's been to me O;
But if I had her in this bonnie green wood,
And she wadna gae maiden free O.

11 The maid bein' in a bush near-by,
She heard him make his moan O;
Says, Here I am in this bonnie green wood,
But I will go maiden home O.

12 Out it spoke the old woman,
Who livèd there near-by O,
Says, What's your business wi' my clothes
That I hang oot to dry O?

13 This was made up in Lincolnshire,
In Scotland to be sung O;
And a' ye young men that hasna
             got marriet,
Beware o' the maskin' rung O.

80

GD 323Bb The music was collected by Greig in July 1908 who noted that Robb's tune is that of 'Lord Thomas of Winchbury'. [Pent].

Editorial Note Lines 8.1–2 absent in the original; replaced by lines adapted from the chapbook version in *Andrew Crawfurd's Collection of Ballads and Songs*, vol. 2 (Emily Lyle, ed.; Edinburgh: The Scottish Text Society, 1996, p. 192), 'The Masking Rung', lines 8.5–6. 'That' (12.4) was given in the original source (*Buchan Observer*, 16 May 1911). 5.1–2 in the tune was originally a crotchet, and 6.5–6 was originally a quaver.

maskin' rung – rod for stirring malt in the mash-tub (used for brewing)

47. The Navvy

ALEXANDER ROBB

The gaf-fer gave to her a ring Which cost him guin-eas three Says, 'Tak ye that my bon-nie lass And be-ware of the nav-vy.' Dur-il-ing, dur-il-ad-die, Dur-il-ing, dur-il-ee.

1   The gaffer gave to her a ring
    Which cost him guineas three
    Says, 'Tak ye that my bonnie lass
    And beware of the navvy.'
    Duril-ing, duril-addie,
    Duril-ing, duril-ee.

2   The navvy gave to her a ring
    Which cost him ae bawbee
    Says 'Tak ye that my bonnie lass
    And lie this nicht wi' me.'

3   The navvy gave to her a gown
    Which cost him shillins nine
    Says 'Tak ye that my bonnie lass
    And aye be kind to mine.'

4   But now my baby it is born
    And sittin on my knee
    And I maun sit and sing to it
    And my navvy's on the spree.

5   But I'll get ribbons to my hair
    And buckles to my cuff
    And I'll gang to see my navvy lad
    He works wi' Donal Duff.

6   Noo my navvy he's come back
    And he's come back in time
    And he's juist as good a navvy lad
    As ever tramped the line.

7   And now my navvy he's come back
    And he has married me.
    And he's juist as good a navvy lad
    As ever was on the spree.

GD 977Ab Greig collected this song in June 1906. There are two versions of the tune, the first having no chorus. The note to Margaret Gillespie's version (B) states that the song was often heard in Savoch district when the Buchan railway was made and that it was introduced by the men building the railways. [Pent].

Editorial Note Tonic lowered from G to F; the semiquavers at 6.4–5 were originally a quaver.

48. The Plooman

ALEXANDER ROBB

It's oh, oh, oh, it's bon-nie oh, To hear them cry Hup, hie, and wo, And
make their hor-ses straight to go, What's bet-ter than a ploo-man? The
ma-son he speaks oot 'O fie' Says 'I can build a cas-tle high The
win' and rain both to de-fy Far bet-ter than a ploo-man.'

(refrain) *It's oh, oh, oh, it's bonnie oh,*
To hear them cry Hup, hie, and wo,
And make their horses straight to go,
What's better than a plooman?

1 The mason he speaks oot 'O fie'
Says 'I can build a castle high
The win' and rain both to defy
Far better than a plooman.'

2 O mason dinna crack sae croose,
We own that ye can build a hoose
But fae the king doon to the moose
Depends upon the plooman.

3 The miller he speaks oot fu' weel
Says I do grind the corn for meal
Says I do grind the corn for meal
For to maintain the plooman.

4 O miller ye should haud yer jaw
Go home and look to your call wa'
There widna muckle dust doon fa'
If it werena for the plooman.

GD 447A. The song was collected by Greig in June 1906. It had been sung in Crimond market when
Robb's mother, born in 1822, was a young girl. The text was said to have been written by John
Anderson, farmer, Upper Boyndlie, and Greig notes that, according to the date given by Robb, it is
not likely to have been written later than 1830 (*Buchan Observer*, 21 February 1911). [M, −4].
Editorial Note Music for refrain only given in original with a note that the text is 'to same music'; text
lyric in refrain line 2 has 'Keep back and Wo' for 'Hup, hie, and wo'; text lyric used for verse 1.

hup, hie, and wo – turn right, turn left and stop;   *croose* – confidently;   *haud yer jaw* – keep quiet;
call (caul) – mill-dam

49. Fair Rosie Ann

ALEXANDER ROBB

Fair Ro - sie Ann sat on her cas - tle wa', Sewing at her sa - tin seam, And

she's a - wa to good green - wood Some nuts for to pu' and bring hame.

1   Fair Rosie Ann sat on her castle wa',
    Sewing at her satin seam,
    And she's awa' to good greenwood
    Some nuts for to pu' and bring hame.

2   She hadna pulled a nut, a nut,
    A nut but barely three,
    When a young man entered into the wood,
    To ruin her fair bodie.

3   Oh cam' ye here to pull my nuts?
    Or cam' ye here to be my slave?
    Or cam' ye here, kind sir, she said,
    For to put me in my grave?

4   I came nae here to pull your nuts,
    Nor I came nae to be your slave,
    But your mantle or your maidenhead
    Some o' them I maun have.

5   It's If ye tak' my mantle, she said,
    My mother can caird and spin,
    But if ye tak' my maidenhead
    There's nae pardon for the sin.

6   Since ye've gotten your wills o' me,
    Your wills o' me ye've ta'en,
    Would you be so good, kind sir, she said,
    As tell to me your name?

7   My name, my name, fair maid, he said,
    My name I'll never deny,
    For I'm Lord Barnet's ae only son,
    And he never had another but I.

8   If ye be Lord Barnet's ae only son,
    There's little between thee and me,
    For I'm Lord Barnet's ae daughter,
    And he never had another but me.

9   Heel weel, heel weel, my sister dear,
    Heel weel, heel weel, on me;
    For I wish my ship she had been wrecked,
    And sunk to the bottom of the sea.

10 Fair Rosie Ann sat in good greenwoods,
    Lamentin' for what she had done,
    When her mother entered into the wood,
    Says, What ails thee, fair Rosie Ann?

11 As I cam' in by yon high high hill,
    And in by yon high castle wa',
    Oh heavy, heavy was the stone
    That on my foot did fa'.

12 O fair Rosie Ann, dry up your tears,
    And come awa hame wi' me,
    For your brother John is new come home,
    Is new come home from sea.

13 Haud your tongue, dear mother, she said,
    Oh haud your tongue frae me;
    For he may be made welcome by a'
                       the hoose,
    But he'll never be made welcome by me.

GD 1395A. Child 52 *The King's Dochter Lady Jean*. The ballad was collected by Greig in March 1909. It was also recorded later by James Madison Carpenter who noted that Robb had learned it from William Booth, a farm servant. Booth was also the source for Robb's 'The Laird o' Elfin' (no. 44). [I].
Editorial Note Tonic lowered from D to C.

heel – conceal

50. The Guid Coat o' Blue

ALEXANDER ROBB

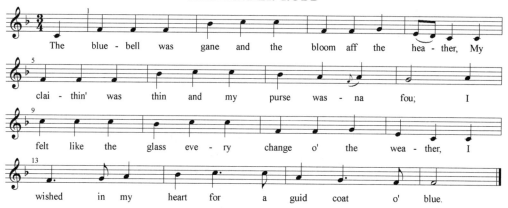

The blue-bell was gane and the bloom aff the hea-ther, My clai-thin' was thin and my purse was-na fou; I felt like the glass eve-ry change o' the wea-ther, I wished in my heart for a guid coat o' blue.

1 The bluebell was gane and the bloom aff the heather,
   My claithin' was thin and my purse wasna fou;
   I felt like the glass every change o' the weather,
   I wished in my heart for a guid coat o' blue.

2 Then fair fa' my wifie sae thrifty and kindly;
   As sune as she kent o' the wind piercin' thro',
   She's gane to the wabster and fittet me finely
   And laid roon my shoulders a guid coat o' blue.

3 Then fair fa' the tailor, our ain honest Sandy;
   He's gien me braw room in't, he ever cuts true
   I'm nae clippet aff like a daft idle dandy
   But happit and tosh in my guid coat o' blue.

4 Noo daft dreary winter may rant, rage and rustle,
   And frae her hail graneries wild tempests brew.
   I care na for her nor her snaw blasts a whistle
   For weel lined wi' plaidin's my guid coat o' blue.

5 Nae mair will I dread the cauld blasts o' Ben Ledi
   Or sigh as the ice covered Ochils I view
   I may hae been cauld but for ance I am tidy
   Sae gausy and tosh in my guid coat o' blue.

6 But weary fa' pride, for it's never contentit
   Ilk ane maun be dressed noo in fine Spanish woo'
   The warld was better at first when I kent it
   Wi' lang plaidin hose and a guid coat o' blue.

7 Lea's me on the Scotchmen, mine ain honest sailor
   Lea's me on auld fashions, I lauch at the new.
   A fig for the fellow wha's made by the tailor!
   Gie me sense and worth and a guid coat o' blue.

8   We fret ower the taxes, and taxes we've mony
    The meal is while's dear and we've ill getting thro'
    But daft silly pride is the warst tax o' ony
    They'll no be content wi' a guid coat o' blue.

GD 660A. The music for this song was collected by Greig in July 1906. [I].
Editorial Note Text lyric has 'a gless ilka' for 'the glass every' (1.3), 'And' for 'I' and 'I'd' in place of 'for' (1.4).

glass – barometer;   *fair fa'* – blessings on;   *wabster* – weaver;   *tosh* – smart;   *gausy* – handsome;
        lea's me on – I favour

51. The Miller o' Straloch

ALEXANDER ROBB

1   I am a miller to my trade, I'm miller at Straloch;
    I'm a curious cankered carlie, my name is Willie Stroth.
    I can play upon the bagpipes wi' muckle mirth and glee,
    For I care for nobody no not I and nobody cares for me.

2   I'm engaged with Dr Ramsay, he's laird owre all our land
    And when he does give call to me I am at his command.
    The only thing that I'm subject to is a pinch of the broon rappee
    And when I do fa' short o' that I'm no good company.

3   My mill's got new machinery, she's something strange to me
    She's of a new construction my eyes did ever see.
    But if I had three roons o' her and a pinch o' the broon rapee
    I care for nobody no not I and nobody cares for me.

GD 452A. The music was noted by Greig in June 1906. He wrote in the *Buchan Observer*, 8 September
    1908: 'Straloch is a property to the north-west of Newmachar Station. The "owreword" [refrain] of
    the song is evidently borrowed from the "Miller of Dee." The tune is an exceedingly common one.
    It is sung to "Drumdelgie" and quite a number of other dities.' [I].
Editorial Note Tonic lowered from Bb to A; alternative note in anacrusis 'e'; text lyric has 'And I' in
    place of 'For I' (1.4).

broon rappee – coarse snuff

52. Robin's Testament

ALEXANDER ROBB

Ye will tak' my twa bon - nie e'en, That eest to blink sae bricht; Ye'll
gie them to yon shew-ster lass, To save her o' can-dle licht. Sing-in
Fee-dle ee-dle in-kin Tin-kin tin-kin Fee-dle ee-dle in-kin tee - rie
Hed - rie ted - rie hed - rie tang Ro - bin sick and wea - rie.

1 Ye will tak' my twa bonnie e'en,
   That eest to blink sae bricht;
   Ye'll gie them to yon shewster lass,
   To save her o' candle licht.
   Singin Feedle eedle inkin Tinkin tinkin
   Feedle eedle inkin teerie
   Hedrie tedrie hedrie tang
   Robin sick and wearie.

2 Ye will tak' my bonnie nib,
   That eest to pickle the corn;
   And gie it to yon little herd,
   To be a tootin' horn.

3 And ye will tak' my twa bonnie wings
   That eest to spread sae wide;
   And ye'll hae them to St. Mary's Kirk,
   To cover her sunny side.

4 And ye will tak' my twa bonnie legs,
   That eest to walk sae trig;
   And ye'll hae them to yon burn bank
   For pillars to the brig.

5 And ye will tak' my bonnie tail
   That eest to cock so fine;
   And ye'll gie it to yon bonnie bride,
   To be her weddin' goon.

6 Ye will tak' your ten owsen,
   And trail me to the hill;
   And pairt sma' and sair a'
   That hungry may get their fill.

7 When Robin had his testament made,
   And had nae mair to say,
   By cam' a greedy gled,
   And snappit him away.

GD 646A. The words and music were acknowledged by Greig in the *Buchan Observer*, 13 October 1908 (see note at no. 45 'The Laird o' Elfin'). [Æ/Dor].

Editorial Note The anacrusis has been bracketed here as it is not included in the first verse; alternative notes 1.3g (quaver), 1.4bflat (dotted crotchet), 3.1bflat. The rhythm has been modified to fit the lyric in the following places: 2.1–3 originally a quaver and two dotted crotchets, 3.3 originally a semi-quaver then a dotted quaver, 7.2–3 originally a crotchet. Greig gives verse 2 with the tune.

eest – used; *shewster* – seamstress; *nib* – beak; *pickle* – peck; *trail* – drag; *gled* – hawk

53. The Harvest Shearin'

ALEXANDER ROBB

Fare-well, love, for I maun leave you, Sor-ry am I nae doots I'll grieve you,

Boun-ding where the bil-lows roar-ing Lea-ving my las - sie all for-lorn.

Fare-well, love, for I maun leave you, Fare ye weel, I maun a - wa'.

1   Farewell, love, for I maun leave you,
Sorry am I nae doots I'll grieve you,
Bounding where the billows roaring
Leaving my lassie all forlorn.
Farewell, love, for I maun leave you,
Fare ye weel, I maun awa'.

2   Don't you hear the colonel crying,
Run, brave boys, keep colours flying,
Colours flying, drums a-beating,
Run, brave boys, they're still repeating.

3   No more we'll go to the harvest shearin'
Hearing the bandsters loudly cheering,
When we was young, lovey, we
          was cheerie,
I was so fond of you, my dearie.

4   No more we'll go to yonder Lomon',
Walking in a summer gloamin',
Underneath the hawthorn bushes,
Hearing the blackbirds and the thrushes.

5   Farewell, father, and farewell, mother,
Farewell, sister, I have no brother,
Farewell, comrades, kind and cheerie,
Again farewell to you, my dearie.

GD 101A. The music was collected by Greig in June 1906. There are four versions of the song in the collection. The word 'Lomon" (4.1) is elsewhere given as 'loaning' (grassy path). [M].

bandsters – sheaf-binders

54. Jock Sheep

ALEXANDER ROBB

1   There was a knicht and a lady bricht
Set trysts amang the broom
The ane to come at twelve o'clock,
And the ither true at noon.
Leatherum thee thou and a'
Madam aye wi' you,
And the seal o' me be abrachee,
Fair maiden I'm for you.

2 He gaed on and she gaed on,
Till they cam' to some coles o' hay,
He said, My dear this is a pleasant place
To spend away the day.

3 He took her by the middle sma',
An' was goin' to lay her doon,
Spare me, spare me, young man, said she,
For rufflin' o' my goon.

4 Spare me, spare me, young man, said she,
For the rufflin' o' my goon,
For it cost my own good father
More than twenty poun.

5 Don't you see yon tower, said she,
Oot owre yon castle wa',
It's there you'll hae your wills o' me,
Amang the sheets sae sma.

6 But when she came to her father's gates,
So merrily she jumpit in,
Says, Stan' ye there thereoot, Jock Sheep,
An' fustle on your thoom.

7 Fustle on your thoom, Jock Sheep,
An' fustle on your thoom,
An' stan' ye there thereoot, Jock Sheep,
An' fustle to the win'.

8 Ye're like a bull my father had,
He gaed amo' the kye,
If a' the bulls had been like him,
The kye wad seen gang dry.

9 Ye're like a cock my father had,
He wore a dooble kaim,
He clapt his wings but never crew,
Young man, ye are like him.

10 Ye're like a ram my father had,
Lay tethered on the loan,
He hang his heid abeen the yowe,
But never ventured on.

11 Ye're like a ram my father had,
He gaed amo' the flock,
He pu'ed the rashes amon' his feet,
And held them like a gock.

88

12 He turned him richt and roon aboot,
   And swore he had gotten the scorn,
   But he wad be aboot wi' her
   At that time o' the morn.

13 He's pitten a mantle aboot his heid,
   A cod upon his wame,
   An' he's awa to good greenwoods
   Like a woman a-travailin'.

14 Then word's gane up and word's gane doon,
   And word's gane roon the toon,
   That there was a woman in good greenwood,
   And she was a-travailin'.

15 This lady's ta'en a mantle aboot her heid,
   Likewise a bottle o' wine,
   And she's awa to good greenwoods
   To see the woman a-travailin'.

16 But when she went to good greenwoods,
   She saw naebody there,
   But the knicht upon his milkwhite steed,
   Kaimin' doon his yellow hair.

GD 302A. The music was collected by Greig in May 1906 and the words in March 1909. This ballad is not well-known. [Pent].

Editorial Note Tonic lowered from D to C. The spelling 'maiden' (1.8) is from the text lyric; the tune lyric has 'maidem'. The following fragment comes after verse 16 in the main collection: 'Noo I've got the wills o' thee,/An' cry lassie, cry'. The suitor, who is baffled in the first part of the song, which is very similar to GD 301 'The Shepherd's Son' (Child 112 *The Baffled Knight*), turns the tables in the second half.

coles o' hay – hay-cocks; *sma* (5.4) – finely textured; *fustle* (whistle) *on your thoom* – take to a useless activity to console yourself after a rebuff; *kaim* – comb; *rashes* – rushes; *gotten the scorn* – been rejected scornfully; *be about* – get even; *gock* – fool; *cod* – pillow; *wame* – stomach

55. Dance to Your Daddy

ALEXANDER ROBB

Dance to your dad-die, My bon-nie lad-die, Dance to your dad-dy, My bon-nie doo.

1 Dance to your daddie,
  My bonnie laddie,
  Dance to your daddy,
  My bonnie doo.

2 Ye'll get a fishie,
  My bonnie missie,
  Ye'll get a fishie,
  When the boats comes in.

GD 1562. Greig collected this song *c*.1909. [Pent].
Editorial Note Tonic lowered from F to D.

doo – dove or dear

56. Daffin Doon

ALEXANDER ROBB

The tai-lor cam' to cloot oor claes, Sic a fine fel-low, He's fulled the hoose richt fu' o' flaes,

Daf-fin doon, daf-fin doon, He's fulled the hoose richt fu' o' flaes, Daf-fin doon dil-ly.

1 The tailor cam' to cloot oor claes,
   Sic a fine fellow,
   He's fulled the hoose richt fu' o' flaes,
   Daffin doon, daffin doon,
   He's fulled the hoose richt fu' o' flaes,
   Daffin doon dilly.

2 The maiden sits ayont the fire,
   Sic a daft hizzy;
   She is the tailor's heart's desire,
   Daffin doon, daffin doon,
   She is the tailor's heart's desire
   Daffin doon dilly.

3 Soon the maiden fell asleep,
   Daffin doon dilly;
   The tailor over her did creep,
   Daffin doon, etc.

4 The maiden waukened in a fricht,
   Daffin doon, daffin doon;
   She thocht her maidenhead had ta'en
                              the flicht,
   Daffin doon, etc.

5 She lookit oot, she lookit in,
   Daffin doon, daffin doon;

   Ay, and in aneath the clockin' hen,
   Daffin doon, etc.

6 She lookit up, sae did she doon,
   Daffin doon, daffin doon;
   Ay, and roon aboot the toon,
   Daffin doon, etc.

7 She lookit in the owsen's sta',
   Daffin doon, daffin doon;
   Ay, and a' the moose-holes in the wa',
   Daffin doon, etc.

8 She's made the tailor pay a fine,
   Daffin doon, daffin doon;
   Or else gie her back her maidenhead again,
   Daffin doon, etc.

9 What wye can I gie ye it again,
   Ye mad, daft hizzy?
   Oh, jist the wye that it was ta'en,
   Daffin doon, etc.

10 He's laid her heid where her feet was afore,
   Daffin doon, daffin doon;
   He's gien her't owre, and owre, and owre,
   Daffin doon, etc.

GD 1438A. Greig noted the music for this song in June 1909. There is only one other version of it in the
   collection, from Margaret Gillespie. [M].
Editorial Note Text lyric has 'flaichs' for 'flaes' (1.3 and 1.5).

daffin – courting;   *cloot* – patch;   *flaes* – fleas;   *clockin' hen* – broody hen

57. Fair Isabel

ALEXANDER ROBB

In fair Lon-don ci-ty lived a ma-son to trade, He had to his daugh-ter a beau-ti-ful maid, The fair-est in face but the fal-sest in heart That e-ver proved love in our neigh-bou-ring part.

1   In fair London city lived a mason to trade,
    He had to his daughter a beautiful maid,
    The fairest in face but the falsest in heart
    That ever proved love in our neighbouring part.

2   While two or three ladies she did wait upon,
    And likewise her mistress she did her adorn,
    And likewise her mistress she did her adore,
    And the finest of clothing upon her she wore.

3   It fell on a day as it happened to be
    That their own steward sought fair Isabel's love,
    But she said I winna mairry ye nor I winna be your wife
    And I swear I'll never mairry ye all the days of my life.

4   But that wouldna satisfy his longing design,
    He was pleased to entreat her with abundance of wine,
    With as much wine as did put her to sleep
    Some time in the night to her bed he did creep.

5   For two or three hours in his arms she did remain
    Until she received her right senses again
    She went from his airms in a passion she flew
    Says, Am I ordained to be ruined by you?

6   But when the time of her appointed drew near
    He said unto her, We'll wed now, my dear,
    But she said, I am no wi' bairn and I winna be your wife
    And I swear I'll never marry ye all the days of my life.

7   So he made a net and he fastened it well,
    Upon the draw-well and he fastened it sure,
    Upon the draw-well and he fastened it sure,
    For fear she should murder her sweet baby there.

8   So it fell on a night as it happened to be
    A light in his bonnie lovie's window he did spy,
    He stood a while to listen while the window she drew
    And something in her apron in the draw-well she threw.

9   So he drew the net caught the bairnie alive,
    And how to do with it he soon did contrive,
    And how to do with it put the bairnie to a nurse
    Which made him pay money just out of his purse.

10 Oh little did fair Isabel's mistress know
    The pain and the anguish she did undergo,
    But in two or three weeks she grew healthy and well
    But still he bore kindness to his bonnie Isabel.

11 It fell on a day as it happened to be
    The child stood a-prattling by its own mother's knee,
    She opened her mouth and she said with amaze,
    Such a beautiful bairnie I saw never a' my days.

12 It fell on a day as they walked in the fields
    He said unto her, Cheer up and be glad,
    Cheer up and be glad for yon bairnie's your own,
    And your innocent murder shall never be known.

13 Oh nothing she spake, oh nothing at all,
    But she went to the house where the bairnie did dwell,
    She went to the house, called the nurse to the door,
    And she killed the bonnie bairnie, left it lying on the floor.

14 So up she was taken and suffered likewise,
    Made the tears like fountains run down from his eyes
    For he loved the mother well, and the bairnie for her sake,
    And now his poor heart is just ready to break.

GD 196A. This song was collected by Greig in September 1907. There are only two versions of it in the collection, version B being from Robb's sister, Miss Annie Robb, and consisting of a tune only. The theme of child murder is found elsewhere in the Scots song corpus, e.g. 'The Cruel Mother' (GD 193, Child 20). [Dor/M].

Editorial Note Tonic lowered from D to C. The title given by Annie Robb of 'Fair Isabel' is used here in preference to the title given with Alexander Robb's version which consists of the opening words: 'In Fair London City'.

suffered – suffered death, was executed

58. There Was a Tree

ALEXANDER ROBB

1 In yon bog there was a tree;
    Eh sic a tree, oh sic a tree;
    And the tree in the bog,
    And the burn rins by yon valley O.

2 And on that tree there was a branch
    Eh sic a branch, oh sic a branch;
    And the branch on the tree,
    And the tree in the bog,
    And the burn rins by yon valley O.

3 And on that branch there was a nest
    Eh sic a nest, oh sic a nest;
    And the nest on the branch,
    And the branch on the tree,
    And the tree in the bog,
    And the burn rins by yon valley O.

4 On yon nest there was a bird –
    Eh sic a bird, oh sic a bird;
    And the bird on the nest,
    And the nest on the branch,
    And the branch on the tree,
    And the tree in the bog,
    And the burn rins by yon valley O.

5 But noo the bird has flown awa
    Eh flown awa, oh flown awa;
    And the bird on the nest,
    And the nest on the branch,
    And the branch on the tree,
    And the tree in the bog,
    And oh, it was a bonnie bog,
    And a bonnie bog for a' that.

GD 1668B. The music was probably noted by Greig around October 1909. Greig mentions, 'Other way with "hill" for "bog" ' and the A version from Mrs Greig received by Duncan has 'in the hill there was a tree'. Mrs Greig knew that the bird flew away at the end but her version lacks the ending. It does, however, include two additions to the sequence: a verse beginning 'an' in the nest there was an egg' after verse 3, and one beginning 'and on the bird there grew a feather' after verse 4. [I].

Performance Note The music of this cumulative song shows verses 1 and 4 fully written out, and gives part of verse 5 showing the variation at the ending.

Editorial Note Greig began by writing the song in 4/4 but four bars later changed to 2/4, and the latter has been used throughout here; alternative note 22.5g. Verses 2 and 3, and 5.2–5, are editorial but follow the general pattern of the song.

59. O Poor Man the Miller

ALEXANDER ROBB

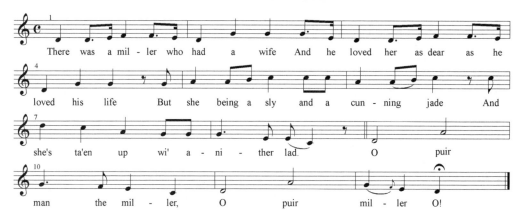

There was a mil-ler who had a wife And he loved her as dear as he loved his life But she being a sly and a cun-ning jade And she's ta'en up wi' a-ni-ther lad. O puir man the mil-ler, O puir mil-ler O!

1   There was a miller who had a wife
And he loved her as dear as he loved his life
But she being a sly and a cunning jade
And she's ta'en up wi' anither lad.
O puir man the miller,
O puir miller O!

2   It fell aboot a Whitsunday
When the miller had his rent to pay,
And he sat up to work his mill,
For the millin' trade was a' his skill.

3   At last he got his mailer made,
He lockit the door, gaed awa' to his bed,
And in at the window he did creep
For his wife he thocht was fast asleep.

4   But when she kent the miller was there,
She wrang her hands and tore her hair,
He said, 'My dear what is the matter?'
'It's I maun die if I getna better.'

5   The miller bein' in a stan',
He took the first cam' to his han',
Says 'My wife is wi' a colic seized
And she thinks a drap o' gin will eas't.'

6   He put his hand to his pocket to pay
                the dram,
A store o' gold cam' first to his han',
Which put the miller in surprise,
And made him on his trousers gaze.

7   In the next pocket he also found
A silver watch and fifty pound,
Which put the miller in surprise,
And then he said, 'O damn their eyes!'

8   The miller he came home again
To gie his wife a hearty dram,
Says 'Come tell to me my heart's delight
Wha was wi' you a' the last night.'

9   'Oh,' says she, 'I can safely tell,
There was naebody here except yersel',
And the spark that was in in the afternoon
And afore night and ye saw him gone.'

10   'Oh,' says the miller, 'ye are a leear,
Or than why came these trousers here?
For this is Spark's as that ye know
And after him ye'll tramp and go.'

11   The miller he's pitten awa' his wife
And coonted his siller baith sma' and great
And she made mair that nicht in her bed
Than ever he did at the mullin' trade.

94

GD 1459A. The music was collected by Greig in July 1907 and the words in May 1908. Robb learned the song from an old man when he was a child. [Dor].

Editorial Note Tonic lowered from E to D; the quavers at 5.3, 5.6 and 7.4 are editorial and were added to accommodate the text. The tune lyric, which Greig gives for verse 7, has 'pounds' for 'pound' (7.2) and 'set' for 'put' (7.3).

got his mailer (melder) *made* – completed the grinding of one customer's load of corn;
  spark – dandified young man

60. A Man Took in His Bed

ALEXANDER ROBB

A man took in his bed and lay, And a' was for a bon-nie may, And he swore he would be dead or day If she did-na lie be-yond him.

1 A man took in his bed and lay,
   And a' was for a bonnie may,
   And he swore he would be dead or day
   If she didna lie beyond him.

2 Young man, she said, ye needna doot,
   It's neither in and neither oot
   Sae near your bonnie back I would creep
   Gin I thocht it was to ease you.

3 He's ta'en her in his airms twa,
   Laid her atween him and the wa'
   And he's gi'en to her a kiss or twa,
   Says, Maid ye lie beyond me.

4 When he had got what he long socht
   And this fair maid to ruin brocht
   He turned about and changed his thocht
   And said, Maid I never loved you.

5 Oh don't you see yon bonnie hoose,
   The maid lives yonder that I'm to choose,
   The maid lives yonder that I'm to choose,
   For I swear I never loved you.

6 Don't you see yon castle in yon wood,
   The maid lives yonder that I'm to wed,
   The maid lives yonder that I'm to wed,
   For, maid, I never loved you.

7 I know the maid of whom you speak,
   The blood is scattered in her cheek

   But I dinna value your love a leek
   Nae mair nor ye dee mine, man.

8 For I may fight and no be slain,
   I may be kissed and no wi' bairn,
   For I'm nae the first that's gotten the scorn
   So tak' ye the wings and flee, man.

9 My father is a wealthy man,
   I've gotten gold and I'm gettin' lan',
   Gin I hae gold I can want a man, –
   So tak' ye the wings and flee man.

10 And if I bear a bairn to thee,
    I'll nurse it tenderly on my knee,
    I'll do it no harm supposin' ye've done me,
    And the gallows game for you, man.

11 But I hae ha's and I hae boors,
    And they are a' mine, but they'll never
                                be yours,
    They are a' mine, but they'll never
                                be yours,
    For, maid, I never loved ye.

12 Your ha's and boors swipe ye them clean,
    Wi' your flatterin' tongue leave me alane,
    And ye can gang to the Isle o' Man,
    For I can live and want ye, –
    And ye can gang to the Isle o' Man,
    For I'm better far withoot ye.

GD 1482. The music was collected by Greig in September 1907. [M].

Performance Note Use bars 5–8 for lines 12.5–6.

boors – bowers

Eliza Clark

c.1849–1934

When Greig recorded songs from Mrs Eliza (or Elizabeth) Clark at the farm of Aucheoch in 1905–6 she was about fifty-five years of age. Born c.1849 in Longside Parish, she was the daughter of John Greig, a nightwatchman, and Elizabeth Greig (née Finnie). Greig was clearly impressed with her musical abilities, commenting on her in a letter to Duncan (28 November 1914): 'Mrs Clark . . . farmer's wife near Brucklay station. Elderly, one of the best singers I have had.' Mary Ann Crichton noted similarly, and offers further information on her:

> As far as I can gather Mrs Clark was a great singer. She had been in service, became housekeeper to Mr Clark, got married – but she had been no saint. She married a second time – a good for nothing – Mr Aitken and then went to Edinburgh to live. . . . She had got her songs from the people round about the district.[1]

The 1891 census places Eliza and her husband James, a farmer born in New Deer, at Aucheoch, Brucklay, and the couple were living at the same address in 1901.[2] They married on 11 December 1890 at Aucheoch, and her occupation then was given as domestic servant.[3] Since they both had the same address at this time, it seems very likely that Eliza worked as a servant to James as Crichton suggests.[4] The records indicate that the couple had no children. At some point after she was in contact with Greig, Eliza married William Aitken, a general labourer, and moved to the town of Musselburgh outside Edinburgh. She died, aged eighty-five, on 13 September 1934 in Musselburgh.[5]

Mrs Clark gave Greig twenty-seven songs. Her repertoire includes five 'A' versions and three songs for which she is the only source. Most of the tunes are dated November 1905 and December 1905. In the case of 307 'The Foundling Baby' D, we have two similar tunes, collected in each of these months. (See illustration shown on the facing page.)

In Argo 10 (pp. 1–21) we have the results of a collecting session with Mrs Clark in April 1906, which most likely took place in her home. It offers us some sense of the sequence of events during the visit. She began by singing 1517 'Adieu to Bogieside' A, then followed with 168 'The Bailiff's Daughter of Islington' C. She quite possibly needed a break after singing the fourteen verses of the latter, and Greig seems to have taken the opportunity to ask about her sources. He noted that Eliza had learned the song she had just sung, and also 173 'The Dublin Heiress' A and 542 'The Happy Days of Youth' A, 'From Watt of Greenburn of Tyrie when a girl – oldish man.' This would likely have been the John Watt who was living at the farmhouse at Greenburn in the parish of Tyrie in 1891 and had been born in Fyvie c.1826.[6] Another note Greig made on the same page indicates that, when she was aged twenty, Eliza learned ' "Foundling Babe" etc.' at Cabra from John Rolly 'very old, 80'. Cabra here probably refers to the area north-west of Fetterangus, and there was a John Rollo, a retired farmer

307 'The Foundling Baby' D, versions a and b

aged eighty, living in Strichen in 1881, who may be the person referred to.[7] The singing then began again with 946 'The Irish Girl' B. At the foot of this page (p. 12) there is the tune of the chorus of the song as given by Arthur Barron. Barron was Greig's son-in-law, who farmed at Mains of Whitehill near the schoolhouse and sometimes accompanied Greig on his collecting trips. Possibly he sang the chorus to jog Mrs Clark's memory of the tune, as her version of it appears on the following page (both tunes are given in the main collection – 946B and C). The next songs to be sung were 603 'Nancy Whisky' F, 225 'The Beggar Man' L, and 401 'Pitgair' C. Above the words of the latter there is a statement indicating that it was learned from her father. Mrs Clark seems to have elected to finish on a comic note, giving 1902 'Cumarashindu',[8] a representation of the Gaelic 'Ciamar a tha si(bh) 'n diugh?' At the foot of that page (p. 21) Greig noted two lines of sol-fa from Arthur Barron with no indication of rhythm. This may possibly represent a variant of Mrs Clark's tune.

The first song collected from Mrs Clark at this April session, 'Bogieside' (Argo 10.1), is shown on the next page.

NOTES

1 *Greig–Duncan*, vol. 8, p. 473.

2 Census records 1891/225/009/031 and 1901/225/018/080.

3 Marriage record 1890/225/20.

4 The claim made in *Last Leaves* p. 282 that Mrs Aitken, Edinburgh, who gave a song to Duncan in 1905 was the same person as Mrs Clark (see *Greig–Duncan*, vol. 8, pp. 516, 526) can now be discounted, since Greig was collecting from her under the name of Mrs Clark at this date.

5 Death record 1934/689/150.

6 Census record 1891/248/00/001.

7 Census record 1881/241/2/4.

8 This was not copied into Greig's music manuscript (Gm) and was mistakenly given as being from an unrecorded source in the main edition, but see remarks in *Greig–Duncan*, vol. 8, p. 473.

'Bogieside'

61. Lord Brechin

ELIZA CLARK

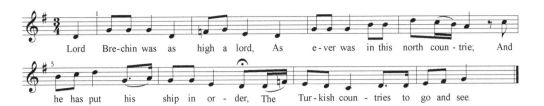

1 Lord Brechin was as high a lord,
  As ever was in this north countrie;
  And he has put his ship in order,
  The Turkish countries to go and see.

2 He sailed east so and he sailed west
  Until he came to the Turkish shore
  And he was taken and put in prison
  Until his life it was nearly gone.

3 There was a tree grew up the prison
  It grew so stout and so very strong
  And he was chained down by the
                        middle
  Until his life it was nearly gone.

4 This jailer had an only daughter
  A fairer creature you never did see
  She stole the keys of her father's prison
  And swore Lord Brechin she would
                        set free.

5 O hae ye houses, or hae ye lands
  Or dis a' Northumberland belang to thee
  Or what would you give unto a
                        young lady
  If out o' prison she could set you free?

6 It's I hae houses an' I hae land
  And a' Northumberland belangs to me
  I would give them all to you young lady
  If oot o' prison ye could set me free.

7 She has ta'en him to her father's cellar
  She has given to him a glass o' wine
  And every health, that she drank to him
  Says, I wish Lord Brechin, that ye were
                        mine.

8 Seven long years I will make a vow
  And seven long years I'll keep it true,
  If ye will wed wi no other woman,
  It's I will wed wi' no other man.

9 She has ta'en him to her father's shore
  She has given to him a ship of fame
  Says Farewell, farewell unto you
                        Lord Brechin
  I'm afraid I'll never see you again.

10 But when seven long years were past
                       and gone
  And other three days will seem to be
  She packed up her gay good clothing
  And swore Lord Brechin, she would go see.

11 And when she came to Lord Brechin's
                       castle
  So nimbly at the bell she rang
  Whose there, whose there, cries the
                      bold young porter
  Whose there, whose there, come tell to me.

12 O, is this Lord Brechin's castle
  Or is his lordship just now in?
  O yes, O yes, it is Lord Brechin's castle
  He is just a-taking his young bride in.

13 You will bid him send a slice o' bread
  A slice o' bread and a glass o' wine
  And not forget on the Turkish lady
  That did relieve him when close confined.

14 Away, away, ran the bold young porter
  Away, away and away ran he
  Away, away ran the bold young porter
  And on his bended knees fell he.

15 What news, what news, my bold
                    young porter
  What news, what news, hae ye brought
                    to me
  What news, what news my bold
                    young porter
  That ye do bow so low to me?

16 There is a lady stands at your gate
  A fairer creature you never did see
  She has as much gold hanging round
                    her brow
  As would buy the lands o'
                    Northumberland.

17 She has a ring on every finger
  And on her mid finger she's got three
  She has as much gold hanging round
                    her body
  As would buy the land o'
                    Northumberland.

18 You are bidden send her a slice o' bread
  A slice o' bread and a glass o' wine
  And not forget on the Turkish lady
  That did relieve you when close confined.

19 Lord Brechin he flew in a passion
  He broke his sword in splinters three
  I'll wager a' my father's lands
  That young Susanna has crossed the sea.

20 Then out did speak his young
                    bride's mother
  She never was heard to speak so free
  I'll surely not forsake my daughter
  Though the Turkish lady has crossed
                    the sea.

21 It is true I made a bride of your daughter
  She's none the better nor the waur o' me
  She came to me with a horse and saddle
  But I'll send her back with a coach
                    and three.

22 So he has ta'en his Turkish lady
  And he did lead her through the room
  And he has changed her name from young Susanna
  Till Lady Brechin of high renown.

GD 1023B. Child 53 *Young Beichan.* Greig collected the music in November 1905. He noted in the *Buchan Observer*, 1 June 1909: ' "Young Beichan" is one of the best known of the old ballads. The name of the hero varies – Brechin, Beikie, etc. . . . The tune is a grand specimen of old-world melody.' [M].

Performance Note Standard Western musical notation can never fully represent the intricacies and subtleties of a performance. The pause in bar 6 is likely to have been prominent in the original rendition and it is suggested that singers exaggerate the length of it before taking a breath for the final phrase.

Editorial Note Tonic lowered from Bb to G; 5.4 originally a dotted crotchet and 5.5 originally a semiquaver grace note – these notes have been rationalised to give a dotted quaver followed by a semiquaver; text lyric has 'good ship' in place of 'ship' (1.3). For 'clothing' (10.3) the manuscript has 'blocking' but this is evidently a miscopying of 'clothing'.

62. Bogieside

ELIZA CLARK

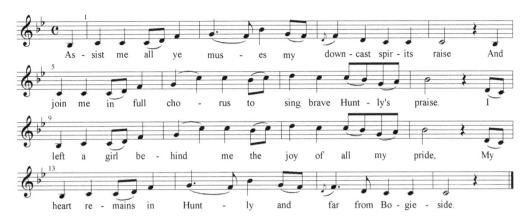

As - sist me all ye mus - es my down - cast spir - its raise And join me in full cho - rus to sing brave Hunt - ly's praise. I left a girl be - hind me the joy of all my pride, My heart re - mains in Hunt - ly and far from Bo - gie - side.

1   Assist me all ye muses my downcast spirits raise
    And join me in full chorus to sing brave Huntly's praise.
    I left a girl behind me the joy of all my pride,
    My heart remains in Huntly and far from Bogieside.

2   All you companions of my youth I bid you all adieu,
    The pleasures of one evening walk I'll walk nae mair wi' you,
    For the pleasures I've enjoyèd here shall in my heart abide
    And I'll sing Farewell to Huntly and Adieu to Bogieside.

3   O all ye comrades of my youth whose memory is most dear,
    And while I think on parting I shed a solemn tear,
    And while my heart it bears to beat till death does me divide
    I'll sing Farewell to Huntly and Adieu to Bogieside.

4   It's down the road to Huntly's lodge with pleasant steps I trod
    And much inspired with rapture to see the girl I loved
    She choosed me in her rambles and choosed me for her guide,
    To walk upon sweet Deveron's banks and around sweet Bogieside.

5   How cheerfully we have wandered to hear the blackbirds sing,
    All in the merry month of May to see the young flowers spring
    The sky being clear and bonnie all in an eveningtide
    We set us down to rest awhile upon sweet Bogieside.

6   May the Powers above protect this girl to whom I've wrote this line
    And bless her with contentment who has this heart o' mine,
    And bless her with contentment and keep her free from pride
    Till I return to Huntly and back to Bogieside.

GD 1517A. Greig received this song in April 1906. In the *Buchan Observer*, 28 January 1908, Greig stated that Mrs Corbet, New Deer, named the author of the song as Jock Riddel, noting that her grandmother knew him well and that he was born on the farm of Craigmill between New Deer and Maud. He apparently went to London and was employed for a time at the Houses of Parliament. Bogieside is to the south of the town of Huntly. Sixteen versions of the song appear in the collection. [Dor/M].

Performance Note Singers may wish to take the verses in the following order in terms of the storyline: 1, 4, 5, 2, 3, 6.

Editorial Note Tonic lowered from D to C; text lyric has 'spirit' in place of 'spirits' (1.1) and 'frae' in place of 'from' (1.4).

63. The Scranky Black Farmer

ELIZA CLARK

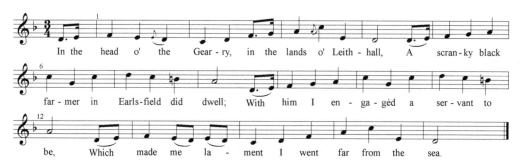

In the head o' the Gear - ry, in the lands o' Leith - hall, A scran-ky black far - mer in Earls-field did dwell; With him I en - ga - gèd a ser - vant to be, Which made me la - ment I went far from the sea.

1   In the head o' the Gearry, in the lands o' Leithhall,
    A scranky black farmer in Earlsfield did dwell;
    With him I engagèd a servant to be,
    Which made me lament I went far from the sea.

2   I engaged wi' this farmer to drive cart and plough
    Hard fortune conveniet an illfated crew
    I one of the number which causes me rue
    That ever I attempted the country to view.

3   In the head o' the Gearry we all did appear
    From various countries some far and some near
    From the parish of Kenethmont, Kilmarnock, Keen Keith
    From Aberlour, Rothiemay and Fordyce.

4   The harvest in our country is both early and late
    And all kinds of drudgery of course we do get
    Our wages are rough and our ale is but pale
    It's the brown bree o' Mollashes that we get for ale.

5   It is early in the morning we rise to the yoke
    The storm nor the tempest can never make us stop
    While the rain it does beat and the rain it down pours
    And still yon black farmer he on us does glower.

6 But the day is expiring and the day it will come
From various countries we all must be going
Bonnie Jeannie must travel, bonnie Babie also
Back to the beyone o' Montgomery must go.

7 So farewell Rhynie and adieu to you Clatt
For I have been wi' you both early and late
Both early and late, both empty and fou,
So farewell Rhyne, I'll bid you adieu.

8 So farewell Babie and adieu to you a'
Likewise to the farmer that lives at Leathhall,
For to serve this black farmer I'm sure it's nae sport
And I will be going to my bonnie sea-port.

GD 357B. Greig received this song in June 1906 and noted that Mrs Clark's rendition was 'uncertain here and there'. Writing in the *Buchan Observer*, 24 August 1909, he stated that the tune is 'a very fine old Dorian – one of the best I know'. The farmer in the story may have been William Ironside, who farmed at Earlsfield until 1863, or Daniel Skinner, who farmed there from then until 1882 and who is known to have been dark in appearance (*Greig–Duncan*, vol. 3, p. 624). [Dor].

Performance Note This song would have been sung in the bothies that housed young male farm workers in the North East, and would likely have been performed stridently and with vigour. It is suggested that performers add 'from' before 'Fordyce' (3.4); and 'to you' before 'Rhynie' (7.1 and 7.4).

Editorial Note Tonic lowered from E to D; grace note 7:1c; alternative notes 14:2f and 14:3g. 'Gearry' is the pronunciation of 'Garioch' (1.1); Greig uses the latter spelling in the tune lyric; alternative tune lyric 'With him I engagèd to drive cairt or ploo,/ Hard fortune conveniet an ill-fated crew' (1.3–4); text lyric has 'makes' in place of 'made' (1.4).

scranky – scraggy, thin; *conveniet* – brought together; *to the yoke* – to harness the horses

64. The Happy Days o' Youth

ELIZA CLARK

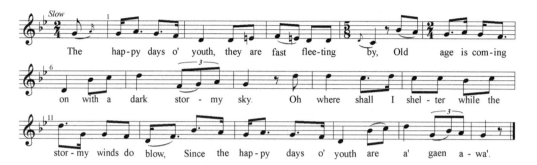

Slow

The hap-py days o' youth, they are fast flee-ting by, Old age is com-ing on with a dark stor-my sky. Oh where shall I shel-ter while the stor-my winds do blow, Since the hap-py days o' youth are a' gaen a-wa'.

1   The happy days o' youth, they are fast fleeting by,
     Old age is coming on with a dark stormy sky.
     Oh where shall I shelter while the stormy winds do blow,
     Since the happy days o' youth are a' gaen awa'.

2   Some say that wisdom comes in manhood's riper years
     But little do they think of the dangers and the cares
     I would gie a' the wealth if any wealth was mine
     For a pleasant summer's morn and a lovely lang syne.

3   It was down among the broom where me and my love met
     The bonnie blooming flowers did bloom around our seat
     The birdies droppèd singing, it was only for a wee
     And they went to their nest in their ain birken tree.

4   The happy days o' youth they canna lang remain
     There is owre muckle mirth and owre little pain
     So farewell to happy youth likewise to mirth and glee
     The young may counter and smile but they are a' gane frae me.

GD 542A. Greig collected the music in November 1905. He noted that there was some uncertainty in Mrs Clark's version and that it was 'not always sung same way'. This is an example of the type of literary song sometimes collected by Greig and Duncan. It was written by Robert Gilfillan (1798–1850). [Dor].

Performance Note The semiquaver followed by the dotted quaver (commonly known as the 'Scotch snap') that first appears in bar 1 should not be interpreted too strictly. 'Blow' should be pronounced 'blaw' (1.3).

Editorial Note The 5/8 time-signature in bar 4 is editorial. An alternative rhythm of a dotted quaver followed by a semiquaver is given at 7.3–4; text lyric has 'they are a' gane awa'' (1.4).

counter – probably for 'court'

John McAllan

*c.*1847–1927

Barnyards of Delgaty

John McAllan was born in Kintore *c.*1847 to William McAllan, a farmer, and Jane McAllan (née McDonald).[1] In 1872, he married Helen Scott at Chapel of Garioch.[2] At the time of the 1891 census, the couple were living at 14 Village Street, Monquhitter, and John was working as a farm overseer.[3] By 1901, he was living at Shevado in New Deer parish and is again listed as a farm overseer.[4] Helen's age at this time is given as forty-four. Two children are mentioned: John aged twenty-four (b. Inverurie) who was working as a chemist's assistant, and Mary Helen aged eighteen (b. Monquhitter). John McAllan died on 4 May 1927 at Glen Cottage, Maud, New Deer, aged eighty.[5]

Greig received seventeen songs from McAllan, Shevado, in September 1907.[6] Mary Ann Crichton, who taught with Greig at Whitehill School, noted in 1919 that 'Mr McAllan was grieve on the Home Farm Brucklay at the time he used to sing for Mr Greig. He has now a farm of his own in district.'[7] Greig received an additional song from him in 1908 as a result of a musical evening hosted by John Mowat at Craigmaud, New Pitsligo. In the *Buchan Observer*, 11 August 1908, he wrote:

Along with some friends I spent a very pleasant evening lately at Craigmaud under the kind roof of Mr and Mrs Mowat. After a round of the farm and a series of valuable lessons in horse and cattle from experts like our host and Mr McAllan we turned in and soon settled down to the old songs. . . . [I] noted the tunes of some of [the song texts that Mowat had given him], along with that of 'Jock the Leg' from Mr McAllan.

The eighteen songs collected from McAllan are as follows: 29 'The Middlesex Flora' D, 48 'Johnnie and the Landlady' A, 84 'The Bonnie Lass o' Fyvie' A, 93 'Donside' A, 151 'Crafty Wee Bony' B, 249 'Gightie's Lady' A, 263 'Jock the Leg and the Merry Merchant' E, 275 'The Beggar Man' I, 347 'The Barnyards o' Delgaty' A, 835 'The Laird o' Drum' C, 942 'Teuchar Howe', 973 'Glenlogie' B, 1055 'The Hireman Chiel' C, 1056 'The Lions' Den' A, 1119 'The Loyal Lovers' B, 1235 'Ellen of Aberdeen' G, 1396 'Bogie's Bonnie Bell' D, and 1517 'Adieu to Bogieside' B. Only one song, 'The Barnyards o' Delgaty', is found in the section on farm songs in volume 3 which is surprising in view of his connection to the land. This is also the only song for which we have any information about when McAllan learned his material, as Greig notes that it was 'heard when a boy'.

NOTES

1 Information from death record 1927/225/30. I have been unable to find his birth record and hence his exact date of birth.
2 Marriage record 1872/179/11.
3 Census record Monquhitter 1891/223/001/003.
4 Census record New Deer 1901/225/002/022.
5 Death record 1927/225/30.
6 *Greig–Duncan*, vol. 8, p. 484.
7 *Greig–Duncan*, vol. 8, p. 484.

65. The Laird o' Drum

JOHN MCALLAN

The Laird o' Drum is a-hun-tin' gane All in a mor-nin' ear-ly; And there he spied a weel-faurt maid; She was shea-rin' her fa-ther's bar-ley.

1 The Laird o' Drum is a-huntin' gane
   All in a mornin' early;
   And there he spied a weel-faurt maid;
   She was shearin' her father's barley.

2 Thou bonnie maid thou weel-faurd maid
   Oh will ye fancy me, O
   Oh will ye fancy the Laird o' Drum
   And let your shearin' be O.

3 I wouldna fancy the Laird o' Drum
   He is far above by degree O
   For I'm not fitted his bride to be
   And his miss I wad scorn to be O.

4 You'll cast aff the goon o' gray
   Put on the silk and scarlet
   And you will be the Lady o' Drum
   And neither miss nor harlot.

5 Your silken goons I canna wear
   They wad rustle at my heels O
   But I will wear the colour o' my ewe,
   For it suits my body weel O.

6 Your china cups I canna wash
   Nor mak' a cup o' tea O
   But I can milk the cow or the ewe
   Wi the cogie on my knee O.

7 My father is an auld shepherd
   Keeps sheep on yonder hill O
   And ilka thing that he bids me do
   I work aye at his will O.

8 He's taen her to the auld shepherd
   Keeps sheep on yonder hill O
   Says, Oh but you have a bonny daughter
   And oh, but I like her weel O.

9 She'll winnow yer corn, she'll sift
                         yer meal
   And drive to mill or kiln O
   And in time o' need, she'll saddle yer steed
   And she'll draw yer boots hersel O.

10 But who will bake my bridal bread
   And who will brew my ale O
   And who will welcome my love in
   It's more than I can tell O.

11 The baker will bake your bridal bread
   The brewer will brew your ale O
   And fa' will welcome your love in,
   You can welcome her in yersel' O.

12 There was four and twenty lairds
                         and lords
   Stood at the gates o' Drum O
   But nane o' them a' put his hand to his hat
   To welcome the shepherd's daughter in O.

13 But he's taen her by the milk white hand
   And he's led her gently in O
   And he's given her the keys into her hand
   And he's styled her Lady o' Drum O.

14 Out and spoke his brother John
   An angry man was he O
   You've married a wife my brother dear,
   She'll be an affront to all your kin O.

15 The first wife that I married
   She was far above my degree O
   I couldna enter the room where she was
   Without my hat down by my knee O.

107

16 Now I've married a wife to win my bread
    But you've married one to spend O
    And as long as my head shall carry my hat
    She'll aye be Lady o' Drum O.

17 When a' was eaten and a' was drunken
    And all were bound for bed O
    The Laird o' Drum and the shepherd's
                              daughter
    They were baith in ae bed laid O.

18 If ye had been as good as me
    As good as the Laird o' Drum O
    We would have walked the streets
                              last night
    Among good company O.

19 I told ye afore ye mairriet me
    Ye were far above my degree O
    But noo that we're mairriet and in ae
                              bed laid
    Ye'll be forced to be deein wi me O.

20 When Adam and Eve our first parents
    Did eat the forbidden tree O
    O where were a' your gentry then
    Am not I just as good as thee O.

21 Gin ye were deid and I were deid
    And baith in ae grave laid O
    And seven lang years had passed
                              and gane
    They wad scarce ken your dust by
                              mine O.

GD 835C. Collected by Greig in September 1907. Greig noted in the *Buchan Observer*, 13 October 1908: 'No ballad is more popular in the north than "The Laird o' Drum." Character and incident have been verified in a way quite unusual with the old ballads. The "Laird" was Alexander Irvine of Drum. His first wife was Lady Mary Gordon, daughter of the Marquis of Huntly, whom he married in 1643. . . . The "weel-faur'd maid" whom he took for a second wife was a Margaret Coutts, daughter of a local shepherd. The Laird died in 1687, and his widow afterwards married Irvine of Cults. She died in 1710 at the age of only forty-five.' [Pent].

Editorial Note Tonic lowered from C to Bb. Text lyric has 'The Laird o' Drum's a hunting gone' (1.1) and 'And he espied a weel-faured maid' (1.3).

ken your dust by – distinguish your dust from

66. I'll Tell You of a Story

JOHN MCALLAN

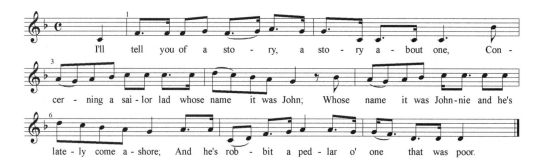

1   I'll tell you of a story, a story about one,
    Concerning a sailor lad whose name it was John;
    Whose name it was Johnnie and he's lately come ashore;
    And he's robbit a pedlar o' one that was poor.

2   He went to the ale-house, he loved as his life
     To see the pretty girl he intended for his wife
     Before that he wad marry her a trial he would gie
     Whether he or his money she wished to receive.

3   He went to the alehouse he used to lodge in
     He looked very poorly, called for a glass of gin
     You're welcome, my dear Jack, the auld wife did say
     Last night my daughter Mally was dreaming of thee.

4   I've come of a sad misfortune, my ship and cargoe's lost
     And in the wide ocean my fortune it is lost
     I am not worth a penny a farthing I am sure
     But I've come to see my Mally although that I am poor.

5   You'll call down your daughter Mally and set her down by me
     And by the melancholy may I have her on my knee
     My daughter Mally is busy Jack and canna come to thee
     So little as I trust Jack, another glance you'll see.

6   Supper being over, poor Jack he hung his head
     He asked for a candle to let him see to bed
     The beds are a' engaged Jack and been for a' the week
     So you for fresh lodgings poor Johnnie ye maun seek.

7   I'll call up my reckoning and it shall be told
     There's five and fifty shillings Jack, you're due to me of old
     There's five and fifty shillings Jack you're due to me of old
     But with this Jack pulled out both his hands full of gold.

8   The sight of the money made the auld wife to rue
     She knew she had offended Jack, she knew not what to do
     Says Ye may be in earnest Jack but I am just in jest
     So by the reputation I love my Johnnie best.

9   I'll call doon my daughter Mally and set her doon by thee
     And by the melancholy ye may have her on your knee
     The green beddie is empty Jack, and been for a' the week
     So you and your Mally may go and take a sleep.

10 Before I'd lodge into your house, I'd lodge upon the street
     For when I wanted money my lodgings were to seek
     For when I wanted money ye'd hae kicked me to the door
     So you are a broad-house keep, I'll try another door.

11 Come all ye jolly sailor lads who plough the raging main
     That win all your money in the cold winds and rain
     Wi' your pockets full o' money, oh ye may rant and roar
     But whenever that your money's deen they'll kick ye to the door.

GD 48A. Collected by Greig in September 1907. The song is given the general title of 'Johnnie and the Landlady' in the collection. [I/M or I/Ph].

Performance Note Greig has underlined the word 'o" (1.4) suggesting that he was puzzled by the sense of it. In version D from Sam Davidson the line runs coherently: 'He was robed as a pedlar and one that was poor.' Similarly, where the text has 'And by the melancholy may I have her on my knee' (5.2), D has 'And for my melancholy I will have her on my knee'. 'My reputation', as in version D, is suggested in place of 'the reputation' (8.4).

Editorial Note Tonic lowered from G to F; text lyric has 'a story' in place of 'of a story' (1.1), 'but one' in place of 'about one' (1.1), 'It's concerning a sailor boy' in place of 'Concerning a sailor lad' (1.2), 'His' in place of 'Whose' (1.3) and 'And robbed a pedlar of' in place of 'And he's robbit a pedlar o" (1.4).

broad-house keep – keeper of a brothel

67. The Bonnie Lass o' Fyvie

JOHN MCALLAN

There was a troop o' I - rish dra - goons Cam'
mar - chin' doon thro' Fy - vie O; And the Cap - tain's fa'en in love wi' a
bon - nie bon - nie lass, Her name it is called pret - ty Peg - gy O.

1   There was a troop o' Irish dragoons
    Cam' marchin' doon thro' Fyvie O;
    And the Captain's fa'en in love wi' a bonnie bonnie lass
    Her name it is called pretty Peggy O.

2   O come doon the stairs pretty Peggy he said
    O come doon the stairs pretty Peggy O
    O come doon the stairs, comb aside your yellow hair
    Tak the last farewell o' your daddie O.

3   O how could I come doon, bonnie laddie she said
    O how could I come doon bonnie laddie O,
    O how could I come doon, while I'm locked into a room
    And a drawwell below my room window O.

4   It's I'll gie you ribbons love, I'll gie you rings
    And I'll gie ye necklaces o' lammer O,
    And I'll gie ye silken gowns, flounced to your knees
    If ye would come doon to my chamber O.

5   I thank you for your ribbons love, I thank you for your rings
    I thank you for your necklace o' lammer O
    I dinna want gowns to suit my degree,
    I wad scorn to be seen in your chamber O.

110

6 A soldier's wife I shall never be
   A soldier never shall enjoy me O
   For I never do intend to go to a foreign land
   So I never shall marry a soldier O.

7 A soldier's wife ye shall never be
   For I'll make you the Captain's lady O,
   I'll make the regiment stand with their hats into their hands
   When they come into the presence o' Peggy O.

8 It's braw being a captain's lady, my dear,
   It's braw being a captain's lady O
   To be into your bed till your breakfast is made
   And dress till dinner be ready O.

9 The colonel he stands on a step on yonder sta
   Cries mount boys, mount and get ready O,
   O tarry, O tarry, another day or two
   Till we see if the bonnie lass will marry O.

10 Out and spoke his brother John
   And oh but he spake angry O
   If she will not go at once we will get sweethearts anew
   There's mony a bonnie lassie into Fyvie O.

11 There is mony a bonnie lass into bonnie Auchterless
   And mony a bonnie lass in the Garioch O
   There's mony a bonnie Jean into bonnie Aiberdeen
   But the flooer o' them a' is in Fyvie O.

12 Long long ere they wan to Old Meldrum toon
   Their captain grew sick and weary O
   And lang lang or they wan to bonnie Aiberdeen
   They got their captain to bury O.

13 It was not the girl's beauty that I did admire
   But she was my only fancy O,
   His name was captain Ned, he died for a maid
   He died for the bonnie lass o' Fyvie O.

GD 84A. Received by Greig in September 1907. Fyvie lies to the south of Turriff. Greig wrote in the *Buchan Observer*, 10 March 1908: 'The tune to which "The Bonnie Lass o' Fyvie" is sung is a vivacious bit of melody, and would make a good march. I have noted it from a number of different singers, and find that the versions do not vary much.' Twenty-six versions of the song appear in the collection. [I].
Performance Note 'Garioch' is pronounced 'Geerie' (11.2).

lammer – amber; *sta* – stall

68. The Lions' Den

JOHN MCALLAN

There were two bro - thers in the ar - my, They've fell in love wi' a la - dy fair; And for to court her was their in - ten - tion, And for to woo her was a' their care.

1 There were two brothers in the army,
 They've fell in love wi' a lady fair;
 And for to court her was their intention,
 And for to woo her was a' their care.

2 The one he was a bold sea captain
 Commanded by Sir Colonel Carr
 The other was a third lieutenant
 On board the Tagrus man o' war.

3 You are two brothers and I do love you,
 You are two brothers and I love you two
 You are both alike in rank and station
 So what can I a poor lady do?

4 She ordered her carriage to be made ready
 Early by the break o' day
 And with these two gallants she o'er the mountains
 Until she came where the lions lay.

5 And when she came up to the door
 She flung her fan in the lion's den,
 Says, 'Which of you wants to gain my favour
 Go fetch to me my fan again.'

6 Out and spake the bold sea captain
 And O he was distressed in mind,
 Says, 'A coward in battle I ne'er was called
 But to face my foes I do nane incline.

7 'There's lions there and they're dangerous creatures
 And all those beasts of different kinds
 So I will not venture my life in danger
 Tho' I your favour should never gain.'

8 Out and spake the third lieutenant
 Wi' a thundering voice both loud and shrill,
 Says, 'I will venture my life in danger
 For to gain my right heart's good will.'

9   He stooped down unto the door,
     The lions they looked so very grim
     But this young man being so well behaved
     His looks they were more fierce than them.

10 He took his sword out frae his scabbard,
     Two of the lions soon did fall
     And when they saw this young man so violent
     Down at their conqueror's feet they lay.

11 He stooped down and the fan he gathered
     His good composure being none dismayed
     While the lady in her carriage trembled
     For fear of him being made the lions' prey.

12 But when she saw this young hero turning
     And unto him being no harm done
     With open arms she did embrace him,
     Says, 'Take the prize lad that ye hae won.'

13 It was not long or the king got notice
     That two of his wild beasts were slain
     But he was not in the least offended
     But gave him honour for the same.

14 He has changed his name from being lieutenant,
     He's made him admiral o'er the blue
     So the next day and they both got married;
     See what the powers of true love can do.

GD 1056A. Collected by Greig in September 1907. Greig noted in the *Buchan Observer*, 23 March 1909: ' "The Lions' Den", or "The Bold Lieutenant", is a popular ballad in the North. . . . The story seems to be an old one. To many readers it will recall Leigh Hunt's vigorous little poem, "The Glove and the Lions". Lions used to be kept at the Tower of London.' Seventeen versions of the song appear in the collection. 'Admiral o'er the blue' (14.2): Admiral of the Blue, i.e. the first grade of Admiral (White and Red being the higher grades). [Æ/Dor].
Editorial Note Text lyric has 'Had faun in love' for 'They've fell in love' (1.2), and 'win' for 'woo' (1.4).

Mary Cruickshank

c.1840–1911

Mrs Mary Cruickshank (née Taylor) was born c.1840 in New Deer.[1] Her father was reputed to be Alexander Taylor, a crofter, and her mother was Margaret Ironside, who later married a farmer named Alexander Watt.[2] At the age of eighteen at New Pitsligo in the parish of Tyrie, Mary married James Cruickshank, aged twenty-seven, a crofter at Greciehill, New Deer. Mary was also living in the New Deer area at the time of the marriage.[3]

According to the censuses from 1881 to 1901, the couple had thirteen children: Alan, Alexander, Margaret, James, Mary, William, Lizzie, Jessie, Isabella, Francis, Robert, George and Hugh.[4] The 1901 census places the family at Smiddyhill, New Deer, where James was working as a blacksmith.

Mrs Cruickshank was described by her son Robert as being 'very musical',[5] and one imagines that this talent would have made her something of an entertainer in this large family. Her daughter, Miss Jessie Cruickshank, seems to have inherited her talents. Greig collected seven songs from her when she would have been in her early thirties. Both contributors lived at Greciehill (now 'Grassiehill' on Ordnance Survey maps), a nearby farm to the south-east of Whitehill, which must have made it easy for Greig to note down tunes for the words of the songs that they sent to him.

In the *Buchan Observer*, 10 May 1910, Greig acknowledged receiving words from Mrs Cruickshank along with the words and tunes for two songs from her daughter. A further contribution followed around 31 May: 'To Mrs Cruickshank, Greciehill, my thanks are due for copies of the following:– "Lord Brechin," "Hynd Horn," "The lass among the heather," "The Wicked Wife," "When will ye wed me," "My Johnnie," "The Bachelor," "I went out in the evening," "Lord Fife," "Tobacco plenty," and parts of "The coat of blue," and "The Duke o' Gordon" – an extensive and welcome budget.'

The tunes of most of these were recorded about a month later (newspaper entry, 7 June 1910): 'From my neighbour, Mrs Cruickshank, Greciehill, I have secured records of quite a number of tunes, for which I am greatly obliged. The list includes – "Hynd Horn," "Lord Brechin," "The Bachelor," "As I went out," "Lord Fife," "The Spanish Lady," "The Village Gate," "The bonnie lass o' Fyvie," "The Lass o' Benachie," "Tobacco Plenty," "Hay Marshall," "When will you wed me?" "The wicked wife," "My Johnnie," "Strichen's Plantins," "The Coat o' blue," "Sally Munro." Mrs Cruickshank also supplies some welcome recollections of the old ballad of "Harlaw".'

A further session was mentioned in the newspaper, 19 July: 'With the advent of summer and better conditions of locomotion I have of late managed to add to my store of tunes. . . . From Mrs and Miss Cruickshank, Greciehill, I have got the following – words and tunes both . . . – all very welcome indeed.' Greig's collecting notebook Argo 13 is entirely devoted to this session. The songs appear in the following order: 875 'Pad the Road' A, 999 'Lord Thomas of Winchbury' G, 1432 'The Devil in the Kist' D, 96 'High Germany' H, 1352 'The Fair Maid of Chelsea', 200 'The Butcher's Boy' C, and 1193 'Barbara Allan' B. Although these are attributed to Mrs Cruickshank in the collection, it is likely that they were the results of the memories of both singers, as Greig implied in his comment above.

Thirty-eight songs from Mrs Cruickshank appear in the collection, and twenty-five have tunes. Although it is said that Mrs Cruickshank 'got her songs when she was young from the singing of others',[6] it is not clear whether she came from a family tradition in singing. She remembered singing 1432 'The Devil in the Kist' D when she was between nine and ten years old, and had learned 1547 'Strichen's Plantins' C from 'old man Willox, Greciehill'.

Mary Cruickshank died on 24 June 1911 at Greciehill at the age of seventy.[7] The last mention of Greig's collecting from her occurs in the *Buchan Observer*, 21 February 1911, where Greig acknowledges receiving a fragment of 'The Maid in Bedlam'.

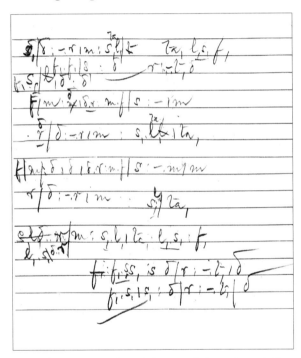

Sol-fa notation of 'Pad the Road' from Argo 13.3

NOTES

1 To date, I have been unable to obtain fresh biographical information on Mrs Cruickshank from members of her family and the article here is thus largely reproduced from my earlier article on her (and Miss Lizzie Crighton) in *Greig–Duncan*, vol. 8, p 554.

2 Death record 1911/225/20.

3 Marriage record 1858/248/3.

4 Census records 1881/225/10/16, 1891/225/010/005 and 1901/225/006/011.

5 *Greig–Duncan*, vol. 8, p. 554.

6 *Greig–Duncan*, vol. 8, p. 554.

7 Death record 1911/225/20.

69. The Spanish Lady

MARY CRUICKSHANK

As I went up thro' E-din-bu-rgh ci-ty, Half-past twelve o'-clock at night,

There I spied a Spa-nish la-dy Dres-sing her-self with can-dle light.

1   As I went up thro' Edinburgh city,
     Half-past twelve o'clock at night,
     There I spied a Spanish lady
     Dressing herself with candle light.

2   She had a basin full of water
     And a towel into her hand
     Five gold rings on every finger
     Like an angel she did stand.

3   Oh she was a charming creature
     What she is I do not know
     But I'll go court her for her beauty
     Whether she be high or low.

4   Madam, I am come to court you
     If your favour I could gain
     If you gently entertain me
     Maybe I'll come back again.

5   Sit ye doon ye're hearty welcome
     Whether ye come back or no
     All I want is a handsome young man
     Whether he be high or low.

6   Madam ye talk much of beauty
     That's a flower will soon decay,
     The fairest flower in all the summer
     When winter comes it doth fade away.

GD 746C. The words were acknowledged by Greig in the *Buchan Observer*, 10 May 1910, and the music, 6 June 1910. There are nine versions of this song in the collection. [M].

Editorial Note Tonic lowered from F to D; the four quavers in bar 2 replace two crotchets – this change has been made in order to accommodate the words.

70. Strichen's Plantins

MARY CRUICKSHANK

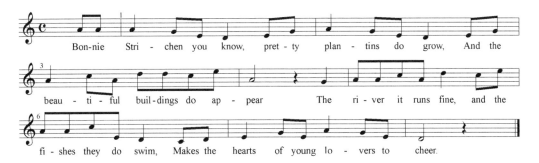

Bon-nie Stri - chen you know, pret - ty plan - tins do grow, And the
beau - ti - ful buil-dings do ap - pear The ri - ver it runs fine, and the
fi - shes they do swim, Makes the hearts of young lo - vers to cheer.

1   Bonnie Strichen you know, pretty plantins do grow,
    And the beautiful buildings do appear
    The river it runs fine, and the fishes they do swim,
    Makes the hearts of young lovers to cheer.

2   It was on an evening clear, as I rambled out
    Pretty plantins to view for a while,
    A voice which I did hear did tingle in my ear
    'Twas a young man embracing his dear.

3   I'm gaun awa' where the stormy winds do blaw,
    And the raging seas roars aye,
    But I say my love, don't mourn, for I hope I'll soon return,
    I'll be back in the end of sweet May.

4   My love she's like a new-blown rose,
    And her teeth's like the ivory in snow,
    Her skin is white as milk, and is soft as any silk,
    Like the wool on young lambs that's new grown.

GD 1547C. The music was collected by Greig around 7 June 1910. Mary Cruickshank had learned the song from an 'old man, Willox, Greciehill'. Greig and Duncan collected a total of thirty-five versions of this song, demonstrating that it was very popular in the North East. Concerning the various places where the song is localised, Greig noted: 'Plenty of singers give us "Forglen" instead of "Strichen"; in fact I should say that I have heard the one about as frequently as the other even in our own immediate neighbourhood, which inclines one to think that possibly Forglen has the better claim to the song, and that it got localised in Buchan by the very easy process of substituting "Strichen" for "Forglen." But the matter cannot now be settled.' He continued: 'Strichen . . . is rich in traditional minstrelsy. In fact, barring Fyvie, it has got more attention at the hands of the folk-songist than any other parish in our north-eastern angle.' (*Buchan Observer*, 10 December 1907) [Pent].

plantins – small woods, plantations

71. Pad the Road

MARY CRUICKSHANK

1   I long I long to see the day when I can call you mine,
    When we both shall be married, and hands together join;
    When we both shall be married, right happy we shall be,
    For ye are the bonnie lassie that's to pad the roads wi' me.

2   To pad the roads with you, young man, – cauld winter's comin' on,
    And my two aged parents they have no child but one;
    And my two aged parents they have no girl but me;
    And I pray you, chise some other fair maid to pad the roads wi' thee.

3   Never mind cauld winter's blast, when the simmer's drawing on;
    But sit ye doon beside me, and I'll sing you a fine song;
    I'll sing you a fine song, my dear, and I'll daut ye on my knee;
    For ye are the bonnie lassie that's to pad the roads wi' me.

4   This couple they've got married now, and lives in yonder town,
    May happiness attend them, and all their friends around;
    May happiness attend them, and their posterity;
    For she's the bonnie lassie that's to pad the roads wi' me.

GD 875A. The song was acknowledged by Greig in the *Buchan Observer*, 19 July 1910. [I or M with inflected 7th].

Editorial Note Tonic lowered from G to F; alternative notes 1.5eb, 6.3g, 7.5d, 11.5d; alternative rhythm at 13.1 of dotted crotchet (replacing following quaver).

pad the roads – travel on foot, looking for work; *chise* – choose

72. Tobacco Plenty

MARY CRUICKSHANK

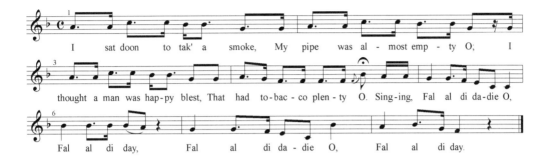

I sat doon to tak' a smoke, My pipe was al - most emp - ty O; I
thought a man was hap-py blest, That had to-bac-co plen-ty O. Sing-ing, Fal al di da-die O,
Fal al di day, Fal al di da - die O, Fal al di day.

1 I sat doon to tak' a smoke,
  My pipe was almost empty O;
  I thought a man was happy blest,
  That had tobacco plenty O.
  Singing, Fal al di dadie O,
  Fal al di day,
  Fal al di dadie O,
  Fal al di day.

2 I sat down to shave mysel'
  Wi' a drap cauld water O
  The soap it bein' scarce at han'
  I took a cold potato, O.

3 I took my pitcher in my hand
  To fetch a pail of water, O
  I hadna gaen a space or twa
  Till it cried clitter clatter O.

4 The shoes that were upon my feet
  A pair o' raggit hose
  My tae gid in a hole o' ane
  I fell and broke my nose.

5 When that I came in again
  Wi' my raggit snout
  My wife she saw the pitcher broke
  Wi' blows she banged me out.

6 Noo a' the ills come ower me noo
  I'll rest mysel contentet
  I'll maybe get some better times
  Than pay the laird his rent.

GD 285B. The song was acknowledged by Greig in the *Buchan Observer*, 31 May 1910. [I, −6].
Editorial Note Tonic lowered from G to F.

space – step; *raggit* – ragged, rough, damaged; *banged* – drove; *than* – then

Georgina Reid

1868–1958

Georgina Reid was born on 27 March 1868 at Jeddock, New Deer.[1] Her parents were John Reid, a farmer, who was born in Fochabers, and Elizabeth Reid (née Murray), who came from Fyvie. The couple married in 1860 at Aberdeen. The 1901 census lists the couple at Collieford, New Deer, along with Georgina, another daughter, Elizabeth, and a son, James. Georgina was working as a dressmaker at this time, and four boarders were listed, including Elizabeth Milne, aged fifty-four, and William Carle (see below), aged twelve.[2]

Greig mentioned Reid in the *Buchan Observer*, 19 January 1909, noting: 'To my good friend and neighbour, Miss Reid, Collieford, I would offer sincere thanks for copies of quite a number of songs and ballads, including "The False Bride", "The Laird o' Drum", "Hame, dearie, hame", "The Longford Murder", "Nancy Whisky", "Bonny Betsy", "The Sailor," etc.' Later, in the newspaper, 23 February 1909, he repeated the titles of these songs (but giving the first as 'The Forsaken Lover') with the note: 'From Miss Reid's singing too I have made records of the tunes, so that altogether I am very much indebted to my kind helper'. Some of the texts in Greig's collecting notebook Argo 9 are written in Reid's own hand. The first two verses of the entertaining nonsense song, 1903 'A Monkey's Wedding', which has words only, are given below.

'A Monkey's Wedding' from Argo 9.29

The dates attached to individual songs as well as the dates when Greig mentions her in the newspaper indicate that she was in contact with him between 1908 and 1910. Thirty-one songs appear from her in the collection including six 'A' versions and three songs for which she is the only source.

Mary Ann Crichton noted of Reid: 'She was accustomed to meeting all classes in farm kitchens and being musical could give pretty accurately what she had heard.' Crichton also states that some of her songs were 'got from parents'.[3] There is no mention of her sources in Greig's notes to the songs apart from 1218 'Oh the Rose' F which was said to have been learned twenty years earlier (probably around 1889) from a man called James Yule who was aged sixty to seventy. Two newspaper cuttings appear to have been supplied by her (see Addenda, 1378 'Come Ye Inksmen' E and 1480 'The Wild Rover' G). Versions of two of her songs 296 'My Guid Kilmarnock Bonnet' and 1466 'The Butcher and the Chambermaid' were also contributed by William Carle who had been brought up in the same household.[4]

On 14 February 1914, not long before Greig's death, Georgina (aged forty-five) married Alex Ironside, a farm servant aged thirty-eight, of New Deer.[5] Later the couple moved to Woodside, Carnousie, Turriff.[6] Georgina died, aged eighty-nine, on 3 February 1958 in the parish of Strichen and was survived by her husband.[7]

NOTES

1 Birth record 1868/225/48. The reading 'Jeddock' is uncertain.
2 Census record 1901/225/004/005.
3 *Greig–Duncan*, vol. 8, p. 501.
4 *Greig–Duncan*, vol. 8, p. 501.
5 The marriage took place in Aberdeen (marriage record 1914/168/1/95).
6 Information from Mary Ann Crichton, see *Greig–Duncan*, vol. 8, p. 501.
7 Death record 1958/241/1.

73. Young Emma

GEORGINA REID

Young Em - ma was a ser - vant girl, She loved young Ed - ward
well; And the rea - son why she lov - èd him, The
rea - son why she lov - èd him, He ploughed the Low - lands low.

1   Young Emma was a servant girl,
     She loved young Edward well;
     And the reason why she lovèd him,
     The reason why she lovèd him,
     He ploughed the Lowlands low.

2   Her parents kept a public house,
     A little way down the shore
     And oft they robbed the sailors
     And heard of them no more.

3   My parents keeps a public house
     A little way down the shore
     And if you chance to go that way
     Don't let my parents know
     That your name it is young Edward
     That ploughs the Lowlands low.

4   Young Edward sat a-drinking
     Till it was time for bed
     But little was he thinking
     That sorrow crowned his head.

5   As Emma lay a-sleeping
     She dreamed a terrible dream
     She dreamed she saw her own true-love
     Lie bleeding in the stream.

6   Young Emma rose put on her clothes
     To her parents' room she went
     Says 'Mother, oh where's the stranger
     Came here last night to sleep.'

7   Oh daughter, dear daughter
     To you I'll tell no lie
     We robbed him and stobbed him
     And sank his body low.

8   Oh parents, cruel parents
     You shall die a public show
     For the murdering of my own true love
     And the sinking his body low.

9   The white fish in the ocean
     Swims o'er my true love's breast,
     His body rolls in motion
     But I hope his soul's at rest.

GD 189A. Greig acknowledged the music in the *Buchan Observer*, 10 May 1910, and the words on 31
     May 1910. [I/M].
Performance Note The repetition of the third line that occurs in verse one is taken to be the pattern
     throughout. In verse 3, an extra two bars are required to accommodate the additional words. Sing
     lines 3.1–4 as normal (but without repeating line 3.3), then 3.5 to bars 5–6 and 3.6 to bars 9–10.
Editorial Note Tonic lowered from G to F; text lyric has 'And she loved' in place of 'She loved' (1.2), and
     'loved' in place of 'lovèd' (1.3); line 1.3 is not repeated in the text lyric.

stobbed – stabbed

74. The Good-Looking Widow

GEORGINA REID

I'm a good-loo-king wi-dow, nae won-der you stare; I've had three men al-rea-dy as sure as you're there; And

oh, for a - ni - ther my hert it is sair, But I'll get num-ber four some mor - nin'. Al -

tho' I'm good-loo-kin', baith hand-some and braw, Al - tho' I'm a wi-dow, that's nae-thing a - va,

Some bon - nie lad - die 'ill tak' me a - wa', And mak' me his bride in the mor - nin'.

1 I'm a good-looking widow, nae wonder you stare;
   I've had three men already as sure as you're there;
   And oh, for anither my hert it is sair,
   But I'll get number four some mornin'.
      Altho' I'm good-lookin', baith handsome and braw,
      Altho' I'm a widow, that's naething ava,
      Some bonnie laddie 'ill tak' me awa',
      And mak' me his bride in the mornin'.

2 The first man I had was a tailor ca'd John,
   He was a swell, and a toff, and a don,
   He'd a wart on his neck where the collar gaed on,
   That he used for a stud in the mornin'.

3 The next man I had was a baker to trade,
   And he was a loafer and very low bred,
   I ne'er kent a man was so fond o' his bed,
   For he wadna rise in the mornin'.

4 The next man I had, oh yes he was man,
   He was some fond o' me, but mair fond o' a dram,
   Oor mairried life didna last very lang,
   He was owre fond o' his mornin'.

GD 1302A. The words and tune were acknowledged by Greig in the *Buchan Observer*, 31 May 1910.
There are four versions of this song in the collection. [I].

Editorial Note Tonic lowered from D to C; bars 9–16 are editorial and replicate bars 1–8 apart from the
rest inserted to accommodate the words in bar 12.

mornin' (4.4) – morning drink

75. A'body's Like to Get Mairriet But Me

GEORGINA REID

As Jean - nie sat doon wi' her wheel by the fire, And thocht on the
days that were fast flee - in' by - Says she to her - sel wi' a hea - vy hoch -
ee - Oh a' - bo - dy's like to get mair - riet but me. Mair - riet but
me, mair - riet but me, Oh a' - bo - dy's like to get mair - riet but me.

1   As Jeannie sat doon wi' her wheel by the fire,
    And thocht on the days that were fast fleein' by –
    Says she to hersel wi' a heavy hochee –
    Oh a'body's like to get mairriet but me.
    Mairriet but me, mairriet but me,
    Oh a'body's like to get mairriet but me.

2   There's Lawrie, the lawyer wad hae me fu' fain
    Though he hae a but and a ben o' his ain
    Afore I'd gae wi' him, I'd far rather dee
    Yon wee stumpin' bodie will never get me
    Never get me, never get me,
    Yon wee stumpin' bodie will never get me.

3   There's Dickie, my cousin, frae London come doon
    Wi' his braw yellow doeskins wad dazzle the toon
    Peer fellow he ne'er got a blink o' my e'e
    Though a'body's like tae get mairret but me.

4   It's hard tae tak shelter at yonder fell dyke
    It's hard tae gang wi' them ye never could like
    It's hard tae leave them that ye fain wad gae wi'
    But it's harder that a' should get mairret but me.

5   There lives a young laddie at yonder dyke-side
    Wha weel deserves ony queen for his bride
    If I had my will it's his ain I wad be
    But a'body's like tae get mairret but me.

GD 1374C. Greig collected the music for this song around 19 January 1909. [I].
Editorial Note Tonic lowered from D to C; alternative note 2.2e. Text lyric has 'I to mysel' in place of
    'she to hersel' and 'Hoch he' in place of 'hochee' (1.3). Since the title 'The Old Maid's Lament' found
    with this song version occurs also as the title of song 15, the repeated ending is given as the title (as
    in other versions of the song in the collection).

wheel – spinning-wheel; *fleein'* – flying; *hochee* – sigh; *stumpin'* – stunted; *doeskins* – breeches;
    peer – poor; *fell dyke* – low wall made of turf

76. Nancy Whisky

GEORGINA REID

I am a wea - ver, a Dub-lin wea - ver, I am a rash and a ro - ving blade, I've got
as much mo - ney in - to my poc - ket, That I maun try the ro - vin' trade.

1 I am a weaver, a Dublin weaver,
I am a rash and a roving blade,
I've got as much money into my pocket,
That I maun try the rovin' trade.

2 Down the city as I was walking,
Oh Nancy Whisky I chanced to meet,
The more I kissed her, the more I
blessed her,
The more I kissed her the more
she smiled,
Till Nancy Whisky, till Nancy Whisky,
Till Nancy Whisky has me beguiled.

3 Down the stair came the landlord,
I asked him for all night to stay,
And Nancy Whisky to bear me company
Until the morning I go away.

4 In the morning when I awakened
I found myself in an unco bed,
I tried to rise but I was not able,
For Nancy Whisky held down my head.

5 Down the stair came the landlady,
I asked her what was to pay,

Just fifty shillings with bygone reckonings,
So pay your money and go your way.

6 I put my hand into my pocket,
And all that money was well paid down,
All that was left to buy me clothing,
All that remained was but a crown.

7 Down the city as I was walking,
Nancy's sister I chanced to smell,
I went in, spent four and sixpence,
All that remained was but a scale.

8 I do not value this crookèd sixpence,
Neither will I lay it up in store,
But I'll go and call another gill,
And then go home and work for more.

9 I'll go back to my cotton weaving,
So quickly I'll make the shuttle fly,
For I'll make more at the cotton weaving
Than ere I did by the roving boy.

10 Come all ye weavers, ye Dublin weavers,
Ye cotton weavers, where'er you be,
And take ye care of Nancy Whisky
She'll ruin you as she ruined me.

GD 603B. Greig acknowledged this song, which also goes under the title of 'The Dublin Weaver', in the *Buchan Observer*, 19 January and 23 February 1909. He wrote of it on 31 August 1909: 'It is gratifying to find a song like this, with so good a moral, enjoying a wide and enduring popularity. . . . Folk-song rarely lends itself to the glorification of drinking but rather discountenances it; and inasmuch as the testimony of folk-song on all questions bearing on the morale of the people carries the greatest weight, we are entitled to maintain that on the subject of drink the popular conscience has been, and is, wonderfully sound.' [Pent].
Performance Note Lines 2.5–6 could be sung to the tune of bars 5–8.
Editorial Note Tonic lowered from F to D.

scale – sixpence

Helen Rettie
1860–1941

Mrs Rettie and her husband Andrew

Helen Rettie (née Cran) – known as Nellie to her friends – lived at West Berryhill farm, Millbrex, Fyvie, together with her husband, Andrew (who contributed several items to the collection). She was born in Fyvie parish in 1860 and died in 1941 in Aberdeen, aged eighty-one. Her mother was Mary Cran (née Ironside) who died in 1876 aged fifty-six.[1] Helen Rettie contributed fifty-five items to the collection, twenty-six with tunes. Mary Ann Crichton said of her: 'Mrs Rettie, Berryhill, Millbrex. (Crofters). Never went outside for songs but picked them all up in the district from old people and from her own mother.'[2] She also speaks of Greig's high opinion of Mrs Rettie: 'Many a time did Mr Greig inconvenience himself to pay this lady a visit. . . . [He] never missed an opportunity of getting her contributions which he valued highly as her memory was exceptionally good.'[3] Mrs Rettie's repertoire includes some unusual items such as 636 'December Cam', a rhyme about Yule; 570 'Glendronach', a text fragment concerning the distillery of that name between Turriff and Huntly; and a saying, 1645 'The Doos o' Dunbennan'.

Greig collected tunes from Mrs Rettie in September 1906 and September 1907. She is first mentioned in the *Buchan Observer*, 11 February 1908, not long after Greig's column began. The frequent mentions of her show that she not only sent Greig a good deal of material, but commonly entered into discussion about the songs. On 28 April 1908, we find that the family appear to have a store of printed material:

> Mrs Rettie, Millbrex, continues to render me valuable help. She sends me copies of 'The Aul Gardener,' and 'Pretty Polly,' kindly promising to let me hear her versions of the tunes when we meet; also her version of 'The Bonny Lass o Fyvie', calling attention to the fact that in it the dragoons are *English* not *Irish*. My correspondent also sends two ballad chap-books; a cutting on 'Children's Rhyme Games'; and a look of a volume of the *Scots Magazine* of date 1809, which contains, among other interesting things, the old song, 'The waefu' want o' siller.' For all which Mrs Rettie has my warm thanks.

A meeting at her home is recorded in the newspaper on 28 July 1908. Greig was taken there by his friend, Mr George Watt of Whinhill:

> I had the pleasure lately of spending a very enjoyable afternoon with Mr and Mrs Rettie, Millbrex. The old songs of course were in evidence, and I was favoured with a number of tunes. From our host I noted 'The Lawyer's Bonnie Peggie,' and from our hostess, who has so often helped me before, I got 'Frendraught,' 'The Girlie and the Oysters,' 'Bay of Biscay,' 'The Auld Gardener,' 'Highland Lads,' 'Auchindor,' 'Pretty Polly,' etc.

Unfortunately, however, the results of this actual session are not found in the collection – and indeed this is true of a number of items from Mrs Rettie mentioned in the newspaper.

The receipt of further items is mentioned on 26 January 1909. Mrs Rettie's relative, John Christie of Turriff, referred to in the article, may well have been influential in terms of her interest in local poetry. His publications include the two poems mentioned below, as well as 'Reminiscences of Drachlaw', which draws on his experiences of being a herd-boy at Drachlaw on Deveronside from 1853–5:[4]

> Mrs Rettie, Millbrex, kindly offers me a look of the poems 'Drachlaw Revisited,' [1906] and 'The Aul' Folk noo awa.' The author, Mr J. Christie, who was my correspondent's granduncle, was a very worthy man, and a great pedestrian, about which latter character-istic she tells a good story. We shall be very pleased indeed to see the pieces referred to. Mrs Rettie also gives me another verse or two of the 'Auld Yule' rhyme which have recurred to memory since her last communication, along with a bit of 'The Battle of the Gallowgate,' an Aberdeen parody of 'The Battle of the Baltic,' – for all which favours she has my sincere thanks.

The final mention of Mrs Rettie is on 24 January 1911: 'I have to thank Mrs Rettie, Millbrex, for copies of "The parson's daughter Jean", . . . "The auld man's mear's deid", and "Jocky and his Owsen".' The last (430) is of particular historical interest. The note to it states: 'In the old herding days the number of the owsen were cut out in notches on the herd's club in the order that they are set down in the rhyme, with a figure of Jocky at the end'.[5] The club was the stick used for driving the cattle.

Helen Rettie knew a considerable number of Child ballads, contributing the following to the collection: 27 'The Mermaid' F (Child 289), 212 'Sweet Willie and Fair Annie' C (Child 73), 232 'The Fire o' Frendraught' B (Child 196), 235 'Sir James the Rose' F (Child 213), 850 'Glasgow Peggy' B (Child 228), 1022 'Hind Horn' A (Child 17), 1231 'Clyde's Waters' F (Child 215), and 1465 'Earl Richard' A (Child 110). The American collector James Madison Carpenter made cylinder recordings of some of these, and also made recordings of the following additional ballads from her: 'The Dowie Dens of Yarrow' (Child 214), 'Andrew Lammie' (Child 233), 'Glenlogie' (238), 'The Laird o Drum' (Child 236), 'Captain Wedderburn's Courtship' (Child 46), 'Lang Johnnie More' (Child 251), 'The Battle of Harlaw' (Child 163), 'The Duke of Athole's Nurse' (Child 212), and 'Bessie Bell and Mary Gray' (Child 201).[6] Greig's collecting clearly had not exhausted her repertoire of interesting old songs.

NOTES

1 *Greig–Duncan*, vol. 8, p. 576.
2 *Greig–Duncan*, vol. 8, p. 575.
3 *Greig–Duncan*, vol. 8, p. 576.
4 See Katherine Campbell, *The Fiddle in Scottish Culture: Aspects of the Tradition* (Edinburgh: John Donald, 2007, p. 88).
5 *Greig–Duncan*, vol. 3, p. 639.
6 See entries for Mrs Rettie in *The James Madison Carpenter Collection Online Catalogue* http://www.hrionline.ac.uk/carpenter

77. Oh! Hard Fortune

HELEN RETTIE

On a fine sum-mer's mor-ning in the sweet month of May, An ar-my of sol-diers went out for to play, When a beau-ti-ful la-dy just chanced to pass by, And one of the drum-mers on her cast his eye. Oh! hard for-tune.

1   On a fine summer's morning in the sweet month of May,
    An army of soldiers went out for to play,
    When a beautiful lady just chanced to pass by,
    And one of the drummers on her cast his eye.
    Oh! hard fortune.

2   He's gone to his captain without more delay
    'Dear honoured captain, for love I maun dee
    For a beautiful lady has chanc'd to pass by
    And if I don't have her, I'm sure I will die.'
    Oh! hard fortune.

3   'You'll go to this lady, an' tell her your pain
    Perhaps she will pity a poor dying swain.
    Tell her "I saw you just now you passed by
    And if I don't have you I'm sure I will die." '
    Oh! hard fortune.

4   He's gone to this lady without more delay
    'Dear honoured lady, for love I maun die
    When that I saw you just now you passed by
    And if I don't have you I'm sure I will die.'
    Oh! hard fortune.

5   'Begone' said this lady, 'pray what do you mean
    My father's a laird o' much fame and renown
    I am his ae daughter, the heiress to be,
    Do you think I will bring myself to misery.'
    Oh! hard fortune.

6   He turn'd aright round and he made a low bow
    'Dear honoured lady I bid you adieu!
    For with my own rapier, I'll soon end the strife
    I'll cut the sweet threads, ev'n the threads o' my life.'
    Oh! hard fortune.

7 'Oh! guilty of murder!' this lady did cry
'Oh guilty of murder! oh, no, no not I
It's a pity such innocent blood for to spill
I'm a lady of honour, just here at your will.'
Oh! happy fortune.

8 Now he's got married to his lady so dear
And he possesses some thousands a year;
He's the richest man in the whole company
He was raised from a drummer a colonel to be.
Oh! happy fortune.

GD 86A. Greig received the music in September 1906 and the words in September 1909. [I/Ly].
Performance Note The sudden change of mood in the last two verses suggests that both these refrains
would be sung 'a tempo'.
Editorial Note Tonic lowered from D to C; text lyric has 'summer' in place of 'summer's' (1.1), 'out to
their play' in place of 'out for to play' (1.2), 'caught his eye' in place of 'cast his eye' (1.4); text missing
lines 3.3–4, supplied from 4.3–4 (except words 'Tell her' which are editorial). 'Oh!' (1.5 and title) is
from the text lyric; the tune lyric has 'O'.

78. Pretty Caledonia

HELEN RETTIE

There was once two Scot-tish lov-ers sat down to make their moan, And
by came a troop o' the north coun-try men, Says: Rise up ye twa lov-ers rise
up an come a-wa' There's com-mis-sion for our pret-ty Ca-le-do-ni-a.

1 There was once two Scottish lovers sat down to make their moan,
And by came a troop o' the north country men,
Says: Rise up ye twa lovers rise up an come awa'
There's commission for our pretty Caledonia.

2 'Oh!' says the lady, 'I'm willing for to pay
Five hundred guineas before I go away
I'll pay it every farthing, I'll pay it ane an' a',
If you'd take me to your pretty Caledonia.'

3 'Oh!' says the sailor, 'her money we will have
And when we are on board we will sell her for a slave
We will sell her for a slave lang ere she win there ava;
An' she'll never get a sicht o' Caledonia.'

130

4   'Oh!' says the captain, but that winna dee
    They dinna sell slaves in our countrie
    They would hang us every one, they would hang us ane an' a',
    If we sold a slave in pretty Caledonia.'

5   'Oh!' says the sailor, 'her money we will take
    And when we are on board, we will heave her over deck
    We will heave her over deck, lang ere she win there ava
    An' she'll never get a sicht o' Caledonia.'

6   They sailed up and they sailèd doon,
    By mony a seaport an' by mony a toon,
    The seas they did beat, an' the win's they did bla'
    An' they couldna get a sicht o' Caledonia.

7   One night the captain dreamed a dream
    There came a voice to him an' said unto him
    'Tak' care o' the lassie that ye brocht here awa
    Or she'll never get a sicht o' Caledonia.'

8   Early in the morning the captain arose
    He put on his clothes to the sailor he goes
    Says: 'Where is the lassie that ye brocht here awa
    For I dreamed she was in pretty Caledonia.'

9   'Oh!' says the sailor, 'she's lying very low
    I've bound her hand and foot ready overboard to throw
    For I hae anither sweetheart, an' that ye weel do know
    An' she'll never get a sicht o' Caledonia.'

10 Straight to the lady the captain did go
    'What is the reason that ye lie here so low
    Oh! what is the reason that ye are servèd so
    For I'm sure you paid your freight for Caledonia.'

11 'Alas! an alake an' ah wae's me
    That ever I was born sic hardships to see
    For he has anither sweetheart, he likes better than me
    An' it makes me sigh an' weep for Caledonia.'

12 'Oh!' says the captain, 'if ye would take in hand
    To wait upon me, when we come to land;
    To wait upon me, an' to be at my command,
    I will take you to our pretty Caledonia.'

13 'Oh!' says the lady I will take in hand
    To wait upon you, when we come to land
    Content wi' my portion, although it be but sma
    If you'd take me to your pretty Caledonia.

14 Straight to the sailor the captain has gone
   He's ta'en by the neck an' overboard him thrown
   'Tak a cup o' cold water although it be but sma'
   You may drink your lassie's health in Caledonia.'

15 They sailed up and they sailed doon
   By mony a seaport an' by mony a toon
   The seas they didna beat, nor the winds they didna blaw,
   Till they were safe arrived in Caledonia.

16 They hadna been there three quarters o' a year
   When in silks an' in satins he made this lassie wear
   In silks and in satins he maks her gang sae braw
   An' she lives the captain's wife in Caledonia.

GD 227A. Greig received the music in September 1906 and the words were acknowledged in the
   Buchan Observer, 17 March 1908. [I/M].
Editorial Note Tonic lowered from G to D.

brocht here awa – brought into this place;   *freight* – fare;   *alake* – alack;   *wae's me* – alas

79. Lass Gin Ye Wad Lo'e Me

HELEN RETTIE

Lass gin ye wad lo'e me, O lass gin ye wad lo'e me, I'd mak' ye la-dy
o' my ha' O lass gin ye wad lo'e me. A can-ty but a cos-ie ben, weel
plen-ished ye may trow me, A brisk a blithe a kind guid-man, O lass gin ye wad lo'e me.

1 (*He*) Lass gin ye wad lo'e me, O lass gin ye wad lo'e me,
   I'd mak' ye lady o' my ha' O lass gin ye wad lo'e me.
   A canty but a cosie ben, weel plenished ye may trow me,
   A brisk a blithe a kind guidman, O lass gin ye wad lo'e me.

2 (*She*) Wealth I've little doot ye ha'e, and bidin' bien and easy
   But brisk nor blithe ye canna be, and you sae auld and crazy.
   Wad mairrage mak' ye young again? Wad woman's love renew ye?
   Awa' ye silly doitet man, I canna winna lo'e ye.

3 (*He*) Witless hizzie, even's ye like, the fient a doit I'm carin',
   But men should be the first to speak, and wanters maun be spierin',
   And lassie, I hae lo'ed ye lang, and noo I'm come to woo ye;
   I'm nae sae auld as clashes gang, I think ye'd better lo'e me.

132

4   (*She*) Doitet body, auld or young, ye needna langer tarry,
    Gin ane be lootin' owre a rung, he's nae for me to marry.
    Gae hame and ance bethink yersel' howe'er ye cam' to woo me;
    And mind me in your latter will, auld body gin ye lo'e me.

GD 813A. Greig collected this song in September 1906. Mrs Rettie learned it from a version that
    appeared in Chambers' *Edinburgh Journal* No. 196, 31 October 1835; the song was written by
    Alexander Laing (*Greig–Duncan*, vol. 4, pp. 320, 546). Mrs Rettie's tune is a version of the one
    commonly used for Burns's 'A Man's a Man'. [I/M].
Editorial Note Tonic lowered from G to F. Tune lyric has 'canty ben' in place of 'cosie ben' (1.3), 'and
    blithe' in place of 'nor blithe' (2.2), 'And woman's' in place of 'Wad woman's' (2.3), 'canna canna lo'e
    me' in place of 'canna winna lo'e ye' (2.4). Text lyric has 'O lass' in place of 'Lass' (1.1), 'lan'' in place
    of 'ha'' (1.2), 'true' in place of 'trow' (1.3).

weel plenished – with everything provided;   *trow* – believe;   *bidin'* – dwelling;   *bien* – comfortable;
    doitet – senile;   *fient a doit* – devil a bit;   *wanters* – bachelors;   *as clashes gang* – as gossip has it;
    lootin' – stooping;   *rung* – stick

80. Drumallachie

HELEN RETTIE

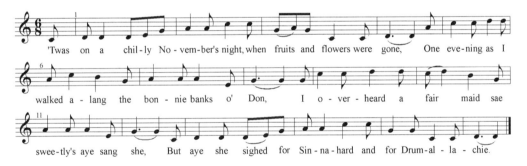

'Twas on a chil-ly No-vem-ber's night, when fruits and flowers were gone, One eve-ning as I
walked a-lang the bon-nie banks o' Don, I o-ver-heard a fair maid sae
swee-tly's aye sang she, But aye she sighed for Sin-na-hard and for Drum-al-la-chie.

1   'Twas on a chilly November's night, when fruits and flowers were gone,
    One evening as I walked alang the bonnie banks o' Don,
    I overheard a fair maid sae sweetly's aye sang she,
    But aye she sighed for Sinnahard and for Drumallachie.

2   Says I, 'My pretty fair maid, why walk you here alone
    Lamenting for some absent love upon the banks o' Don?
    The reason o' your grieving come tell it a' to me,
    And why you sigh for Sinnahard and for Drumallachie.'

3   'Peter was my true love's name, he lived on the banks o' Don,
    He was as fair a young man as e'er the sun shone on;
    The cruel wars o' Scotland hae ta'en my love frae me,
    Which makes me sigh for Sinnahard and for Drumallachie.'

4 Says I, 'My pretty fair maid, if ye'll gie me your han'
  On the bonnie banks o' Don I hae baith hoose and lan'
  To you alane I'll gie them a' if ye wad be my bride
  And forsake yon bonnie laddie that lived upon Donside.'

5 Says she, 'Young man your offer's fair, but you I must deny,
  For the sake o' one young man I am to live and die.
  In the space of seven years black shall cover me,
  For him who's far frae Sinnahard and frae Drumallachie.'

6 When I saw my true love weep, I could no longer stan',
  But I turned aright and round about says, 'Jeannie I'm the man.
  Now for your constant true love you're free frae every care,
  Since we hae met upon Donside we will pairt nae mair.'

GD 1043D. Greig received the music in September 1906 and the words in February 1907. He wrote in the *Buchan Observer*, 28 April 1908: 'The plot is an exceedingly common one with the old balladist, and never fails to interest and please. We think, however, that in the case of [this] song . . . the main charm will be found to reside in the happy combination of the two place-names, Sinnahard and Drumallachie.' These places lie on either side of the River Don in the Kildrummy area of Aberdeenshire. The song concerns Peter Watt and Betsy Taggart, who later married, and Duncan interviewed Mr Watt in 1908 and got the story from him. When Mr Watt was working at the farm of Drumallachie in the 1850s he shot a hare on another man's land under the instruction of his master, and when Watt was charged for this, and about to be arrested for non-payment of legal fees, he 'left the district, changed his name, and went to work on the Great North of Scotland Railway near the Bridge of Spey' and stayed there for two months. He then returned and married Betsy Taggart and was eventually successful in forcing his master to pay most of the legal expenses as he had promised. Betsy Taggart was working as a housekeeper at the Mill of Brux quite close to Drumallachie at the time and the song was composed by a farm servant called James Hepburn who had worked with Watt at Milton of Cairncoullie. Some versions have 'cruel laws' where this text has 'cruel wars' (3.3); the former is more appropriate to the theme of the song. [Dor/M].

Editorial Note Tonic lowered from E to D; the anacrusis is editorial. Text lyric 'she' is editorial (1.4). 'Drumallachie' (1.4 and title) is from the text lyric; the tune lyric has 'Drumalachie'.

James W. Spence

1867–1928

James W. Spence

James Wattie Spence was born on 1 August 1867 at Rose Croft, Millbrex, Fyvie, to Thomas Spence, a crofter, and Helen Spence (née Gould).[1] He died in February 1928 at Fernbank, Maud, aged sixty.[2] The Spence family was living at Rose Croft in 1881,[3] but the 1891 census lists James at Gellibrae, New Deer, where he was a boarder and was working as a merchant's assistant, very likely to James Fowler who was also lodging there. The head of the household was James Milne, a farmer.[4] By 1901, James was back at Rose Croft and working as a crofter. He was married to Maggie (née Gray), born Monquhitter, and had two children, Lizzie, aged three, and James, aged eleven months. Also present at the time of the census were his father, Thomas Spence, and his (James's) sister, Eliza Spence, aged thirty-five, who was working as a stocking knitter.[5] Spence contributed one hundred and twenty-two songs to the collection. Tom McKean notes: '[He] shows a rounded, well-developed repertoire, thoroughly typical for its size and featuring the entire range of local song – bothies, humorous songs, romantic lyrics and great ballads – of North East, South West, Irish, English origin.'[6]

Greig collected from Spence in three consecutive years – July and August 1905, April and August 1906, and September 1907 – and again after a lapse of time in 1912.[7] In addition, Spence sent items to Greig that were acknowledged in the *Buchan Observer*. On 25 February 1908,

135

Greig wrote: 'From Mr J. W. Spence, Fyvie, I have received a big budget of songs and ballads which he has kindly been copying out for me for some time past. The consignment represents a very substantial addition to my stock of words; and I would thank Mr Spence very cordially for his kind and valuable help.' Two weeks later he is acknowledged again: 'Mr J. W. Spence, Fyvie, kindly forwards his versions of "Jock o' Braidiesley" and the "Battle of Harlaw" at my request.'

The notebook called 'Watt', which contains items from John Quirrie and other contributors, has sixteen items from Spence that were collected in August 1906, including 1132 'The Braes o' Strathdon' A (see next page). It was particularly interesting for Greig to collect from J. W. Spence, who had learned songs from his father, and also to be able to record songs from Thomas Spence himself. The repertoire recorded from Thomas consisted of six songs all noted down in Argo 22 (September 1907). The songs appear in the following order: 160 'The Duke of Athole's Nurse' E (p. 9), 266 'The Yorkshire Farmer' A (p. 11), 93 'Donside' G (p. 12), 858 'Haud Awa, Bide Awa' B (p. 13), 134 'Highland Harry' C (p. 13), for which Greig identifies the tune as 'Green Grow the Rashes O', and 236 'Erin-Go-Bragh' E (p. 28). Greig also noted in Argo 3, p. 13, that Thomas Spence 'knew Shaw &c. Colliehill & A. Kindness', characters in the song 'Pitgair' given here from John Quirrie.

All of the songs from Thomas were recorded from James, with the exception of one (no. 134). Concerning 160 'The Duke of Athole's Nurse', Greig wrote in a letter to Duncan on 1 October 1911: '[The song] came from Spence, Fyvie, and wd. be the version of his father, a substantial man of nearly 90, who sang me the tune bravely and well.'[8] Thomas Spence was born at Methlick in 1822 to Thomas Spence and Mary Spence (née Bruce), and Greig's estimate of his age was accurate since he died in 1912 in Turriff aged ninety.[9] A comparison of their versions of this ballad shows that the tunes are very similar, although Thomas gave only four stanzas of it (three of them incomplete), whereas James gave fifteen.

At two other recording sessions, captured in Argo 3 and Argo 7, it is clear that Arthur Barron was present as Greig noted a single item from him on each occasion. Millbrex was a considerable distance from Greig's home, and it seems likely that Barron had taken him there, perhaps in his farm gig. Mary Ann Crichton credits Arthur Barron with putting Greig in touch with the Spences.[10]

NOTES

1 Birth record 1867/222/B/33.
2 Death record 1928/225/6.
3 Census record 1881/222/B/001.
4 Census record 1891/225/007/010.
5 Census record 1901/222B/001/005.
6 *Greig–Duncan*, vol. 8, p. 590.
7 *Greig–Duncan*, vol. 8, pp. 472, 514.
8 *Greig–Duncan*, vol. 8, p. 472.
9 OPR 1822/221/4 and death record 1912/247/34.
10 *Greig–Duncan*, vol. 8, p. 472.

'The Braes o' Strathdon'

81. The Rigs o' Gorrachree

JAMES W. SPENCE

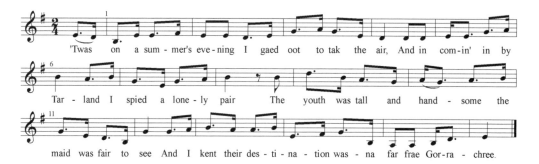

'Twas on a sum-mer's eve-ning I gaed oot to tak the air, And in com-in' in by Tar-land I spied a lone-ly pair The youth was tall and hand-some the maid was fair to see And I kent their des-ti-na-tion was-na far frae Gor-ra-chree.

1 'Twas on a summer's evening I gaed oot to tak the air,
    And in comin' in by Tarland I spied a lonely pair
    The youth was tall and handsome the maid was fair to see
    And I kent their destination wasna far frae Gorrachree.

2 The moon bein' clear, the nicht bein' calm, I heard what they did say
    And for to watch their movements as they walked on their way
    I wrapped my plaid aboot my heid and set my pipe agee
    Just for to watch their movements aroon by Gorrachree.

3 Aboot halfway up the avenue they both sat doon to rest
    He took her in his arms says 'My dear I like you best'
    A maid he might have laid her doon, she's still a maid for me
    But a maid again she'll never tramp the rigs o' Gorrachree.

4 Now Sandy, lad, ye'll ne'er deny the ill that ye hae done
    My bonnet ye hae broken doon, my hair flees wi' the win
    My maidenhood has got a fright and gane awa frae me
    And the session clerk will come to ken the rigs o' Gorrachree.

5 'Oh' says Sandy, ye needna care a fig
    For there's mony a bonnie lassie has gane aff on the rig
    And on mony a' ane's the joke been played and fairer far than thee
    So come all ye rigin' maidens, remember Gorrachree.

6 Aboot this couple's destinations inquiry I hae made
    The maid she comes frae Aberdeen, she acts as chambermaid
    The youth he hunts the beggar wives and sets them agee
    And caes the country roon and roon, syne hame by Gorrachree.

GD 1468A. The music was collected by Greig in August 1906. [Æ/Dor].
Editorial Note Tonic lowered from A to E; text lyric has 'And comin' for 'And in comin'', and 'lovely' for 'lonely' (1.2).

agee – to one side; *rigs* – ridges of land; *on the rig* – on the spree; *rigin'* – teasing; *caes* – travels

82. Bethelnie

JAMES W. SPENCE

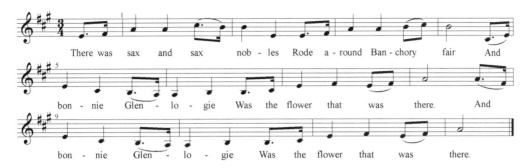

There was sax and sax nob - les Rode a - round Ban - chory fair And
bon - nie Glen - lo - gie Was the flower that was there. And
bon - nie Glen - lo - gie Was the flower that was there.

1   There was sax and sax nobles
Rode around Banchory fair
And bonnie Glenlogie
Was the flower that was there.
And bonnie Glenlogie
Was the flower that was there.

2   There was nine and nine of them
Sat at the king's dine,
And bonnie Glenlogie
Was the flower o' twice nine.

3   There was nine and nine maidens
Sat in the king's ha',
And bonnie Jeannie Gordon
Was the flower o' them a'.

4   Doon cam' Jeannie Gordon
She cam' trippin' doon stairs,
And she fancied Glenlogie
Above all that was there.

5   She called on his footboy
That walked by his side,
Says, 'What call you that young man
Or where does he bide?'

6   He's styled Glenlogie
When he is at home,
But he's o' the gay Gordons,
And his name is Lord John.

7   Glenlogie, Glenlogie,
Ye'll be constant and kind,
For I lay my love upon you,
And I'll tell you my mind.

8   He's turned round smartly,
As the Gordons do all,
I'm obliged to you, love Jeannie,
But I'm promised awa'.

9   She called to her maiden
To make her a bed,
She'd some fine sheets and blankets
They were quickly down spread.

10   Down came her father
He came tripping down stairs
Says, 'Oh what ails ye Jeannie
That ye are lyin' there?'

11   He's a nice little fellow
With a dark rolling eye,
If I get na Glenlogie
For him I will die.

12   Her father had a chaplain,
A man of great fame,
He wrote a braid letter
And pennèd it well.

13   Glenlogie, Glenlogie,
Be constant and kind
And let not this virgin
Now die in her prime.

14 When Glenlogie got the letter
   He was among men,
   It's out spake Glenlogie
   What does young Lemon mean?

15 Ye'll saddle the black horse,
   Go saddle the brown,
   Bonnie Jeannie o' Bethelnie
   Will be dead ere I win.

16 Lang or the black horse was saddled
   And o'er to the Green,
   Bonnie Glenlogie
   Was three miles him lane.

17 When he came to Bethelnie,
   There was nobody there,
   But ae bonnie lassie
   Sat combing her hair.

18 If ye be the maiden
   Tak' me by the han'
   And ye'll lead me to the chamber
   Jeannie Gordon lies in.

19 O pale and weary was she
   When he gaed in,
   But red and rosy grew she
   When she saw it was him.

20 O where does your pain lie,
   Does it lie in your side?
   O where does your pain lie,
   Does it lie in your head?

21 Glenlogie, O Glenlogie,
   Ye are far frae the place,
   For the pain that I lie under
   Lies below my left breast.

22 Come turn to your side, Jeannie,
   Come turn to your side,
   For the morn I'll be the bridegroom,
   And ye'll be the bride.

23 Now Jeannie's got married,
   And her tocher doon told,
   Bonnie Jeannie o' Bethelnie
   Was scarce sixteen years old.

24 Bethelnie, O Bethelnie,
   Ye shine where ye stand,
   May the heather bells around you
   Shine o'er Fyvie's land.

GD 973A. Child 238 Glenlogie. The music was collected by Greig in August 1905 and the words were received in January 1907. Greig wrote in the *Buchan Observer*, 12 January 1909: 'Glenlogie is one of our most popular ballads. It is found in widely varying forms, but would seem to belong originally to the north.' There are nineteen versions of it in the collection. [Pent].
Editorial Note Tonic lowered from Bb to A.

him lane – alone; *tocher* – dowry

83. The Braes o' Strathdon

JAMES W. SPENCE

As I was a-wal-king one eve-ning in May, Down by yon flow-ery gar-dens I care-less-ly did stray; I spied a pret-ty fair maid, she was stan-ding a-lone, And blea-ching her clothes on the Braes o' Strath-don.

1 As I was awalking one evening in May,
Down by yon flowery gardens I carelessly did stray;
I spied a pretty fair maid, she was standing alone,
And bleaching her clothes on the Braes o' Strathdon.

2 I stepped up to her as I meaned to pass
Says, You're bleaching your clothing, my bonnie young lass
Tis twelve months and better, since I had a mind
To go and get married if you are inclined.

3 To marry, to marry, I am far far too young
Besides all ye young men have so flattering tongues
My parents would chide me and right angry be
If I were to marry a rover like thee.

4 Oh hold your tongue bonny lass and do not say no
You don't know the pains love that I undergo
Consent, dearest lassie, consent and be mine
And we will live happy on the braes o' Strathdon.

5 Oh get ye gone young man, I care not what you say
I think you'd be better to go on your way
For I am far happier while I stand here alone
Than with you and yours on the braes o' Strathdon.

6 He turned himself round about, the tear in his e'e
Says 'May you have a good one whoever he be
I'll go court another, leave you standing alone
I'll soon find another on the braes of Strathdon.'

7 Come back dearest laddie, ye hae gained my heart
Till death separate us we'll never mair part
We'll never mair part love till the day that we dee
May a' good attend us wherever we be.

8   Now ye have consented but it's quite out of time
     Since the last words ye spoke love, I have altered my mind
     The clouds are fast lowering, I'm afraid we'll have rain
     So they shook hands and parted on the braes o' Strathdon.

9   Come all ye young fair maids wherever ye be
     Never slight a young man for his poverty
     By the slighting of this young man I'm afraid I'll get none
     I'll be doomed to live single on the braes of Strathdon.

GD 1132A. The song was collected by Greig in 1906. He notes that it is very popular in the north and that the tune 'is one of the finest airs we have' (*Buchan Observer*, 31 March 1908). [Pent].
Editorial Note Text lyric has 'Ableaching her clothing' for 'And bleaching her clothes' (1.4).

84. Cameloun

JAMES W. SPENCE

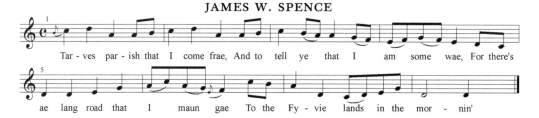

Tar-ves par-ish that I come frae, And to tell ye that I am some wae, For there's ae lang road that I maun gae To the Fy-vie lands in the mor-nin'

1   Tarves parish that I come frae,
     And to tell ye that I am some wae,
     For there's ae lang road that I maun gae
     To the Fyvie lands in the mornin'.

2   At Cameloun I did arrive
     A pair of horses for to drive
     And ilka morn to rise at five
     And ca' the fan in the mornin'.

3   I hadna weel begun to sleep
     When the foreman he began to creep
     And oot o's bed he sprang to's feet
     Cries 'Losh boys rise for it's mornin'.'

4   To ca' the fan they set me tae
     Which I began richt cannily
     And took a look fu' they wid dee
     In the Fyvie lands in the mornin'.

5   We hae a bailie stoot and stark
     It sets him weel to work his wark
     But owre his heid he's drawn a sark
     As lang's himsel' in the mornin'.

6   I hadna long been at the ploo
     When I began to couck and spue
     The nicht afore I'd been some foo
     Sae I had a dowie mornin'.

7   Tarves parish is lang and wide
     Tarves parish is fu o' pride
     But in this cauld corner I'll nae langer bide
     Gin I had Whitsunday mornin'.

GD 389Aa. The music was collected by Greig in July 1905. He noted that this is a characteristic specimen of the ploughman song and that Spence gave the author's name as R. Cooper (*Buchan Observer*, 17 March 1908). Cameloun is near Fyvie Castle. [Dor].
Editorial Note Text lyric has 'It's Tarves' for 'Tarves' (1.1). The inclusion of 'It's' in this verse together with the first word of each of verses 2–6 suggests that the opening grace note would normally be an anacrusis.

some wae – rather sad; *fan* – instrument for winnowing grain; *stark* – strong; *couck* – retch; *dowie* – woeful

Sam Davidson

1864–1951

Sam Davidson

Sam Davidson, a farmer at Auchedly, Tarves, was a well-known figure in his local area who frequently performed on stage. He was born in 1864 at Northseat, Auchedly, to Samuel and May Davidson (née Godsman),[1] and died in 1951 in Aberdeen.[2] In 1938 he recalled:

> I have attended many musical evenings both in the district and further afield. I think I have sung in all the schools within twenty miles of my home and there again I formed many pleasant friendships. It was when I was singing one evening at Cuminestown that I met for the first time Gavin Greig of New Deer whose friendship I prized highly.[3]

This meeting likely took place prior to September 1902, when the first of Mr Davidson's songs (the words of 391 'The Weary Fairmers' A) entered the collection. The first mention of Davidson in the *Buchan Observer* is on 3 March 1908:

> My musical friend Mr Sam. Davidson, Tarves, kindly sends me copies of two old tunes. Mr Davidson has helped me from time to time in this way, some of my earliest records in fact having been made from his singing. I remember the last time we met was at the New Deer Cattle Show where my friend was acting as a judge. After his official duties were over we adjourned to a tent (there was nothing stronger about than ginger ale), where I

took down from his 'sowthin' one or two fine old tunes. I spare nobody and am hardest on my friends.

Greig was grateful to Davidson not only for contributing his own songs to the collection, but also for giving him the loan of a farm-servant's notebook, which contained thirty-eight songs. He wrote in the *Buchan Observer*, 7 April 1908: 'I only wish other people who may have MS. Collections would favour us with a look of them.' Notebooks containing words were common amongst singers of this period in the North East, and a good number have survived to the present day. Greig commented on one song as follows: 'Looking through a manuscript book of songs kindly lent by a farm servant, I have just come on one called "The Term" [700 C] which moves me deeply. It is in fact one of the most touching pieces of verse I have ever come across.' (*Buchan Observer*, 26 May 1908) A local song, which concerns a young man who goes out drinking in the village but ends up being forced into a fight, is 576 'The Tarves Rant' B, for which Davidson supplied a tune and one verse:

> Gae ear to me, you gay young lads that mean to tak' a spree;
> I'll tell to you a story withoot a word o' lee;
> My name I will not mention, it's hardly worth my while,
> I dinna like to harm mysel', or spend my time in jile.

Nineteen songs from Davidson appear in the collection. One of these was 1899 'Maggie Gordon' from Argo II (supplement to Argo 2), noted in 1904, which Greig did not write out as a fair copy. Greig's note 'Apply Mrs J Webster Tarves' indicates that Davidson was putting him on to a neighbour of his who would be likely to know more of the song. 'Maggie Gordon', which is not found elsewhere in the collection, is better known as 'Maggie Jardine'. A version of this music-hall song, sung by John Strachan, is available in the School of Scottish Studies Archives, University of Edinburgh.[4]

Sam Davidson was the last precentor in Tarves church before the installation of the church organ in 1882. Mr Arthur Watson from Tarves remembered Davidson and recollected that he sang at concerts and in the local church choir. He was also an instrumentalist: 'Sam liked to play the big Bass Fiddle, and would carry it on his back, on foot and bicycle the three miles from Northseat, to the village of Tarves, for any fiddle concert in the Village Hall.'[5]

NOTES

1 Birth record 1864/243/14.
2 Death record 1951/168/3/443.
3 See *Greig–Duncan*, vol. 8, p. 555.
4 SA1952.25.A8; cf. also the commercial recording 'The Best of John Mearns' (Ross Records, 2006, CDGR210).
5 Information from *Greig–Duncan*, vol. 8, p. 556. I am most grateful to Mr Watson for his kind help.

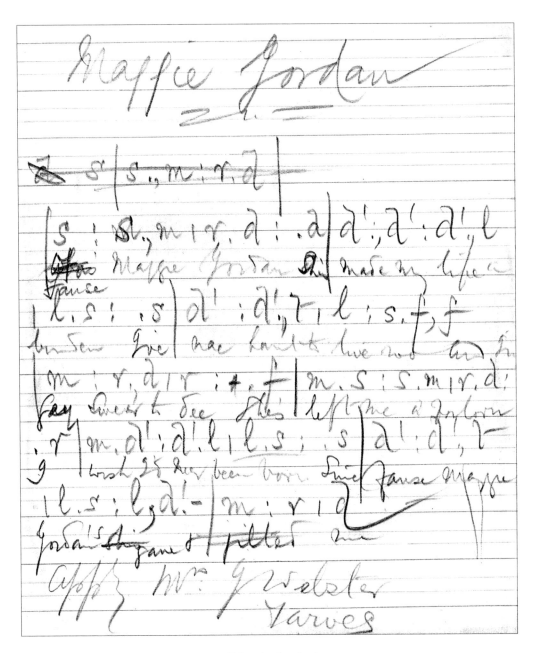

'Maggie Gordon'

85. The Fyvie Ploughman

SAM DAVIDSON

Come lis-ten all ye plough-man lads in Fy-vie's lands do dwell, I mean to sing the plough-man's praise, tho' I'm nae ane my-sel'; For they're the lads gars bar-ren lands, grow in a ver-dure green; They'll mould the lands like un-to us, and sow their seeds in spring.

1 Come listen all ye ploughman lads in Fyvie's lands do dwell,
   I mean to sing the ploughman's praise, tho' I'm nae ane mysel';
   For they're the lads gars barren lands, grow in a verdure green;
   They'll mould the lands like unto us, and sow their seeds in spring.

2 In summer and in winter months in autumn and in spring
   When going to and from the plough they whistle and they sing.
   Though the winter months be dreary they will brave the winter's blast
   The seeing o' their dearie 'twill warm the winter's frost.

3 The seeing o' their sweetheart is not to be denied
   Nor to such regulations I would not have them tied.
   But I would have you deal justly and not deceivers be
   Nor cheat the bonnie lassie that lays her love on thee.

4 She'll kindly sit doon by your side, her hand laid on your knee
   And sweetly smile into your face, her heart it's a' to thee
   And when you fold her in your arms the time it does beguile
   And when you do embrace her you do forget your toil.

5 To gie the ploughman justice is the thing I mean to dee
   Wi' twa or three exceptions to guide his penny fee.
   The lass that gets a ploughman tho' poor perhaps he be
   She'll never want a sixpence when he has ane to gie.

6 Remember well ye fairmers all there's men as good as thee
   And don't think you're obliging them while that they're serving thee.
   For there's fields of speculation all around as you may see
   And there is emigration to tak' them o'er the sea.

7 Remember then ye fairmers all there's men as good as thee
   And if you treat them kindly they will serve you faithfully.
   They will do their work wi' pleasure, time will extended be
   And you will increase their treasure by largely paying their fee.

GD 420A. The music of this song was collected by Greig in 1904. He noted in the *Buchan Observer*, 17 March 1908: 'Fyvie may be expected to have its ploughman songs. One of these sounds the praises of the ploughman. The sentiments are good, although the verse is at times a little lame.' [Dor/M].

Editorial Note Text lyric has 'that dwell' in place of 'do dwell' (1.1), 'They are the lads makes barren heath' in place of 'For they're the lads gars barren lands' (1.3), and 'They mould their lands like to the sands' in place of 'They'll mould the lands like unto us' (1.4). The tune lyric has 'Fyvie' in place of 'Fyvie's' (taken from the text lyric) (1.1). The title is from the text lyric; the tune has 'The Ploughman Lad'.

guide – manage economically

86. The Term Time

SAM DAVIDSON

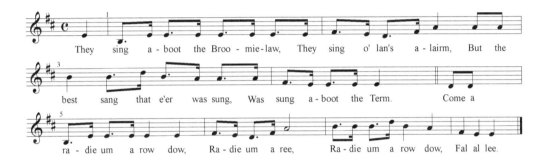

1 They sing aboot the Broomielaw,
   They sing o' lan's alairm,
   But the best sang that e'er was sung,
   Was sung aboot the Term.
   Come a radie um a row dow,
   Radie um a ree,
   Radie um a row dow,
   Fal al lee.

2 The term time is comin', lads,
   And we will a' win free,
   And wi' the weary fairmer
   Again we winna fee.

3 First there comes the market,
   And then there comes the term,
   So a' ye weary fairmers
   Dinna be alairmed.

4 They'll tap ye on the shouther
   And say 'Lad are ye to fee?'

And they'll tell ye a lang story
Perhaps it's a' a lee.

5 He'll pit his han' intae his pouch
   And he'll pu' oot a shillin',
   And he'll say the siller's unco scarce,
   Eh! the leein' villain!

6 They'll tell ye every jot o' work
   That ye hae tae perform,
   But then when ye gang hame tae them
   There'll be a ragin' storm.

7 On cauld kail and pitawtis
   They feed ye like a pig,
   When they ait at their tea and toast
   Or hurl i' their gig.

8 Wi' broad-tailed coats and Quaker hats
   And whups below their airm
   They dunt and ride on horseback
   When they get a fairm.

147

9 Wi' broad-tailed coats and Quaker hats,
   And spurs upo' their heels,
   Altho' ye ca' the country roon
   Ye winna get sic chiels.

10 And noo my sang is ended,
    A warnin' tak' frae me,
    And wi' the weary fairmer
    Be sure and dinna fee.

GD 391A. Words collected by Greig in September 1902; music in September 1907. The song's general title in the collection is 'The Weary Fairmers'. [Pent]. Robert Ford's *Vagabond Songs and Ballads of Scotland* (Paisley: Alexander Gardner, 1899, p. 249) has 'An' sound out an alarm' at 1.2, and states that the song 'has been sung as enthusiastically at foys and other gatherings, by those who meant to "fee again" for another term as by those who did not. Farmers' sons, even, have been wont to sing it with as much birr [enthusiasm] in the big houses above as the ploughmen in the bothies below' (p. 251).

Editorial Note Tonic lowered from G to E.

term – period of employment; *weary* – miserable; *to fee* – available for hire; *shouther* – shoulder; *pouch* – pocket; *kail* – cabbage, greens; *pitawtis* – potatoes; *hurl* – drive; *Quaker hat* – round hat with a low crown and an upturned brim; *dunt* – stamp about

87. Ythanside

SAM DAVIDSON

As I cam' in by Y-than-side, Where gen-tly flows the rol-ling tide, A bon-nie lass passed by my side, Her looks did me en-snare.

1 As I cam' in by Ythanside,
   Where gently flows the rolling tide,
   A bonnie lass passed by my side,
   Her looks did me ensnare.

2 This maid she was a beauty bright
   As ever trod the Braes o' Gight
   I could hae spent the lea lang night
   Wi' her on Ythanside.

3 I turned me round to Fyvie's belles
   And my poor heart ga many a knell
   I spiert the road to St John's Wells
   With courage stout and bold.

4 The maid she turned without delay
   And thus to me began to say
   I scarcely go two miles this May
   Young man I'll tell you plain.

5 But gin ye gae back the gate ye cam
   I'll get a man till show you hame
   Out ower yon bonny flowery glen
   And hame by Ythanside.

6 I thanked the maid and turned right bold
   The flocks were driving to the folds
   And many a lively tale she told
   Just as we passed along.

7 Till at length we reached her father's home
   Sae bashfully as I gaed ben
   Thinks I mysel I am frae hame
   Altho' on Ythanside.

8 But the people a' they seemed discreet
   And ilka ane aboot did creep
   The auld gudewife brought ben a seat
   And bade me to sit doon.

9   I sat me down the folk to please
     They treat me well wi' bread and cheese
     The bairnies a' flocked round like bees
     That wis a blithesome sight.

10 I sat me there right weel content
     The auld gudeman for news was bent
     To view the maid was my intent
     The truth I'll tell you plain.

11 But the servant lads began to spit
     And gather a' up to their fit
     Thinks I My lads ye're gyan to flit
     An' a' boun' for your beds.

12 Then up I started straight outright
     And bade them a' a blithe gude night
     And spiered the road to Mains o' Gight
     To which the man replied.

13 I'll show you by the barn door
     Judge ye gin our twa hearts was sore
     To think to part to meet no more
     Although on Ythanside.

14 I held the fair maid by the hand,
     The time was short we had to stand,
     I got a kiss upon demand
     These words to me she said.

15 When you come back this road again
     It's wi' you I will gyan
     And I gied fustling through the lane
     And hame by Ythanside.

GD 951A. Greig collected this song in 1904. [Æ/Dor].
Editorial Note Tonic lowered from G to E; text lyric has 'pleasant' for 'gently' (1.2), 'weel faur'd maid'
   for 'bonnie lass' (1.3), and 'Whose looks' for 'Her looks' (1.4).

lea lang – whole;   *gate* – way;   *till* – to;   *gudewife* – woman of the house;
   gudeman – man of the house;   *fit* – feet;   *fustling* – whistling

88. Buy Broom Besoms

SAM DAVIDSON

    Buy broom besoms
    Buy them when they're new,
    Fine heather reengers,
    Better never grew,

    Besoms for a penny,
    Reengers for a plack,
    Gin ye dinna buy them
    Lift them to my back.

GD 489A. Greig collected this song in April 1905. [M, -6].
Editorial Note Tonic lowered from F to C. Greig has written 'Rangers' (1.6) with 'ee' added above the
   letter 'a'.

broom besom – a broom for sweeping made with twigs of broom;   *reengers* – scourers;
   plack – small copper coin

Robert Alexander

1835–1917

Robert Alexander was born on 18 January 1835 in Towie parish in Aberdeenshire, the son of James Alexander, a farmer, and Garden Alexander (née McRobbie), who came from Strathdon.[1] He died on 17 October 1917 in the parish of Rubislaw in Aberdeen, aged eighty-two.[2]

Stewart Milne, Longside of Blair, Whiterashes, near Old Meldrum (who had been a member of Duncan's congregation at Lynturk) wrote to Duncan on 14 July 1906, saying:

> As you have not yet got down to make Longside a song-searching centre I have thought of sending a line or two to remind you of your task. There is a retired farmer, an old precentor living near, who I think will be able [to] recall several old songs, and possibly some of them may be new to you. He is willing to give audible specimens of both words and music.[3]

Duncan recorded tunes at Quarrylea, Whiterashes, from Robert Alexander and from his unmarried daughter, Beatrice, in September 1906, and returned in December of that year and in April 1907 to note additional tunes. Meantime, Milne was taking down the words of Alexander's songs in two notebooks.

Extract from 'The Exciseman in a Coal Pit'

Robert Alexander contributed sixty songs to the collection, ten of which were family songs that came from his mother, while other songs were learned from a variety of sources, including some in the farming context to which he belonged.[4] He had a particularly large number of narrative songs in his repertoire, including 282 'The Exciseman in a Coal Pit', part of which is shown here, for which he gave the only version in the collection.

NOTES
1 OPR 1835/245/2.
2 Death record 1917/168/3/579.
3 The manuscript number of Milne's letter to Duncan (which is written in shorthand) is 998/16/154.
4 See article on Robert Alexander by Andrew R. Hunter in *Greig–Duncan*, vol. 8, p. 549.

89. The Haughs o' Newe

ROBERT ALEXANDER

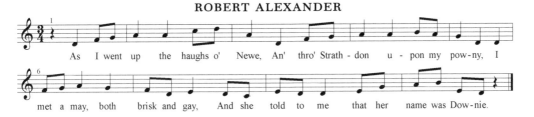

As I went up the haughs o' Newe, An' thro' Strath-don u - pon my pow-ny, I met a may, both brisk and gay, And she told to me that her name was Dow-nie.

1   As I went up the haughs o' Newe,
    An' thro' Strathdon upon my powny,
    I met a may, both brisk and gay,
    And she told to me that her name was Downie.

2   Her face so fair an her coal black hair
    Her eyes they shone like ony lamber
    I viewed her charms fae top tae toe
    Till my heed grew light and my feet did stammer.

3   I said 'Fair maid, from whence come ye
    Where is your home or father's dwelling.'
    'In yonder glen sir, I'll tell you plain
    A hunter is my father's calling.'

4   It's of your glens I am afraid
    And likewise of your occupation
    Bit if Downies be such beauties rare
    There's few of them into oor nation.

5   Your Gaelic tongue I cannot speak,
    Because my mother never learned
    But to dance a reel I'll do it genteel
    With anyone in a' Strathearn.

6   I will range the fairs baith far an near
    An a between Aboyne an Tarland
    I'll do me up an to Corgarf
    For there I'm sure I'll find my darlin.

7   For the like o her's nae to be seen
    In a Strathspey nor yet Strathearn
    She far excells our Cuttie's Jean
    Lives jist as ye gang ower the Cairn.

GD 1238. The music was collected by Duncan in September 1906 and the words by Stewart Milne in
    October/November. The song was learned by Alexander from his mother who was brought up in
    Towie. The 'Cairn' (7.4) is the 'Cairn o' Mounth' according to William Christie, and Duncan noted
    that 'Cuttie was a public house at the foot of the Cairn'. [Dor].
Performance Note Duncan gives the pronunciation 'Newe = Nyow' (1.1) and also gives the spelling
    'powny' (for pony) in the tune lyric (1.2), indicating that the word rhymes with 'Downie'.
Editorial Note Tonic lowered from E to D; text lyric has 'maid' for 'may' (1.3).

lamber – amber;   *into* – in

90. The Shepherd, or Andrew Roo

ROBERT ALEXANDER

1   A shepherd keeps sheep on yon mountain sae high,
    Faldril ay, faldril addie.
    A shepherd keeps sheep on yon mountain sae high,
    A pretty fair maid she came trippling bye,
    Wi' my rairy, tairie, faldril ee,
    Faldril ay, faldril addie!

2   'O shepherd, O shepherd what makes you look wae?
    Ye look as though you hadn't got breakfast today.'

3   'O pretty maiden what makes you say so?
    You'l see I've got breakfast before that you go.'

152

4   He changed his plaid, his crook, his dog,
      And he changed his name frae Roo to Hogg.

5   He winked on an eye just as though he'd been blind
      An' he happ'd on one leg, trailed the other behind.

6   When six months were over this girl came through
      And she sought for a shepherd they called Andrew Roo.

7   'O pretty maiden ye're surely mista'en,
      For there ne'er was a shepherd here called by that name.'

8   Ye're much o' the colour, ye're much o' the hue
      If you werena half blind, I would swear it was you.'

9   'O lassie gang back the road that ye cam'
      Gae father your babe on some other man.'

GD 1467A. The words were noted by Stewart Milne in January or February 1907 and the music was
noted by Duncan on 29 April 1907. [Æ/Dor].
Editorial Note Tonic lowered from E to D; text lyric has 'kept' in place of 'keeps' (1.1 and 1.3), 'Falderile
falderaladie' (1.2), and 'Wi' my rari tari falderale falderala falderaladie' (1.5–6).

91. Oysters

ROBERT ALEXANDER

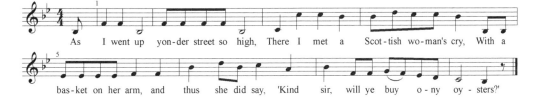

As I went up yon-der street so high, There I met a Scot-tish wo-man's cry, With a bas-ket on her arm, and thus she did say, 'Kind sir, will ye buy o-ny oy-sters?'

1   As I went up yonder street so high,
      There I met a Scottish woman's cry,
      With a basket on her arm, and thus she did say,
      'Kind sir, will ye buy ony oysters?'

2   'Oysters' said she, 'Oysters' said he
      'How many oysters for one pennie.'
      'You shall have more than one, two, three
      According to the size o my oysters.'

3   'O waiter' said he 'O waiter' said he
      'Have you any room for this girlie an me
      That we may eat an drink an merry merry be
      Wi oor white breed an wine to oor oysters.'

4 'O yes' said the waiter 'that I can do
I have got room for this girlie an you
Where ye may eat an drink an merry merry be
Wi your white breed an wine to your oysters.'

5 They werna weel in nor yet sitten doon
When she picked his pockets of five hundred pown
When she picked his pockets of five hundred pown
Left him nothing but a basketful of oysters.

6 'O yes' said that waiter 'her I did see
I saw the girlie you brought in with thee
She's up yonder street and she's down yonder lane
Left you nothing but a basketful of oysters.'

7 'O then' said the gentleman 'I'm nae worth a groat'
'O then' said the waiter 'I'll have your coat,
O then' said the waiter 'I'll have your coat
For your white breed an wine to your oysters.'

8 O I've been in England an I've been in France
But I never met with siccan a mischance
For a Scottish woman's learned an Englishman a dance
And she's learned him the wye to bye oysters.

GD 304C. The music was noted by Duncan in September 1906 and the words were noted by Milne in October/November 1906. The song was learned by Alexander in Culsalmond. Greig wrote of the song in the *Buchan Observer*, 12 October 1909: '[It] is a lively ditty and very popular. The sum stolen from the gentleman varies in different copies from five hundred to ten thousand pounds. We have taken the lowest figure as being sufficiently big for even an Englishman to be carrying about with him, and quite enough for "the creelie and the oysters". The tune, which I have recorded several times, is lively and stirring, and more modern in style than the average folk-tune.' [I].
Editorial Note Tonic lowered from D to Bb; text lyric has 'There I heard a Scottish woman cry' (1.2).

groat – coin worth fourpence; *wye* – way

92. Aul' Langsyne

ROBERT ALEXANDER

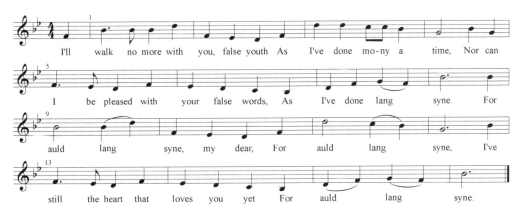

I'll walk no more with you, false youth As I've done mo-ny a time, Nor can I be pleased with your false words, As I've done lang syne. For auld lang syne, my dear, For auld lang syne, I've still the heart that loves you yet For auld lang syne.

1   I'll walk no more with you, false youth
    As I've done mony a time,
    Nor can I be pleased with your false words,
    As I've done lang syne.
    For auld lang syne, my dear,
    For auld lang syne,
    I've still the heart that loves you yet
    For auld lang syne.

2   'Another fair maid fills your arms
    The place that once was mine
    She's enjoying the pleasures of
                your sweet charms
    As I've done many a time.

3   'But may she flourish in your arms
    And ever happy be
    She's innocent, she's ignorant
    How ye deceivèd me.

4   'But if ever I do hae a hoose
    That I can call it mine
    Ye's aye be welcome into it
    For aul' langsyne.'

5   He's taen her in his airms twa
    An' gien her kisses nine
    An' after that he's married her
    For aul' langsyne.

GD 1143A. The music was noted by Duncan in September 1906 and the words in October/November 1906 by Stewart Milne. The song was learned by Alexander in Culsalmond *c.*1846. [I].
Editorial Note Tonic lowered from C to Bb.

auld lang syne – old time's sake

155

93. The Exciseman in a Coal Pit

ROBERT ALEXANDER

I know that young folks like to hear a new song Of some-thing that's fun-ny and

not ve-ry long; Con-cer-ning an ex-cise-man the truth I will tell, Who

thought one night he was lan-ded in hell. An' sing fal de dal day, dal dad-die i-doo.

1   I know that young folks like to hear a new song
      Of something that's funny and not very long;
      Concerning an exciseman the truth I will tell,
      Who thought one night he was landed in hell.
      An' sing fal de dal day, dal daddie i-doo.

2   The exciseman went out for to look for his prey
      He met two or three smugglers upon the highway
      And gauging there liquors they had got to sell
      The exciseman got drunk for the truth I will tell.

3   He got so drunk that he fell to the ground
      And like a fat sow he was forced to lie down
      Just nigh to a coal pit the exciseman did lie
      When four or five colliers by chance passed by.

4   They shouldered him up and they carried him away
      Like a pedler's pack, without any delay
      And into a bucket they handed him down,
      This jolly exciseman they got underground.

5   The exciseman awoke in a terrible fear
      Up started a collier, says 'What brought you here?'
      'Indeed Mr Devil I don't very well know
      But I think I am come to regions below.'

7   'O what was you then in the world above?'
      'O I was a gauger, and few did me love
      But indeed Mr Devil the truth I will tell
      For since I've got here I shall be what you will.'

8   'O then' said the collier 'it's here ye'll remain
      Ye'll never get out of this dark cell again
      For the gates they are shut and they'll bind you secure
      All this you must suffer for robbing the poor.'

9 'O Mr Devil have pity on me
   I'll ne'er go a-robing the poor ye shall see
   If you would look over as you've done before
   I'll ne'er go a-robbing the poor any more.'

10 'Then give us a guinea to drink with demand
   Before ye get back to a Christian land'
   'O yes Mr Devil,' the gauger did say
   'For I long to get back to see the light of day.'

GD 282. The words were noted by Stewart Milne in October/November 1906 and the music by Duncan in December 1906. Alexander had learned the song from a 'travelling character in early days'. [M, with inflected third].

Editorial Note Tonic lowered from E to D; text lyric 1.1 has 'folk' in place of 'folks' (1.1), and the word 'he' is not present (1.4); a quaver has been split into two semiquavers in bar 5 to accommodate the words.

Isaac Troup
1853–1938

Isaac Troup with his wife Christina

Isaac Troup was born at East Cranloch on 2 December 1853 to Isaac Troup, a mason, and Margaret Troup (née Neish).[1] He came from a musical family and his brothers Alexander and George also contributed to the collection. On 23 June 1883, at Cults in the parish of Kinneth-mont, he married Christina Gall and the couple had twelve children.[2]

The photograph below of Ythanwells shows Gowanlea (bottom right) where Isaac Troup lived when he retired.[3] The farm of East Cranloch, where he spent his working life, is not shown, but lies just beyond the manse to the top left of the photo.

On 2 November 1906, Troup attended a lecture that Duncan gave on folk-song in the Public

158

Letter from Isaac Troup to Alexander Keith, 2 September 1925

Hall, Alford, and spoke about it enthusiastically to his neighbour, James Alexander, who contacted Duncan to suggest that he meet with the Troup brothers.[4] Duncan followed up the suggestion and collected in Ythanwells on 11 September 1907, and 29 June and 3 September 1908. Thirty-one songs from Isaac appear in the collection. Carpenter recorded material from

Ythanwells, showing Gowanlea

Isaac and Alexander and from another brother called James at Ythanwells *c.*1930.[5] Isaac Troup died on 9 March 1938 at the age of eighty-four.[6]

Mrs Mary Hay, a granddaughter of Isaac Troup, remembered her grandfather, who died when she was aged seventeen. She grew up at Sunnyside, Ythan Wells, and recalled him singing songs such as 'Come Under my Plaidie' at the fireside, but said that he also sang in public at events like children's concerts. He did not play any instruments as far as she could remember.[7]

A letter from Troup to Alexander Keith dated 2 September 1925 (opposite) describes his contact with Duncan as well as his own musical abilities.

NOTES

1 Information from article on Isaac Troup by Rosalind Cheyne, *Greig–Duncan*, vol. 8, p. 592, and from marriage record 1883/212/4.

2 Marriage record, and information from Mrs Mary Hay, Turriff (interview 5 February 2004, El2004.04). I am most grateful to Mrs Hay for her kind help.

3 Information from Mrs Mary Hay.

4 *Greig–Duncan*, vol. 8, p. 592.

5 See *The James Madison Carpenter Collection Online Catalogue* http://www.hrionline.ac.uk/carpenter

6 Death record 1938/202/9.

7 Information from Mrs Mary Hay.

94. I Am a Miller to My Trade

ISAAC TROUP

1 I am a miller to my trade, an' that fu' weel ye ken, O,
   I am a miller to my trade, an' that fu' weel ye know;
   I am a miller to my trade, an' mony's the sieve o' meal I've made,
   Coortit mony's the bloomin' maid among the sacks o' meal, O.

2 Merrily the stone goes round, rightly goes she full, O,
   Merrily the stone goes round, when grinding peas or corn,
   Merrily the stone goes round, when the grain is dry and sound,
   A better trade was never found since ever I was born, O.

3 It was upon one night in June, that I being alone, O,
   It was upon one night in June a maid came past the mill;
   Said she, 'In passing by the linn, I heard your merrily clapping din,
   I thought to mysel' I would come in to see your ain dear sel', O.'

4 Says I, 'My lass, you're welcome here, and aye will be the same, O,
   Says I, My lass, you're welcome here, I'll welcome you again,
   Says I, My lass, you're welcome here, an' what's your news and I maun spier
   If ye'll consent to be my dear about the even time, O.'

5 The laughing lass she gave a smile, and says, 'I dinna ken, O.'
   The laughing lass she gave a smile, and says, 'I canna tell';
   The laughing lass she gave a smile, and says, 'Young man, just wait a while,
   And gin my heart ye fairly win, ye'll get me to yoursel', O.'

6 I kissed her lips fu' sweet and wee, sweeter far than honey,
   I kissed her lips fu' sweet and wee, it seemed that I was blest,
   I kissed her lips fu' sweet and wee, until the tear came in her ee
   'I'll lea' my mother a' for thee, and always love thee best, O.'

161

7   That night we named the wedding day, that night that I kissed fairly,
    That night we named the wedding day, it seemed that I was blest;
    The time it soon did slip awa, a year as weeks een or twa,
    And then did come the wedding day of my ain lovely Jean, O.

8   And now we've lived a married life, and happy we've been together,
    Now we've lived a married life, and happy may we be;
    So now we've lived a married life, I've got a canty carefu' wife,
    She always shines in company, she's not like some I see.

9   Dear freens, ye must excuse me noo, my hands are turnin' sore,
    Dear freens, you must excuse me noo, my thooms are turnin' lang,
    Dear freens, you must excuse me noo, for my arms are turnin' blue,
    I've got a wife, and so may you: what think ye o' my sang, O?

GD 1489A. The song was collected by Duncan on 11 September 1907. Duncan noted: 'Learnt from some
masons about 1874. . . . Mr Troup states that the song was always sung with the action of turning
the left hand from side to side, and striking each side alternately with the right, so as to imitate the
sound of the mill.' [Æ/Dor]. In the note to version C from William Wallace, Duncan stated: 'Mr
Wallace explained that the song was generally sung with an imitation of the mill sound by two
people, one striking on the top of one closed hand with the other, and on the table alternately;
while the other person imitated the sound of the hopper by a glass tumbler rolling round on a table,
and striking a spoon as it passes.'
Editorial Note Tonic lowered from G to E; text lyric has 'And coorted' for 'Coortit' (1.4).

linn – waterfall

95. The Thiggin' Song

ISAAC TROUP

The aul' year's deen an' the new's be-gun, Be-soo-thin', be-soo-thin; An
noo the beg-gars they are come, An' a-wa by soo-thin toon.

1   The aul' year's deen an' the new's begun,
    Besoothin', besoothin';
    An noo the beggars they are come,
    An' awa by soothin toon.

2   Rise up, gweedwife, an' binna sweer,
    An' deal your charity to the peer.

3   It's nae for wirsel 't we stan' for,
    Bit seekin' charity for the peer.

4   Ye'll tak' th' peck bit nae the muttie,
    An' deal your charity lairge an' lucky.

5   Yer door is open an' we'll come in,
    An' we'll return wi' little din.

6   In meal an' money gin ye be scant,
    We'll kiss yer lasses or we want.

GD 642A. The music was noted by Duncan on 11 September 1907 and the words were derived by both Duncan and Greig from Troup's version of the song that appeared in the *Aberdeen Free Press*, 26 October 1906, p. 10, col. 1. The song was sung at New Year in the North East by groups of young men going round 'thigging' or begging oatmeal or cash on behalf of the poor. [Æ/Dor].

Editorial Note Tonic lowered from B to A; text lyric has 'have' for 'are' (1.3), and 'besoothan' for 'by soothin'' (1.4).

gweedwife – woman of the house; *binna* – be not; *sweer* – reluctant; *wirsel* – ourselves;
muttie – measure for grain equal to about a quarter of a peck

96. Greenland

ISAAC AND ALEXANDER TROUP

A - gain for Green - land we are bound, We leave you all be - hind, With tim - bers firm and hearts so warm We'll sail be - fore the wind.

1 Again for Greenland we are bound,
   We leave you all behind,
   With timbers firm and hearts so warm
   We'll sail before the wind.

2 We do not go to face our foe
   Upon yon raging main;
   We only sail to catch the whale,
   We'll soon return again.

3 We leave behind us on the shore
   All whom we love most dear,
   We leave our sweethearts and our wives
   All weeping on the pier.

4 The weeping baby's hushed asleep
   With its bosom full o' pain;
   Dry up your tears for half a year,
   We'll soon return again.

5 A blowing breeze came from the south,
   All sails they seemed asleep;
   Three cheers more, and we left the shore,
   And we floated on the deep.

6 In tarry dress we'll reach Dromness,
   Perhaps we go on shore;
   When water's less or the landsmen's scarce,
   We always takes in more.

7 At length we safely reach the ice,
   And quickly crowns all sail
   With the boat well manned, a gallant band,
   For to pursue the whale.

8 Till dark and dreary grows the night,
   And stars begin to burn,
   With the valiant crew, and hearts all true,
   For the ship she does return.

9 When the ship's got load, and homewards
   And past yon Orkney Isles,   [bound,
   With a flowing cup, brimmed to the lip,
   The time we had beguiled.

10 When the shore comes in our view,
   The pilot boat draws near,
   We see our sweethearts and our wives
   All waiting on the pier.

11 When the ship's got moored and safe
   And all paid off on shore,   [secured,
   With plenty o' brass and a bonny lass,
   We make the taverns roar.

12 To Greenland's frost we'll drink a toast,
   To it we hold most dear,
   We'll cross the main to it again,
   And we'll take a trip next year.

GD 10A. The music, which Isaac had learned from his father 'long ago', was collected by Duncan on 3 September 1908. The words came chiefly from Alexander Troup. Greig stated that this was the most popular of all the North-East whaling songs (*Buchan Observer*, 27 July 1909). 'Dromness' (6.1) is used for Stromness in Orkney where the ships from Aberdeen stopped on their way to and from the whaling (*Greig–Duncan*, vol. 1, p. 499). [Æ].
Editorial Note Tonic lowered from E to D; text lyric has 'To' for 'We' (1.2), and 'all' for 'so' (1.3).

crowns – crowd, set

97. Broadlan' Lan'

ISAAC TROUP

I am a young gentleman délights in hunting, A - mong yon high moun-tains lies far i' the sooth, An' there I fell in love wi' a bon - ny young las - sie, An' O gin I hid 'er in Broad - lan' hoose. Broad - lan' hoose! Broad - lan' hoose! And O gin I hid 'er in Broad - lan' hoose!

1   I am a young gentleman délights in hunting,
    Among yon high mountains lies far i' the sooth,
    An' there I fell in love wi' a bonny young lassie,
    An' O gin I hid 'er in Broadlan' hoose.
    Broadlan' hoose! Broadlan' hoose!
    An' O gin I hid 'er in Broadlan' hoose!

2   Her face it is fair without any stain,
    Her weel made foot and her lily-white han';
    And when I look to her, my heart it's in pain,
    And oh gin I had her in Broadlan' lan'.
    Broadlan' lan', Broadlan' lan',
    And oh gin I had her in Broadlan' lan'.

3   But in a short time, her apron grew short,
    Her petticoats they wadna meet by a span;
    But oh the fine fellow, he gave me his hand,
    Says, 'I'll make you the lady o' Broadlan' lan'.'
    Broadlan' lan', Broadlan' lan',
    Says, 'I'll make you the lady o' Broadlan' lan'.'

4   Her father and mother they gave her advice
    For to stay at home in the lan's o' the sooth,
    For all his prosuasion had proved all in vain,
    'For he's nae the laird o' Broadlan' lan'.
    Broadlan' lan', Broadlan' lan',
    For he's nae the laird o' Broadlan' lan'.'

5   The gentlemen they stood all in a course
    To see how the lady wad manage her horse,
    The laird gaed a boo, wi' his hat in his hand,
    Says, 'You're welcome, my dear, to Broadlan' lan'.'
    Broadlan' lan', Broadlan' lan',
    Says Ye're welcome, my dear, to Broadlan' lan'.

6   'Your face it is fair, without any stain,
    Your weel made fit and your lily white hand;
    And when I look to you my heart it's in pain,
    But you're now the lady o' Broadlan' lan'.'
    Broadlan' lan', Broadlan' lan',
    But you're now the lady o' Broadlan' lan'.

GD 1494A. This song was collected from both Isaac and Alexander Troup and the music was taken down by Duncan on 29 June 1908. It had been learned from their father and mother. Duncan commented that 'the remarkable notes at the opening of the refrain were specially tested, and were uniformly sung as noted'. Apart from a fragment from William Scott in *Greig–Duncan*, this is our only known version of the song. [Æ].

Performance Note 'Broadlan' should be pronounced 'Broadlin' according to Duncan's comments.

Editorial Note Tonic lowered from C to A.

98. The Banks o' Inverurie

ISAAC TROUP

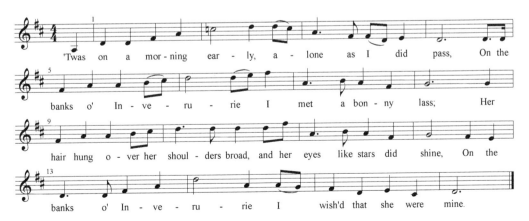

'Twas on a mor-ning ear-ly, a-lone as I did pass, On the banks o' In-ve-ru-rie I met a bon-ny lass; Her hair hung o-ver her shoul-ders broad, and her eyes like stars did shine, On the banks o' In-ve-ru-rie I wish'd that she were mine.

1 'Twas on a morning early, alone as I did pass,
  On the banks o' Inverurie I met a bonny lass;
  Her hair hung over her shoulders broad, and her eyes like stars did shine,
  On the banks o' Inverurie I wish'd that she were mine.

2 I did embrace this fair maid, with all the haste I could,
  Her har hang over her shoulders broad like to the threads of gold
  Her cherry cheeks and rubby lips and her eyes like drops of dew,
  On the banks of Inverurie I'm glad to meet with you.

3 Hold off your hands young man she said and do not trouble so
  For after kissing then comes wooing after wooing woe.
  My tender heart might be betrayed, and me beguiled be
  On the banks of Inverurie I'll walk alone said she.

4 You think young man I know you not your thoughts are all in vain
  For ye are come of gentle blood sprung from a barbarous train
  I know your occupation for good it may not be
  On the banks of Inverurie to flatter maids like me.

5 Oh no my pretty fair maid, the truth I'll not deny,
  It was on Inverurie banks twelve maids beguiled have I.
  But now I'll not begin this thing my charmer with thee
  On the banks of Inverurie, my wedded wife you'll be.

6 He's put a horn to his mouth and blew it loud and shrill.
  There was fifty-five wellarmed men, who drew their master till,
  It's here we used to flatter maids, but noo that wanno de
  On the banks of Inverurie I've found my wife said he.

7 You'll take this pritty fair maid set her on horseback high
  Unto some parson we will ride be married presently
  But now I'm bound to sing this lines until the day I dee
  To give the prais to Inverurie banks where first I did her see.

GD 1263A. The music was noted by Duncan on 3 September 1908 and the words were forwarded to
   him in December 1908 from Overton, Glenfoudland. The song had been learned by Alexander
   Troup from his mother. Greig noted in the *Buchan Observer*, 11 February 1908: 'The air to which the
   "Banks of Inverurie" is sung is particularly fine. It seems to be of Gaelic origin.' [I with inflected
   VII].
Editorial Note Tonic lowered from E to D; text lyric has 'It was' for ' 'Twas' (1.1), and 'hang' for 'hung'
   (1.3).

train – strain, family

99. Tam Broon

ISAAC TROUP

Let the king tak the queen and the queen tak the jeck, And we shall all be merry boys, since we're a drunken set. Here's to you, Tam Broon, Here's to you, my jolly loon, Here's to you with all my heart, An we shall have a bottle or two before that we do part. Here's to you, Tam Broon.

1 Let the king tak the queen and the queen tak the jeck,
   And we shall all be merry boys, since we're a drunken set.
   Here's to you, Tam Broon,
   Here's to you, my jolly loon,
   Here's to you with all my heart,
   An' we shall have a bottle or two before that we do part.
   Here's to you, Tam Broon.

2 Let the jeck tak the ten, and the ten tak the nine,
   And we shall all be merry boys, since we are drinking wine.

3 Let the nine tak the eight, and the eight tak the seven,
   And we shall all be merry boys, as we go to Newhaven.

4 Let the seven tak the six, and the six tak the five,
   And we shall all be merry boys, since we are all alive.

5 Let the five tak the four, and the four tak the three,
   And we shall all be merry boys, since we do all agree.

6 Let the three tak the two, and the two tak the one,
   And we shall all be merry boys, and end where we began.

GD 571. The music was noted by Duncan on 29 June 1908. This song, sometimes known as 'The Card Song', was learned by Isaac Troup from his father. Troup explained that it 'was acted with four persons round a table, the singer signalling to each of the four in succession'. The signalling was done by raising a glass in a toast. Peter Kennedy in *Folksongs of Britain and Ireland* (London: 1975, p. 630) gives further information on the song's performance: 'each member of the company contributed a suitable rhyme as he drained his glass before the whole party joined in the chorus'. [I/M].

Editorial Note Tonic lowered from G to F; the semiquavers in bar 16 were originally a quaver and were altered to accommodate the words; tune lyric has 'Lat' for 'Let' (1.1); text lyric has 'And with you we'se have' for 'An' we shall have' (1.6); Duncan has written 'knave' below 'jeck' in the tune lyric (1.1) since Troup gave this as the meaning of 'jeck' (i.e. 'jack').

Robert Chree

1852–1915

Robert Chree, who worked as a slater, was born, lived and died in Glenbuchat in Strathdon. His parents, who were unmarried, were John Chree, Sunnybrae, and Elizabeth McGregor, Ledmacay. Robert was born on 22 September 1852.[1] He died, aged sixty-three, on 3 October 1915 at the Mill of Glenbuchat.[2] Chree did not marry. The 1891 census places him as living at Sunnybrae with his father,[3] who was then a general merchant. The 1901 census shows him boarding at Kirktown of Glenbuchat along with Alexander Reid, a blacksmith, and his family.[4]

Duncan collected fourteen songs from Chree, all in 1906. The tunes were recorded as a batch in January in Alford, and additional words were taken down later in the year.[5] Duncan's noting of the tune and first verse of 'Kilbogie Toon' is reproduced below. His shorthand note at the end runs: 'Robert Chree, learned from Margaret Kellas, in Glenbuchat, about 40 years ago. He has all the words.' Duncan took down the words from Chree's dictation on 12 June 1906.[6]

'Kilbogie Toon'
(or 'Macdonald of the Isles')

NOTES

1 OPR/1852/240/3.
2 Death record 1915/200/3.
3 Census record 1891/200/1/11.
4 Census record 1901/200/1/4.
5 *Greig–Duncan*, vol. 8, p. 516.
6 *Greig–Duncan*, vol. 4, p. 560.

100. Kilbogie Toon

ROBERT CHREE

First when I cam to Kil - bo - gie's toon, Wi' my short coat an' my tar - tan plai - die,

First when I cam my bon-ny love to see, She lay in her bed till her break - fast was rea - dy.

1   First when I cam to Kilbogie's toon,
     Wi' my short coat an' my tartan plaidie,
     First when I cam my bonny love to see,
     She lay in her bed till her breakfast was ready.

2   When she got up, and put on her clothes,
     She said she had been on the hill wi' her daiddy,
     But weel kent I by her milk white hands
     She lay in her bed till her breakfast was ready.

3   When her breakfast was set doon,
     It was set doon and it was made ready,
     Oot spake her mother unto her,
     Have ye any regard for a Highland laddie?

4   It's I wid gie you all my silk goons,
     All my silk goons and my Glasgow plaidie,
     It's I wid leave them a' wi' you,
     And gae far far awa wi' my Highland laddie.

5   It's they went oot to tak a walk,
     To tak a walk till the dinner was ready,
     He's mounted her on his high horse back,
     And she's far far awa wi' her Highland laddie.

6   The first true love that they did meet,
     She said, Who is this that you hae wi' you?
     It is my sister, he did reply,
     And I'm takin her to the Highlands wi' me.

7   They rode on and farther on,
     There was nothing there fittin for a lady;
     There was nobody there for to welcome her hame
     But an aul carl and a cankered wifie.

8   The one o' them called her Lowlan Kate,
     The other called her Lowlan Jinny,
     But she gae them a far properer name,
     It was her Highland mam and her Highland daiddy.

9   They rode on and farther on,
     There was nothing there fittin for a lady,
     There was nothing there for to lay her on
     But a wee puckle heather and his Highland plaidie.

10 First when I cam to the Highlands wi' you,
     My stays wad hae laced like any lady,
     But noo they winna meet up and awa,
     It's wi' ower lang lyin' wi' a Highland laddie.

11 In my father's ha' there's sheets and blankets anew,
     They're a sewed and made ready,
     And wid'n they be richt angry to see
     Me lyin here wi' a Hielan laddie?

12 In the Highlands there's flocks and sheep anew,
     They are very thick and many,
     It's ye'll get woo, and ye can spin,
     And make you a blanket instead of a plaidie.

13 Flocks and sheep they're good and good enough,
     Corn stacks are muckle better;
     They will stand in drift and snaw,
     When the sheep will die wi' the wind and the weather.

14 In the Highlands I've got fifty acres o' land,
     It's a' ploughed and sown already,
     I am Ardonald of all the Isles,
     And why should not Peggy be called my lady?

15 In the Highlands I've got fifteen milk cows,
     They're a' tied to the sta's already,
     I am Ardonald of all the Isles,
     And why should not Peggy be called my lady?

16 A coach and six to me prepare:
     A coach and six they soon made ready;
     A coach and six to me prepare,
     And we'll go once more and see your daiddy.

GD 851A. 'Kilbogie Toon' was recorded by Duncan in 1906 (see above). Chree learned it when he was ten years old. Kilbogie is probably identifiable as the place of this name in Clackmannanshire. [Dor/M].

Performance Note Duncan stated: 'Perhaps it would better indicate the accent to put bar in the *middle* of the above measures'. This suggests that the third as opposed to the first beat of each bar should be stressed in performance.

Editorial Note Tonic lowered from E to D; text lyric omits first 'her' (1.4); Duncan suggests that line 6.1 should probably take the form 'His first true love when they did meet' and that 'Ardonald' (15.3) 'may represent a corruption of some such form as Sir Donald or Lord Donald'.

puckle – bit of; *anew* – enough

101. 'Twas in the Month of August

ROBERT CHREE

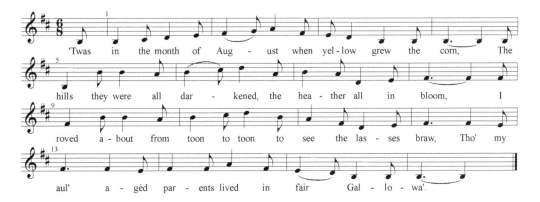

'Twas in the month of Aug - ust when yel - low grew the corn, The hills they were all dar - kened, the hea - ther all in bloom, I roved a - bout from toon to toon to see the las - ses braw, Tho' my aul' a - gèd par - ents lived in fair Gal - lo - wa'.

1 'Twas in the month of August when yellow grew the corn,
   The hills they were all darkened, the heather all in bloom,
   I roved about from toon to toon to see the lasses braw,
   Tho' my aul' agèd parents lived in fair Gallowa'.

2 Then into Glasgow toon I came, and doon upon a green,
   There was thousands of bonny lasses there to be seen,
   There was one amongst the rest, the flower ootowre them a',
   The bonniest lassie hereabout or yet in Gallowa'.

3 I steppèd up unto her for to enquire the way,
   The way I knew right well, to see what she would say;
   'You seem to be a stranger lad, wi' me you'll come awa,
   And I will show you straight the way doon by the Broomielaw.'

4 Alang with this fair maiden I instantly did go,
   Doon by the Clyde where the purling streams do flow;
   She was a charming bonny lass, the flower ootowre them a',
   Gweed spare her life, she'll be my wife in fair Gallowa'.

5 But unto this fair maiden I happened for to say,
   'It's a pity I have taken you so far out of your way;'
   But smiling in my face she said, 'I'm nae sae far awa,
   I bide wi' my auld mither here doon by the Broomielaw.'

6 I courted this fair maid by night and by day,
   Until the time appointed I had to go away;
   'It's tak your choice, my bonny lass, to bide or come awa,
   And I will show you straight the way to fair Gallowa'.

7 The road it is lang, love, the hills they are high,
   No friends nor relations have I to be nigh,
   And you'll rue the same, love, when I am far awa,
   You wi' your auld mither here, and me in Gallowa'.'

8   I turned me around for to go away,
    Sae strong as she invited me to stay anither day;
    This couple they've got married now, and live thegither braw,
    And now she lives a happy wife in fair Gallowa'.

GD 949A. The tune was noted by Duncan in January 1906. Chree had learned the song, which is known
    as 'Fair Gallowa" in the collection, in his youth. [Æ].
Editorial Note Tonic lowered from D to B; 'agèd' (1.4) is taken from the text lyric, the tune lyric has
    'aged'.

Gweed – God

102. The Sailing Trade

ROBERT CHREE

The sai - ling trade is a wea - ry life, It's be - rea - vèd me o' my heart's de - light; It's
left me here in tears to mourn, Just wai - ting for my Wil - lie's re - turn.

1   The sailing trade is a weary life,
    It's bereavèd me o' my heart's delight;
    It's left me here in tears to mourn,
    Just waiting for my Willie's return.

2   It's where he's gone I cannot tell,
    Nor in whose arms my love doth dwell,
    But who enjoys him at this same time
    Enjoys the fairest of all mankind.

3   The grass grows green where my love's been,
    The little birds sing in ilka tree,
    The nightingale in her cage doth sing
    To welcome Willie in the spring.

4   She's causèd them to make a boat
    That on the ocean she might float,
    And view the French ships as they passed by,
    And still enquire for her sailor boy.

5   She had not sailèd long on the deep,
    When a French ship she chanced to meet,
    'Oh captain, captain, pray tell me true,
    Is my true love on board with you?

6 'Amber is the colour of his hair,
His cheeks like roses, his skin so fair,
His lips like lilies all steeped in wine,
Ten thousand times they been joined to mine.'

7 'It's your true love an' he is na here,
He is drownèd in the depths, I fear,
It was just last night, as the wind blew high,
It was then we lost a fine sailor boy.'

8 The sailors they were all dressed in black,
The sailors they were right mournfully,
With their silken screen on their topmast high,
The wind did blow with a pleasant gale.

9 This fair maid she went to her home,
She has called for paper, and she has penned this song,
At ilka word she did shed a tear,
And at ilka line cried, 'Willie dear!'

10 As she was walking on the quay,
A row of sailors she chanced to see,
With their jackets blue and their troosers white,
Just mind her on her heart's delight.

11 She wrang her hands, she tore her hair,
Just like a lover in despair,
Oot owre a rock herself she's thrown,
'How could I live, and my darling gone?'

GD 1245A. The tune was noted by Duncan in January 1906. The song was learned by Chree *c.*1894 in Leochel-Cushnie from an Agnes Bain (said to have moved to South Africa). There are twelve versions of this song in the collection. [I/M].
Editorial Note Tonic lowered from F to C.

screen – black scarf as a sign of mourning

William Wallace

1849–1925

William Wallace's birth was recorded on 6 January 1849 in the parish of Leochel Cushnie. His parents were James Wallace and Ann Wallace (née Smith).[1] The 1891 census places him at the Episcopal Church Manse in Leochel Cushnie, along with the Reverend George M. Grassick, Grassick's wife, and their three children. Also present were Ellen Pithie, a visitor; Betsy M. Young, a kitchen maid; Jessie Reid, a house maid; and Jessie Young, a nurse.[2] Wallace was working as a farm servant at this time. In 1901, at the age of forty-nine he was living at Hillock in Leochel Cushnie and working as a ploughman. His employer was Charles Bruce, and Mary Smith, a housekeeper, was also present in the house.[3] This pattern of living with many unrelated people was typical of Wallace's lifestyle, and seems to account for his various song sources detailed below. Although neither of the census records places him at Woodcot, Leochel Cushnie, where he was living at the time that Duncan collected from him, his mother, Ann, was living there in 1891 and died there in 1900 at the age of seventy-one.[4]

Thirty-nine songs were collected from Wallace between 1908 and 1911. At the first of these, 1461 'Will the Weaver' B, Duncan stated: 'Noted from William Wallace (Woodcot), 4th August 1908. This and the following airs from William Wallace were noted at Culmellie, where he is shepherd.'[5] Sometimes Duncan made the journey to Culmellie, which is about five miles from Lynturk, but on other occasions Wallace visited him at the Manse. The sol-fa notation of a tune that Duncan collected on 26 August 1908 is given on the next page.

Just prior to one of the collecting sessions in 1908, Duncan recorded from a friend of Wallace's called John Bain who lived at Tillybrig, Dunecht, and the links between them can be seen particularly in the case of two songs. Both singers had learned 286 'Jock Tamson's Tripe' (versions B and E) from John Goodall, Haybogs, Tough. Duncan was surprised to find that Wallace sang it 'note for note' as Bain did. 318 'The Wife o' Kelso' (versions A and B) was also noted by Duncan from the pair, Bain having learned words and tune from William Wallace.

Duncan's notes to individual songs give a detailed picture of where Wallace obtained his material and it can be seen that his informants were largely male. His major sources were John (or Jake) Crawford who lived at Holyhead and was beadle at Leochel church (170D, 746D, 1262C, 1459D); a man McHardy, a gamekeeper at Craigievar (1239B, 1531A, and possibly 318A); John Milner, a shoemaker near Leochel Church (321A, 1462G); and a Cromar man (1512A and 1699A). Other sources were his mother (195C); John Goodall, East Haybogs, Tough (286E); James Reid, Liggerdale (349A); a Lumphanan shepherd (450); Alex Fraser, a farm-servant, residing in a cottage near Cowford (867C); Miss Morrison in Leochel (974D); a farm-servant, John MacKenzie, engaged at Carnaveron (1169B); Robert Farquharson, game-keeper at Craigievar (1199M); George Reid, farm-servant, Alford/Leochel (1361B); James McHardy, a shepherd from Ordihoy, Corgarff (1480B); a man Duncan at Clova (1489C), and

John Murray, Macharshaugh (1538A).[6] The earliest date given in the collection at which he learned a song is *c.*1866 (see 746 'The Spanish Lady' D) when he would have been around seventeen, and the latest is *c.*1888 when he would have been around thirty-nine (see, for example, 318A).

William Wallace did not marry and died on 2 January 1925 at Shielfield, Leochel Cushnie, aged seventy-four.[7]

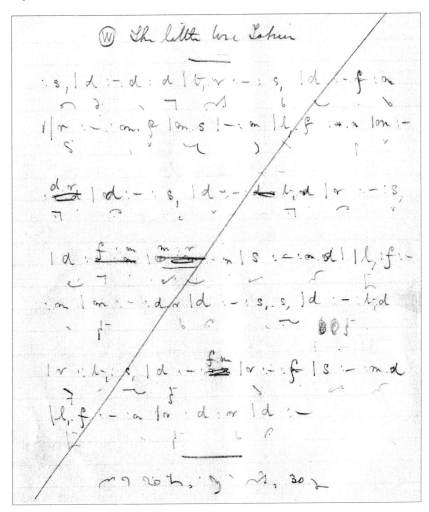

'The Wee Little Tottum'

NOTES

1 OPR 1849/214/2.
2 Census record 1891/214/002/007.
3 Census record 1901/214/005/003.
4 Death record 1900/214/8.
5 *Greig–Duncan*, vol. 8, p. 521.
6 Information from Dw 5.173. The place-name, which is written in shorthand, is uncertain.
7 Death record 1925/214/1.

103. The Fair o' Balquhither

WILLIAM WALLACE

1. As I was comin' hame fae the fair at Balquhither,
   I met a bonny lass, she was fairer than the heather;
   I asked her where she dwelt as we jogged along together,
   'By yon bonny mountain side,' she replied, 'among the heather.'

2. 'O, lassie, I'm in love wi' you, you hae sae monie charms,
   Lassie, I'm in love wi' you, my bosom for you warms,
   The blythe blink o' your ee, and your person being so clever,
   I wad fondly wed with thee, you're my lassie through the heather.

3. 'Oh dinna think, young man,' she said, 'I believe what ye hae spoken,
   Dinna think, young man, that I'd be so easy taken,
   For I'm happy and I'm weel wi' my father and my mither,
   It wad tak a cannie chiel for to wyle me fae the heather.'

4. 'Oh dinna be sae saucy, oh dinna be sae cruel,
   But grant to me one kiss o' thee, one kiss o' thee, my jewel.'
   'If I would grant ye een, you'd be sure to ask anither;'
   But they've kissed and kissed again; she's my lassie through the heather.

5. 'Now since that we've stayed sae lang, and spent oor time together,
   Surely ye will me convoy a mile amang the heather,
   For my father he will fret and my mither she'll abuse me,
   For the staying here so late, and I've nothing to excuse me.'

6. 'Oh never mind the aul' folk, for they will aye be girnin',
   But think ye on the laddie whose heart for you is burnin',
   I'll tak ye to mysel', fae your father and your mither,
   Along with me to dwell in a hoose aside the heather.'

7. So now this couple's married, and they live baith thegither,
   In a cantie wee wee hoose on the hill aside the heather;
   And aye when they think on the time, the time they met thegither,
   He sings till her, 'Ye're mine, ye're my lassie fae the heather.'

GD 873A. The tune was noted by Duncan on 4 August 1908 and the words in September 1908. [I].
Editorial Note Tonic lowered from D to Bb; text lyric has 'o" in place of 'at' (1.1). 'Aside' (7.2) is a correction from manuscript.

blink – look; *clever* – handsome; *girnin'* – grumbling

104. The Gauger

WILLIAM WALLACE

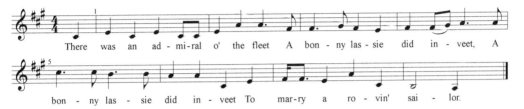

There was an ad - mi - ral o' the fleet A bon - ny las - sie did in - veet, A bon - ny las - sie did in - veet To mar - ry a ro - vin' sai - lor.

1 There was an admiral o' the fleet
A bonny lassie did inveet,
A bonny lassie did inveet
To marry a rovin' sailor.

2 'Oh,' said the lassie, 'that widna dee,
My mither she wid angry be,
My mither she wid angry be
For to mairry a rovin' sailor.'

3 'Then what contrivance shall we take,
Or what contrivance shall we make,
Or what contrivance shall we take
For to beguile your mother?'

4 'It's ye'll pit off that troosers blue
And put on clothing light and new,
And put on clothing light and new,
And come to the toon like a gauger.'

5 The first time he cam to the toon,
Blythe and lauchin' cam he in,
Says, 'Hae ye ony maut or gin?
For here come I, the gauger.'

6 'Oh,' said the lassie, 'come awa,
For maybe we hae a cask or twa,
For maybe we hae a cask or twa,
If this be you, the gauger.'

7 He sought it up, so did he doon,
But ne'er a drap o' the gin could be fun',
But ne'er a drap o' the gin could be fun',
For he hadna the wiles o' the gauger.

8 'O bonny lassie, ye'll tell me
Where a' the maut and the gin can be,
If I dinna get the gin, I will tak thee
For beguilin' o' me, the gauger.'

9 'Oh,' said her mither, 'that's weel deen,
For she's aye ready wi' ilka een,
For she's aye ready wi' ilka een,
And especially wi' you, the gauger.'

10 Sae gin that day month was past and deen,
The lassie awa wi' her gauger's gane,
The lassie awa wi' her gauger's gane,
And she's married a rovin' sailor.

GD 1015B. The music was noted by Duncan on 24 August 1908 and the words on 28 September 1911. Wallace had forgotten the source but indicated that the song had been common around the 1890s. [I/Ly].
Editorial Note Tonic lowered from D to A. 'The Gauger' and 'The Rovin' Sailor' are given as alternative titles with both the tune and the text. The word 'If' (6.4) has been corrected from manuscript.

maut – malt

105. The Barrin' o' the Door

WILLIAM WALLACE

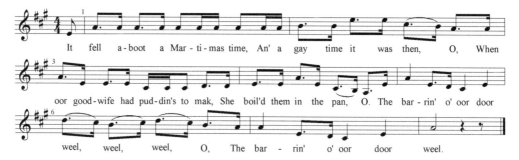

It fell a-boot a Mar-ti-mas time, An' a gay time it was then, O, When oor good-wife had pud-din's to mak, She boil'd them in the pan, O. The bar-rin' o' oor door weel, weel, weel, O, The bar-rin' o' oor door weel.

1   It fell aboot a Martimas time,
    An' a gay time it was then, O,
    When oor goodwife had puddin's to mak,
    She boil'd them in the pan, O.
    The barrin' o' oor door weel, weel, weel, O,
    The barrin' o' oor door weel.

2 The wind blew caul' fae north to sooth,
    It blew into the floor, O,
    Said oor goodman to oor goodwife,
    'Get up and bar the door, O.'

3 'My hand is in my hoosewifeskip,
    Goodman, as ye may see, O,
    If it should na' be barred this hunner year,
    It'll no be barred by me, O.'

4 They made a paction 'tween them twa,
    They made it firm and sure, O,
    That the een that spak the foremost word
    Should rise and bar the door, O.

5 By there cam twa gentlemen
    About twelve o'clock at night, O,
    And they could neither see hoose nor ha'
    Nor coal nor candle light, O.

6 'It's whether is this a rich man's hoose,
    Or whether is it a poor, O?'
    But the never a word would een o'
              them speak
    For the barrin' o' the door, O.

7 It's first they ate the white puddin',
    And then they ate the black, O,
    Muckle muckle thocht oor goodwife,
    But never a word she spak, O.

8 Said the een unto the other,
    'Here, man, get oot your knife, O,
    And ye'll tak aff the aul' man's baird,
    While I kiss the goodwife, O.'

9 'It's there is no water in the hoose,
    And what'll we do than, O?'
    'What ails ye at the puddin' bree
    That's boilin' in the pan, O?'

10 It's up then spak the aul' goodman,
    And an angry man was he, O,
    'Would ye kiss my wife before my een,
    Scaud me wi' puddin' bree, O?'

11 'Up then gat oor auld goodwife,
    Gied three skips on the floor, O,
    Says, 'Goodman, ye've spoken the
              foremost word,
    Ye'll rise and bar the door, O.'

GD 321A. Child 275 *Get Up and Bar the Door*. The music was collected by Duncan on 17 September 1908 and the words on 28 September 1911. The song was learned from a shoemaker, John Milner, in Leochel, pre 1871. [I, −6].
Editorial Note Tonic lowered from Bb to A.

hoosewifeskip – housekeeping; *scaud* – scald

106. The Wee Little Tottum

WILLIAM WALLACE

Some says to get mar-ried it's no the best plan, But I ne-ver was hap-py till I got a man. When I got a man, I soon got a wean, A wee lit-tle tot-tum to tod-dle its lane. To gang tod-dlin' but an' gang tod-dlin' ben, A wee lit-tle tot-tum to tod-dle its leen.

1   Some says to get married it's no the best plan,
    But I never was happy till I got a man.
    When I got a man, I soon got a wean,
    A wee little tottum to toddle its lane.
    To gang toddlin' but an' gang toddlin' ben,
    A wee little tottum to toddle its leen.

2   When Jamie comes hame as tired as can be,
    He is no sooner set than it's placed on his knee;
    But tired though he be, what need he complain,
    When the wee little totum gangs toddlin' its leen?
    It gangs toddlin' but, etc.

3   When supper is over, we then go to bed,
    And in Jamie's arms I lay down my head,
    I lay down my head as couthie's can be,
    And the wee little totum lies we him and me.
    It gangs toddlin' but, etc.

4   Then we rise in the mornin' as merry's the lark,
    When Jamie to his business, and I my hoose work,
    I my hoose work, to keep trig but and ben,
    And the wee little totum that toddles its leen.
    It gangs toddlin' but, etc.

5   In a bonny wee hoose upon yon braeside,
    It's there that my Jamie and me doth reside,
    It's there that we bide and we never complain,
    'Cause we've twa three little totums toddlin' their leen.
    They gang toddlin' but and gang toddlin' ben,
    Lang may the wee totums gang toddlin' their leen.

GD 1072A. The tune was noted by Duncan on 26 August 1908. The song was learned by Wallace c.1878. There are five versions of this song in the collection. [I]

Editorial Note Tonic lowered from G to F; text lyric has 'say' for 'says' (1.1), 'was so happy' for 'was happy' (1.2), 'It's when I' for 'When I' (1.3), 'and' for 'an' gang' (1.5), and 'that toddles' for 'to toddle' (1.6).

wean – child; *tottum* – small child; *toddle its lane* – walk by itself; *couthie* – comfortable; *their leen* – by themselves

107. The Back o' Benachie

WILLIAM WALLACE

1 At the back o' Benachie I saw a skate flee,
   To my fair fal de diddle fal de dandy, O,
   There was fower and twenty flukies a-pickin' at a pea,
   To my teerin oorin eerin oorin andy, O.

2 There was fower and twenty pairtricks yokit in a pleuch,
   And little robin redbreast haudin' weel eneuch.

3 Fower and twenty tailors chasin' at a loose,
   Up cam the hinmost een, and took her to his piece.

4 There was fower and twenty hielanmen chasin' at a snail,
   Up cam the hinmost een an' trampit on her tail.

5 The snail shot oot her horns like ony hummle coo;
   Said the stoot and hardy hielanmen, 'We'll a' be stickit noo'.

6 As I cam by the mill, the psalms was singin' there,
   And as I cam by the kirk, an' the meal was grin'in' there.

7 Oot cam a maiden, she was the miller's midder,
   She was riddlin' at her green cheese, and siftin' at her butter.

8 Then oot cam the miller, they ca'd him Gibby Reid,
   Wi' his bonnet on his bottom, an' his breeks on his heid.

9 They saiddled the soo wi' the saiddle on wrong,
   And he rade upon the rump, wi' the tail in his haun'.

GD 1699A. The song, which has been given the general title 'Quo the Man to the Jo', was collected by Duncan on 6 October 1911 and had been learned by Wallace *c*.1871 from a Cromar man. The tune is also commonly used for 'The Bonnie Lass o' Fyvie'. Greig noted: 'There is the topsy-turvy kind of fun which is . . . primitive in character and makes instant appeal to the ordinary mind. [This song] illustrates this sort of humour, and seems to have some affinity with the nursery rhyme.' (*Buchan Observer*, 3 March 1908). [I].

Editorial Note Tonic lowered from A to G; tune lyric had 'four' in place of 'fower' (1.3); text lyric has 'neerin' for 'eerin' (1.4). 'Cam' (8.1) is a correction from manuscript.

flukies – flounders;   *a-pickin'* – pecking;   *pairtricks* – partridges;   *pleuch* – plough;   *haudin'* – holding up;   *loose* – louse;   *to his piece* – for his snack;   *hummle* – hornless;   *stickit* – stabbed;   *midder* – mother;   *riddlin'* – sieving

George Garioch

c.1824–1917

George Garioch was born c.1824 at Coull in Aberdeenshire to John Garioch, a farmer, and Martha Garioch (née Milne). In June 1863, he married Isabella Robb, a domestic servant aged twenty-five, at Collieston in the parish of Lumphanan.[1] George was farming at Drumreoch, Leochel Cushnie, at this time. Isabella was from Collieston and her parents were Charles Robb and Christina Robb (née Berry). Four children are listed in the 1891 census: Isabella aged twenty-seven,[2] George aged twenty-five, Charles aged twenty-two and John aged sixteen.[3] Duncan's shorthand shows that he pronounced the surname 'Geery', as is common practice in the North East.

On 24 and 29 July and 21 August 1907, Duncan recorded from George Garioch and his unmarried daughter Isabella, who were living at Drumreoch, about seven miles from Lynturk.[4] On 20 September 1911, he made further recordings from the pair. He commented that: 'Mr Garioch is eighty-eight years of age at this date, but sang several tunes ["Ellen of Aberdeen", "Allan MacLean", "Irish Molly"] to me with surprising clearness', and also repeated 'Sir Neil and McVan' and 'The Battle of Harlaw' 'with wonderful fluency and correctness'.[5] Isabella contributed 1480 'The Wild Rover' D at the end of this session. She and her father had sung 992 'The Bonnet o' Blue' B jointly at the opening of Duncan's first recording session in 1907. Duncan also drew five items dated between 1858 and 1860 from a manuscript book of songs belonging to John Garioch, Greystone, Leochel Cushnie, George's brother.[6]

Thirty-one songs were recorded from George Garioch. He learned songs from his mother and father as well as from a host of other sources including an old soldier, a niece, an Irishman, a harvest hand, a boy and a servant girl. One item was a very early memory: 1022 'Hynd Horn' F was 'learnt from his mother at Greystone of Hallhead ... not later than 1830', when he would have been about six years old.

George Garioch died on 23 August 1917 at Drumreoch, aged ninety-three, and his daughter Isabella died on 20 February 1940 at Bogloch Cottage, Lumphanan, aged seventy-six.[7]

NOTES

1 Marriage record 1863/220/5.
2 Census record 1891/214/002/007.
3 Birth record 1863/214/51.
4 *Greig–Duncan*, vol. 8, p. 520.
5 Note to GD 217 'Sir Niel and MacVan' B; Dw 6.32.
6 *Greig–Duncan*, vol. 8, p. 523.
7 Death records 1917/214/8 and 1940/220/1. His great-grandson, George Garioch, Perth, had no knowledge that he was a singer (telephone conversation, 16 August 2003).

108. Allan Maclean

GEORGE GARIOCH

It's from the North coun - try My course I did steer, See - king
af - ter e - du - ca - tion, For I loved it most dear.

1   It's from the North country
     My course I did steer,
     Seeking after education,
     For I loved it most dear.

2   There was Peter, and William,
     And Donald, and me,
     We went a' to the college
     Free students to be.

3   But there happened a wedding
     At Westfield nearby,
     We went a' to the wedding
     Pretty girlies to spy.

4   I being a stranger,
     And my acquaintance but sma,
     I fixèd on Sally,
     The queen o' them a'.

5   She dancèd so neatly,
     While the drink it went round;
     I says, 'Pretty Sally,
     Isna't time to go home?'

6   I says, 'Pretty Sally,
     Will ye go to the broom?'
     'Oh yes,' she says, 'Allan,
     We'll go very soon.'

7   There was Peter, and William,
     There was Donald, and me,
     We went a' to the green broom,
     Our lovies wi' 's.

8   In spite o' her weepin'
     I did her beguile,
     In spite o' her cryin'
     I did her betray.

9   Sally went home,
     It was late in the night,
     Her father he rose
     And he struck up a light,

10   Says, 'Where have you been Sally,
     So late in coming home?
     I fear with the students
     Among the green broom.'

11   'Oh yes,' she says, 'father,
     The truth it is plain,
     I was at the green broom
     Wi' Allan Maclean.

12   'It's Allan Maclean,
     He's a Highlandman bright,
     He's abusèd me sorely
     At the wedding this night.'

13   Her father in a passion
     To the college he went,
     And without any favour
     Gave in his complaint.

14   Says, 'Have you any student
     Called Allan Maclean?'
     'Oh yes,' says the regent,
     'We have one o' that name.'

15   'It's Allan Maclean,
     He's a Highlandman bright;
     He's abused my daughter
     At the wedding last night.'

16 'If this be true,' says the regent,
  'That you tell to me,
  It's as for her sake
  High hangèd he's be.'

17 It's the rest they were callèd on
  The truth to declare,
  'And be sure you say nothing
  But what you can swear.'

18 'It's we will say nothing
  But what we can swear;
  He was at the broom with her,
  But we wasna there.'

19 Allan was callèd on
  The truth for to see;
  He says, 'The best proof that ye'll get's
  The youngest o' three.

20 'The morn's our graduation,
  And Tuesday's our ball,
  And from our royal college
  Exclude him we shall.'

21 'Exclude, exclude,
  It makes my heart sore;
  I'll never, I'll never,
  See the Alton no more.

22 'My goon it is bonny,
  My books they're all new;
  They are all to be torn,
  And what shall I do?

23 'My books they're all torn
  And thrown ower the wall,
  And my goon o' broad scarlet
  Was torn in the hall.

24 'My father he's a minister,
  And he preaches at hame,
  My mother died in Caitness,
  And I daurna gang hame.

25 'I set oot for a minister,
  But that will not do,
  So it's right for a doctor
  I now must pursue.

26 'It's Chairlotte the Royal,
  It's she is lyin' tee,
  She taks in goods and passengers,
  And she'll maybe tak me.

27 'For I'm going to Glasgow
  Strange faces to see,
  Next voyage to Jamaica
  A doctor to be.

28 'Ye'll keep weel your mind, Sally,
  Keep it a' weel to me,
  And let no other young man
  Be sharer wi' me.

29 'For if ever I return again,
  As I hope I shall,
  I will mairry Sally Beverley
  In spite of you all.'

GD 1403A. The song was noted by Duncan on 20 September 1911. It was learned by George Garioch *c.*1851. Greig wrote in the *Buchan Observer*, 30 May 1911: 'Few folk-songs are more popular in the North-East than "Allan Maclean". I have a number of records of it, with plenty of variants. . . . As an absolute melody . . . I incline to place it first among our folk-tunes.' Mr Garioch later remembered the following additional stanza:

  It's neither heightened your honour,
  Nor reesit [raised] your fame,
  You've blaudit [damaged] a' my character,
  And spoilt my good name.

Version 1403N, collected by Duncan from Mrs Taylor, indicates that the above verse would come just before Garioch's verse 26. Garioch gave the name of the girl in the song as Sally Beverley and said: 'She pled for the student. When she failed, she gave the regent [lecturer/student adviser] a kick. I have heard that she was dressed in a green manky [calamanco] coat.' [I].

Editorial Note Tonic lowered from D to C. Verse 8 is taken from 1403B John Bain, verse 9; the original had 'In spite of her weepin'/I did her betray.'

broad scarlet – probably red scarlet;   *lyin' tee* – ready to sail

109. The Donside Lassie

GEORGE GARIOCH

I once had a sweet - heart on Don - side did dwell, There
was nane in Scot - land that could her ex - cel; I coor - ted this fair crea - ture by
night and by day, Till by the French wars I was for - cèd a - way.

1   I once had a sweetheart on Donside did dwell,
    There was nane in Scotland that could her excel;
    I coorted this fair creature by night and by day,
    Till by the French wars I was forcèd away.

2   To join the Scottish standard, the brave Forty-twa,
    When we went to Egypt to fight wi' them noo;
    We blazèd our pistols on Egypt's bloody plain,
    Our commander was Sir Wellington, of Portugal and Spain.

3   We fought many a battle, ere the wars closed again,
    Fought many a brave hero for honour and for fame;
    But now the wars they're over, and I leave Spain,
    Hoping for to see my native aul' Scotland again.

4   When I arrived on the banks of the Don,
    I sought for my Nelly, but I found she was gone,
    I lookèd at the place where she used to stay,
    But they told me she had left that, and crossèd the Spey.

5   Then with courage like a soldier, by the light of the moon,
    The road she had taken I thought of right soon,
    Through wild woods and valleys, through cold frost and snow,
    For a fortnight and better I constant did go.

6   But one night, being wearied, I set myself doon,
    I spied a small cottage by the light of the moon,
    I was hungry and thirsty, I marched there wi' speed,
    I was thinking of getting lodging and a small piece of breid.

7   But oot there speaks an aul' wife, says, 'Ye canna be here,
    You seem an old soldier, so off you may wear;'
    'Oh yes, I'm a soldier, I never will deny,
    But to row me oot o' quarters I will you defy.'

8 But looking around me, who did I spy
   But my ain dearest Nelly, she was sitting close by
   I says, 'My dearest Nelly, it's how dae ye do?
   Since we parted on the Donside, I've sought much for you.'

9 It's Nelly looked round wi' a heavy rolling eye,
   Says, 'Is this my dearest Jamie, whom the wars stole away?'
   'Oh yes, it's your Jamie, he's still true and alive,
   And from the wars he's got his lasting reprieve.'

10 It's 'Oh,' exclaimed Nelly, 'and what shall I do?
   I am going to be married just in a week or two,
   And this is the young man that's sitting close by,
   That I'm to be married with, I never will deny.'

11 It's 'Oh,' exclaimed Jamie, 'ye ken what to do,
   Ye must now choose one of the two;'
   She flew into his arms, says, 'Jamie, I'm for you,
   For ye hae been langest constant and true.'

GD 93B. The song was noted by Duncan on 24 July 1907. It was learned by George Garioch near Fraserburgh *c.*1857 from a Rayne man. Greig wrote of the story in the *Buchan Observer*, 28 April 1908: 'The French wars of a hundred years ago have left us a legacy of soldier songs. Of these "Donside" is one of the most popular. The theme is a common one. A young fellow becomes the victim of the press-gang, and is forced away from home and sweetheart. He is so long away that the girl, despairing of his return, listens to the overtures of another lover. The soldier, however, returns in the nick of time and claims the girl, who is still true at heart.' [Æ/Dor].
Editorial Note Tonic lowered from G to E.

the brave Forty-twa – the Black Watch; *wear* – set; *row* – drive

110. Hirrum Tirrum

GEORGE GARIOCH

The nicht is caul', I can-na stay, Let's kiss an' par-ted be An'
I'll come back the mor-n's nicht, My dear, if ye'll ag-ree. Wi' a
hir-rum tir-rum tow de ad-die, Hir-rum tow de ree.

1 The nicht is caul', I canna stay,
   Let's kiss an' parted be
   An' I'll come back the morn's nicht,
   My dear, if ye'll agree.
   Wi' a hirrum tirrum tow de addie,
   Hirrum tow de ree.

2 'It's I'll come back the morn's nicht,
   If ye wid be as kin',
   Fan a' the lave gang to their beds,
   To rise and lat me in.'

3 'To rise and lat ye in, young man,
   It's fat I winna dee
   For it's nae for maids o' modesty
   To trust young men like thee.'

4 'Ye rashly speak, my bonnie lass,
   O' men o' modesty,
   Ye never had occasion yet
   For dreedin' ill o' me.'

5 'It's true I've little reason had
   Since we did idder ken
   To speak o' injured modesty
   Or slight false-hearted men.

6 'So if ye will a promise make
   Ye will behave yoursel',
   Ye may come in maist onie time,
   For oh I like ye weel.'

7 'What ither promise wid ye hae
   Than I've already gien?
   I've sworn by all the powers of love
   That's working o' my mind.'

8 'Ye'll come canny by the west window
   And canny doon the loan,
   And fan ye come to the kitchie door,
   Cast canny aff your sheen.'

9 'Ye'll tak the lifter i' your hand,
   I'll hae the door barred by,
   And ye may come in maist onie time,
   And kiss me far I lie.'

GD 773A. The song was collected by Duncan on 24 July 1907. George Garioch learned it from Peter
   Murray at Tillyorn c.1847. [Æ/Dor].
Editorial Note Tonic lowered from E to D.

dreedin' – fearing;   *idder* – each other;   *loan* – grassy path;   *lifter* – latch

111. The Twa Emperors

GEORGE GARIOCH

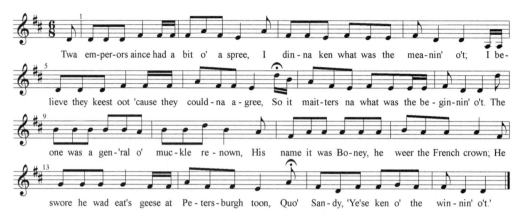

Twa em-per-ors aince had a bit o' a spree, I din-na ken what was the mea-nin' o't; I believe they keest oot 'cause they could-na a-gree, So it mait-ters na what was the be-gin-nin' o't. The
one was a gen-'ral o' muc-kle re-nown, His name it was Bo-ney, he weer the French crown; He
swore he wad eat's geese at Pe-ters-burgh toon, Quo' San-dy, 'Ye'se ken o' the win-nin' o't.'

1 Twa emperors aince had a bit o' a spree,
 I dinna ken what was the meanin' o't;
 I believe they keest oot 'cause they couldna agree,
 So it maitters na what was the beginnin' o't.
 The one was a gen'ral o' muckle renown,
 His name it was Boney, he weer the French crown;
 He swore he wad eat's geese at Petersburgh toon,
 Quo' Sandy, 'Ye'se ken o' the winnin' o't.'

2 Bony tooted his horn to gather his clan,
 Till his wizzen was sair wi' the blawin' o't;
 He had four hundred thousand men under command,
 Sae wasna that a gay beginnin' o't?
 It's Sandy was eerie to see sic a thrang,
 The swords, guns and halberds all marchin' alang,
 He thought it was time to raise his gang,
 To help him a hitch wi' the thinnin' o't.

3 Quoth he, 'Neebour Bony, take this counsel I'll gie,
 For strife it's nae mous to be tiggin' wi't;
 And dinna be shakin' your pikestaff at me,
 For fear ye be dung o' the riggin' wi't.
 For though I dinna fear at sharp weapons ava,
 Gin ye come my way, ye may get a blaw
 Wi' a piece o' ice or some grippit snawba'
 That 'ill lay ye a month i' your biggin' wi't.

4 'O Sandy, dinna ware your good counsel on me,
 For I'm nae just in the way o' needin' o't,
 And lightly my pikestaff, but wait yet a wee,
 I'll gar your lungs ring wi' the whizzin' o't.

So they boldly pursued him fae hillock to howe,
Fae toonie to toonie, fae knappie to knowe,
Till at length they arrived at the walls o' Moscow,
Sair dung wi' the pushin' and the blawin' o't.

5   Says Bony to's men, 'You're baith hungry and dry,
But you're no very far fae the slakkin' o't,
There's plenty o' biscuits and brandy forbye,
And ye's get it a' for the takin' o't.
But Bony stood all the while scratchin' his pow,
Till he near clawed a hole in the wiggin' o't,
For to see a' his brandy get up in a lowe,
Fan he made himself sure o' the swiggin' o't.

GD 149A. The song was collected by Duncan on 29 July 1907. It was learned by George Garioch in his teens from an old soldier (John Falconer) who belonged to Tarland. Greig noted in the *Buchan Observer*, 1 December 1908: 'The story relates to Napoleon's Russian campaign of 1812 – his invasion of that country, the burning of Moscow by the Russians themselves, and the disastrous retreat of the French army. We consider it about as forceful an effort of the vernacular as has ever been achieved in the north.' Six versions of this song, which has the general title 'Sandy and Nap', appear in the collection. It was written by William Lillie of Inverugie soon after the events it describes. [I/M].
Editorial Note Tonic lowered from F to D.

keest – fell; *wizzen* – throat; *eerie* – alarmed; *help him a hitch* – give him a hand; *mous* – joke;
  tiggin' – meddling; *dung* – hit; *riggin'* – back; *dinna fear at* – am not afraid of;
  lay ye a month i' your biggin' – lay you up at home for a month; *ware* – waste;
  lightly – make light of; *lungs* [for 'lugs'] – ears; *knappie* – hillock; *knowe* – knoll;
  sair dung – exhausted; *pow* – head; *slakkin'* – relieving; *clawed* – scratched;
  wiggin' – hair; *lowe* – flame

Alexander Mackay

1857–?

Alexander Mackay was born on 25 August 1857 at Linthaugh in the parish of Auchindoir. His parents were George McKay, a farm servant, and Christina McKay.[1] The 1881 census lists Alexander, his parents, and his siblings, William, Anne, and Maggie, at West Lodge, Breda, Alford. His father was a quarry worker and a crofter of five acres at this time and Alexander was working as an agricultural labourer.[2] By 1891, Alexander, then a quarry worker, was married to Mary Ann McKay and was living in the parish of Tullynessle and Forbes at Waterside Cottage.[3] In 1901 he and his family were living at Bridge Cottages in the same parish, where McKay was working as a flesher and van driver. Seven children are listed in the census: Robert, Mary Anne, Annie, Emily, Georgina, Maggie and Flora.[4] Mackay is referred to in the collection as a butcher in Alford and contributed forty-one songs. Duncan recorded tunes from him on 21 February 1907 and again on 7, 11 and 13 March in that year, and later noted down words in 1909. The first tune recorded was of the well-known deer-poaching ballad, 250 'Johnnie o' Braidisleys' A, which had been learned by Mackay in the Castle Forbes area c.1867. An example of Duncan's sol-fa notation – 404 'The Lothian Hairst' A, collected on 13 March 1907 – is shown on the next page.

In Mackay's case we know a good deal about when, where and from whom he learned his repertoire. The earliest songs seem to have been 99 'The Banks of the Nile' B from Alexander Laing, a servant at Castle Forbes, and 1284 'The Scolding Wife' B, which were both learned around the age of seven. 356 'Sleepy Toon' B was sung in farm kitchens in his boyhood. This is not a family repertoire and probably reflects time spent on different farms in the course of both his father's and his own employment. One song, 960 'The Farmer's Boy' F, was learned from a broadsheet. Mackay's song sources were both male and female and spanned a range of ages: e.g. 1012 'The Lass o' Benachie' E learned c.1867 at Auchnagathle from a cattleman's wife, 106 'Jamie Foyers' A learned c.1867 from a young man called Jamie Galt, 1042 'Cairn o' Mount' I learned c.1874 from Mrs Cobban, wife of the farmer at Boggieshalloch, and 1701 'Speculation' A from a boy at Terpersie about 1879 or 1880. In 1888, at around the age of thirty, Mackay learned 1130 'Glasgow Green' A from a young woman in Aslown. Other sources not already mentioned include a maidservant at Dorsell, Al. Murray who was a blacksmith at Balquharn, a young man from Udny and a man who had been feed in Morayshire. His most important single source was Alexander Laing of Castle Forbes, who is described as being 'a very old man' when Alexander Mackay was a boy.[5] The map shows the locations in the Alford area where Mackay learned his songs.[6] Mackay was living at Burnbank, Alford, when his mother died in 1913, but later emigrated to Canada and was living at 15 Ward Street, Toronto, in 1925.[7]

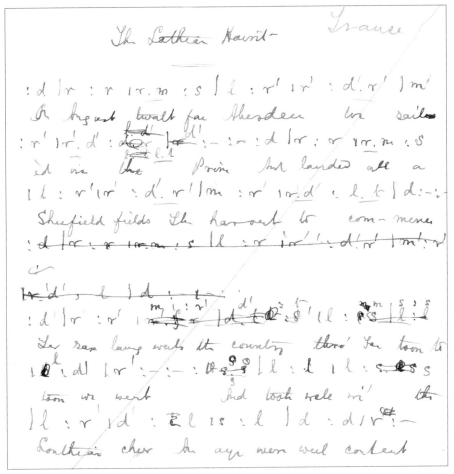

'The Lothian Hairst'

Map showing locations in the Alford area where Alexander Mackay learned his songs

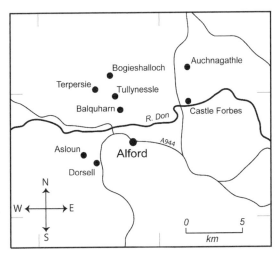

NOTES

1 Birth record 1857/172/41.
2 Census record 1881/171/1/1.
3 Census record 1891/246/002/005.
4 Census record 1901/246/003/001.
5 See note to GD 99 'The Banks of the Nile' B.
6 The place-name spellings used are those found on current Ordnance Survey maps.
7 Death record 1913/171/A/2; *Greig–Duncan*, vol. 8, p. 519.

112. Lord Thomas, or the Brown Girl

ALEXANDER MACKAY

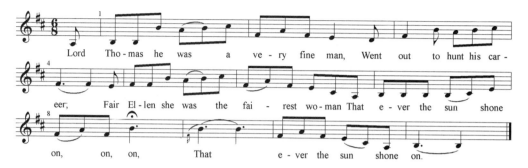

Lord Tho-mas he was a ve-ry fine man, Went out to hunt his car-eer, Fair El-len she was the fai-rest wo-man That e-ver the sun shone on, on, on, That e-ver the sun shone on.

1 Lord Thomas he was a very fine man,
Went out to hunt his career;
Fair Ellen she was the fairest woman
That ever the sun shone on, on, on,
That ever the sun shone on.

2 Come riddle me, riddle me, mother,
         he said,
Come riddle me all in one;
'Tis whether fair Ellen shall be my bride,
Or I'll bring you the brown girl home.

3 The brown girl she has got houses
         and land,
Fair Ellen she has none;
Take my advice, my son so dear,
And bring me the brown girl home.

4 When he came to fair Ellen's gate,
He gave a loud ring to the bell;
And there were none so clever there
As fair Ellen to welcome him in.

5 What news, what news, Lord Thomas,
         she said,
What news have ye brought to me?
I have come to bid you to my wedding,
It's very bad news to thee.

6 Come read my riddle, my mother, she said,
Come read my riddle in one;
It's whether I'll go to Lord Thomas's
         wedding,
Or whether I'll tarry at home?

7 Some might be your friend, she said,
And others might be your foe;
Take my advice, my daughter dear,
To Lord Thomas's wedding don't go.

8 But she dressed herself in scarlet red,
Her merry men all in green;
And everyone, as she passed them by,
They took to be some queen.

9 'Twas when she came to Lord Thomas's
         gate,
She gave a loud ring to the bell,
And there were none so clever there
As Lord Thomas to welcome her in.

10 Is this your bride, Lord Thomas,
         she said,
Is this your bride for to be?
O yes, but I would not give your
         little finger
For all her whole bodie.

11 The brown girl had a little penknife,
And O it was wondrous sharp,
And between the breastbone and
         the side
And she piercèd fair Ellen's heart.

12 What aileth thee, fair Ellen? he said,
   You are looking so pale and wan;
   You used to be the fairest woman
   That ever the sun shone on.

13 O are you blind, Lord Thomas, she said,
   So blind that ye do not see?
   For do ye not see my very heart's blood
   Running trinklin down to my knee?

14 Lord Thomas he had a very broad sword,
   And O it was wondrous sharp,
   And between the breastbone and the side
   And he piercèd the brown girl's heart.

15 Ye will lay the brown girl at my feet,
   Fair Ellen close to my heart:
   Did ever ye see three lovers did meet,
   And part as these lovers did part?

GD 212A. Child 73 *Lord Thomas and Fair Annet*. This song was collected by Duncan on 13 March 1907. It was learned by Alexander Mackay in 1874 from a maidservant in Dorsell. There are five versions of the ballad in the collection under the general title 'Sweet Willie and Fair Annie'. Duncan noted: 'There are two types of the ballad, in one of which [as here] the first lover is killed by her rival, "the brown girl," while in the other she dies of sorrow on the evening of the wedding.' [Æ/Dor].

Performance Note The words of the refrain should reflect the last line of each verse.

Editorial Note Tonic lowered from E to B.

his career – probably for 'the King's deer';   *riddle me* – answer my question;
all in one – probably 'at one attempt';   *clever* – quick; *trinklin* – trickling

113. Robin the Smuggler

ALEXANDER MACKAY

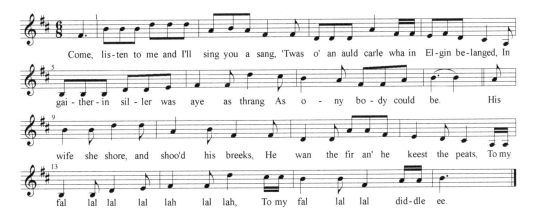

1   Come, listen to me and I'll sing you a sang,
    'Twas o' an auld carle wha in Elgin belanged,
    In gaitherin siller was aye as thrang
    As ony body could be.
    His wife she shore, and shoo'd his breeks,
    He wan the fir an' he keest the peats,
    To my fal lal lal lal lah lal lah,
    To my fal lal lal diddle ee.

193

2   The bonnet he wore was the bonny sky blue,
      A hamil spun coat o' the very same hue,
      The troosers he wore and queetikins too,
      For a plain hamil carle was he.
      He had a coo and twa stirks that lowed in the byre,
      A meerie that cared na for moss nor for mire.

3   He had a bit cairt made o' good fir rungs,
      A teuch timmer aixle and good teuch sprungs,
      It rattled and scraiched like a thousand tongues,
      'Twas heard owre muir and lea.
      Likewise he had an auld bit barrow,
      A coulterless plough and a tineless harrow.

4   He lived in a hoosie, 'twas far in the hill,
      He had nae neebours near him, he thocht it nae ill
      To conceal in his pantry a cantie bit still,
      And files he would practise 't a wee.
      The drappie he brewed was the pure mountain bead,
      The Forres and Elgin folk liked it gweed.

5   And aye as the Tuesdays and Fraidays cam roon',
      The cairtie was packit wi' peats for the toon,
      Wi' a keg in the middle and Meg o' the croon,
      And awa to Elgin gaed he.

6   Twa ell lengths afore auld Robin made haste,
      Owre hicht and owre hillock faur a wagon could rest,
      He ruggit and tuggit the cairt and the beast,
      For a pushin' auld body was he.

7   The peats they were o' the black and the broon,
      They were thrifty and gweed, and weel kent through the toon,
      And naebody grudged their siller half croon
      For 's weel packit loadie to gie.
      And files he would gie a bit fir to the peat,
      It saired them for licht along wi' the weet.

8   The cairt being teemed the beast got a rest,
      Wi' a ripachie shaif aye she did her best,
      The hames teen aff and the halter made fast
      To the tram for security.
      And aye she wad nicher good-e'en to her fellows,
      For weel did she ken a' the horses o' Kellas.

9   This couple wad saunter some ferlies to spy,
      To gaze on the muckle kerk steeple so high,
      Or into the shops some orras to buy;
      Nae hoose fae expense can be free.
      Some congo for Meggie, as we may suppose,
      Some sneeshin' for Robin to tickle his nose.

10 Noo fan this auld couple had seen a' their folk,
   And coft a' their orras and crackèd their joke,
   Awa they went, got the beast to the yoke,
   And jogged along cannily.
   She needed nae worl to punish her sprite,
   'Twas aneuch gin she eence got her heid to the height.

11 'Twas week after week and auld Robin was seen,
   A mair hamil carle there couldna hae been,
   Though his hair was withered, his hert was green,
   For a kindly auld body was he.
   But he has na been seen noo in Elgin for lang,
   Nor een in his room, and sae ends my sang.

GD 261. The song was taken down by Duncan on 21 February 1907. He noted at the time: 'Learnt
twenty-two years ago, from a man who had been feed in Morayshire and got it there. . . . This air
is a version of "Muirland Willie".' The *Elgin Courant and Courier*, 24 March 1939, published a
version of this song called 'The Kellas Peatfutherer', where it is said that it was written by James
Simpson from Mortlach *c.*1850, and that its subject was Robert Milne (1792–1870), a crofter at
Newton of Kellas (*Greig–Duncan*, vol. 2, p. 554). Kellas is near Elgin in Moray. [Æ/Dor].

Performance Note Verses 5 and 6 have four rather than six lines and the tune for these requires some
modification. Suggestion: omit bars 9–12.

Editorial Note Tonic lowered from D to B; alternative notes 1.5a and 1.6a. Text lyric has 'fal lal lah' for
'fal lal lal' (1.8).

shore and shoo'd – cut and sewed; *wan* – gathered; *keest* – cut and dried; *hamil* – plain, homely;
 queetikins – gaiters; *stirks* – bullocks; *byre* – cowshed; *meerie* – mare;
 moss – boggy ground; *bit* – small, little; *rungs* – spars; *teuch* – strong;
 scraiched – screeched; *tineless* – prongless; *mountain bead* – whisky; *ruggit* – dragged with
effort; *saired* – served; *teemed* – emptied; *ripachie shaif* – handful of unthreshed grain;
 hames – collar; *teen aff* – taken off;*tram* – cart shaft; *nicher* – neigh; *ferlies* – wonders;
 orras – odds and ends; *congo* – tea; *sneeshin'* – snuff; *coft* – bought

114. The Banks o' Don

ALEXANDER MACKAY

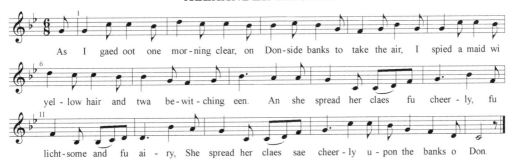

As I gaed oot one mor-ning clear, on Don-side banks to take the air, I spied a maid wi
yel-low hair and twa be-wit-ching een. An she spread her claes fu cheer-ly, fu
licht-some and fu ai-ry, She spread her claes sae cheer-ly u-pon the banks o Don.

1 As I gaed oot one morning clear, on Donside banks to take the air,
   I spied a maid wi yellow hair and twa bewitching een.
   An she spread her claes fu cheerly, fu lichtsome and fu airy,
   She spread her claes sae cheerly upon the banks o Don.

2   I said to her, 'My bonny lass ye're early on the dewy grass,
    And spierit gin she wad take a pass doon by the waterside.
    For there's nane can match your beauty your gay and verdant beauty,
    There's nane to match your beauty on a' the banks o Don.'

3   She says, 'I'd rather gang my leen I never followed a lad but een,
    And that was Jamie that hyows the steen, and makes oor toon sae bra'.
    For I winna leave my laddie my bonny mason laddie,
    I winna leave my laddie for a' the ere I saw.'

4   'My bonny lass, you're surely mad to trust a rovin' mason lad,
    He'll go and leave ye dool and sad for ony thing ye know.
    So ye'll come alang my dearie my bonny blithesome dearie
    Ye'll come alang my dearie I'll aye be true to thee.'

5   I coaxed a while, she gaed consent, and doon Don's floory banks we went,
    I own the day was gaily spent ere we land at Aberdeen.
    And she soon forgot her laddie, her bonny mason laddie,
    She soon forgot her laddie, upo' the banks o Don.

6   At Aberdeen we land in time, far we got whisky, rum, or wine,
    The session clerk made oot a line that siccar't us fu weel.
    And aye sin seen my Mary my rosy cheekit Mary,
    And aye sin seen my Mary to me has proved richt leal.

7   Now all ye lads that dee repair in search o wives at Kirk or Fair
    Be sure to take the morning air upon the banks o Don,
    To woo a bonny lassie, a bonny blue-eyed lassie,
    To woo a bonny lassie to sleep wi you at een.

GD 1130A. Alexander Mackay learned this song *c*.1888 from a young woman in Aslown. Duncan noted
    it on 21 February 1907 and added the information that it was often sung on Donside. It is a version
    of 'Glasgow Green' that has been adapted and localised. [Dor/M].
Editorial Note Tonic lowered from D to C; a crotchet and a quaver have been inserted at bar 8 in place
    of a dotted crotchet to accommodate the words.

pass – walk;   *my leen* – alone;   *hyows* – hews;   *steen* – stones;   *dool* – sorrowful;
    siccar't – secured, i.e. married

115. The Lothian Hairst

ALEXANDER MACKAY

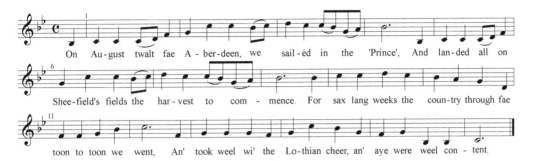

On Au-gust twalt fae A - ber-deen, we sail-èd in the 'Prince', And lan-ded all on Shee-field's fields the har - vest to com - mence. For sax lang weeks the coun-try through fae toon to toon we went, An' took weel wi' the Lo-thian cheer, an' aye were weel con - tent.

1   On August twalt fae Aberdeen, we sailèd in the 'Prince',
    And landed all on Sheefield's fields the harvest to commence.
    For sax lang weeks the country through fae toon to toon we went,
    An' took weel wi' the Lothian cheer, an' aye were weel content.

2   Oor gaffer, Willie Mathieson, fae sweet Deeside he came;
    Oor foreman came fae that same place, and Logan was his name.
    O' brisk young lads some half a score; oor lasses were but few;
    While Logan herded what he had, and kept a decent crew.

3   I followed Logan on the point, sae weel as he laid it doon,
    Sae nobly as he led the squad ower mony a thistly toon.
    My mate and I got little chance for Logan's watchful eye,
    Oor fancy chaps could get nae chance, auld Logan was sae sly.

4   He cleared the bothy every night before he went to sleep,
    He would not leave behind him one, so strick his rule he keeped.
    And when we lan' at Aiberdeen, he weel deserves a spree,
    A' for the herding us sae weel, from Louthian tumes we're free.

5   But noo the corn is a' cut doon, and we are on the pier;
    Farewell, ye Louthian feather beds, and a' the Louthian cheer.
    Farewell, Mackenzie, Reid, and Ross, and all the joyful crew,
    Chalmers, Shepherd, Logan, Jack, and royal Stewarts too.

6   O' a' the lads that's in oor squad, to take them one by one,
    Commend me to the Deeside lads, for it's them that leads the van.
    And I mysel', a Hielan' lass, wad seek nae better cheer
    Nor a Deeside lad in a Louthian bed, and a nicht as lang as a year.

GD 404A. Duncan noted this song, which Mackay learned from 'a maid-servant at Asloun twenty-four years ago', on 13 March 1907. The song was said to have been written around the 1850s by a Highland lassie who was part of a band of Deeside harvesters (*Greig–Duncan*, vol. 3, p. 633). There are ten versions of this song in the collection. [Dor/M].

Editorial Note Tonic lowered from E to C. Text lyric has 'from' in place of 'fae' and 'we sailed upon' in place of 'we sailed in' (1.1), 'Sheefield' in place of 'Sheefield's' (1.2), 'from' in place of 'fae' (1.3).

hairst – harvest;   *twalt* – twelfth;   *tumes* – probably for 'loons' (lads)

116. Van Diemen's Land

ALEXANDER MACKAY

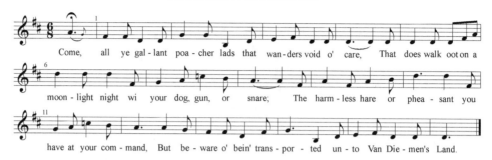

Come, all ye gal-lant poa-cher lads that wan-ders void o' care, That does walk oot on a moon-light night wi your dog, gun, or snare; The harm-less hare or phea-sant you have at your com-mand, But be-ware o' bein' trans-por-ted un-to Van Die-men's Land.

1   Come, all ye gallant poacher lads that wanders void o' care,
    That does walk oot on a moonlight night wi your dog, gun, or snare;
    The harmless hare or pheasant you have at your command,
    But beware o' bein' transported unto Van Diemen's Land.

2   There was Tom Brown from Glasgow, John Wilson, and poor Joe,
    They were three gallant poacher lads the country weel did know,
    The harmless hare and pheasant they had at their command,
    They were seven lang years transported unto Van Diemen's Land.

3   The very same day we landed upon that fatal shore,
    The keepers came round us, full half a score or more;
    They drew us up like horses, and took us into command,
    And they yoked us in the plough, my boys, to plough Van Diemen's Land.

4   The houses that we lived into were built of clod and clay,
    With rotten straw for bedding – we dare not answer nay;
    Aroon' our camps are blazing fires – we slumber when we can;
    They guard the wolves and tigers here still on Van Diemen's Land.

5   There was a girl from sweet Dundee, Jean Stewart was her name;
    She was seven lang years transported, we all did know the same.
    Our keeper bought her liberty, and married her right off hand,
    And she gave us good usage here still on Van Diemen's Land.

6   One night that I did slumber I had a pleasant dream,
    That my true love was along wi' me doon by yon purlin' stream.
    In Scotland I was roaming wi' her at my command;
    But I awoke quite broken-hearted here still on Van Diemen's Land.

7   Oh, if I had five hundred pounds laid doon into my hand,
    I wad give it all for liberty, if that I could command;
    To Scotland I'd return again, and be a happy man
    I wad bid farewell to poachin', and to Van Diemen's Land.

GD 252A. This song, which tells of convicts being transported to Tasmania, was noted by Duncan on 21
    February 1907. The song, like 'Robin the Smuggler', was learned by Mackay from a man who had
    been feed in Morayshire, but was first heard from his father around 1877. [M].
Editorial Note Tonic lowered from F to D; alternative note 12.3a.

George F. Duncan
1860–1927

George Forrest Duncan was born on 14 June 1860 at Whitehill, New Deer, to William Duncan and Elizabeth Duncan (née Birnie), and was a brother of James Bruce Duncan.[1] He was the youngest of the family of eleven, the others being Elizabeth (b. 1839), Margaret (b. 1841), John (b. 1843), William (b. 1846), James Bruce (b. 1848), Alexander (b. 1849), Jane (b. 1852), Mary (b. 1854), Robert (b. 1856) and Leslie (b. 1858).[2] George was a school teacher and the 1891 census places him at the village of Tongue in Sutherland, along with his wife Charlotte Gordon Duncan (née Campbell). The couple had married in 1887 at Kirkton, Farr.[3] Charlotte was born at Farr in Sutherland and spoke Gaelic. The couple had two sons, William G. F. Duncan and Leslie Duncan, both of whom were born in Tongue.[4] Also living with the family was George's unmarried sister, Jane, who was working as an assistant teacher. The Gaelic air of 1816 'Mo Run Gil Dileas' was learned by George in Melness and reflects his time in the Sutherland area, as does 1489 'I am a Miller to my Trade' F received from Daniel Sutherland, also from Melness. By 1901, George and his family were living at 42 Wilton Gardens in the Maryhill area of Glasgow, along with another son, Robert G. C. Duncan, aged eight, who was born in Tongue.[5] Charlotte Duncan died in 1921, aged sixty-one, in the district of Rutherglen[6] and in 1923, at the age of sixty-two, George married Annie Summers Barr, aged thirty-five, whose father was a property agent.[7]

George wrote two letters to Alexander Keith from Red House, Fenwick, by Kilmarnock, Ayrshire, on 18 and 28 September 1925, in which he states that he was a schoolmaster in Orkney, Aberdeenshire, Sutherland, Staffordshire and Glasgow, and notes that a neighbour in Whitehill, Mary Gillan, was the source of some of his songs.[8] In the collection itself, however, she is mentioned in the case of only one song – 275 'The Beggar Man' B. She was clearly an interesting character: 'Mary Gillan . . . lived with her mother, Bell Henderson, known in the district as a witch about two hundred yards from our house. . . . She had a great collection, but I only remembered some of them.'[9]

Sixty-six songs from George F. Duncan appear in the collection. Almost half of these are jointly attributed to his sister Margaret Gillespie or to James B. Duncan or to all three. George collected from his parents early on in life and describes this in one of his letters to Alexander Keith (18 September 1925): 'I should mention that at the age of fifteen, while at home on my father's farm, hearing the ballads so often sung, it occurred to me that they ought to be preserved, and I took a number of them down from their singing then.'[10] Like his brother, George was fluent in shorthand and used this to write out song texts.

James B. Duncan noted down tunes from George when they met and also received songs from him by letter. George F. Duncan died on 14 January 1927 at Hillhead in Glasgow.[11]

NOTES

1 Birth record 1860/225/75.
2 Information from *Greig–Duncan*, vol. 8, p. 525.
3 Marriage record 1887/050/1/3.
4 Census record Tongue 1891/056/005.
5 Census record Maryhill, Glasgow, 1901.
6 Death record 1921/654/65.
7 Marriage record 1923/644/12/72. Their address is given as 13 Jedburgh Avenue, Rutherglen.
8 *Greig–Duncan*, vol. 8, p. 525.
9 18 September 1925, 2732/30/27.
10 As note 9.
11 Death record 1927/644/12/65.

117. When Charlie First Cam to the North

GEORGE F. DUNCAN

When Char-lie first cam to the North, The man-ly looks o' my
High-land lad-die Garr'd il-ka Scot-tish heart to burn To
guard the lad wi' the tar-tan plai-die.

1 When Charlie first cam to the North,
   The manly looks o' my Highland laddie
   Garr'd ilka Scottish heart to burn
   To guard the lad wi' the tartan plaidie.
      Garr'd ilka Scottish heart to burn
      To guard the lad wi' the tartan plaidie.

2 But when King George did hear o' this,
   That he was come north to heir his daddy,
   He sent Sir John Cope to the north
   To catch the lad wi' the tartan plaidie.

3 But when Cope cam' to Inverness,
   O, Charlie he was south already,
   And fairly he did conquer all,
   By sportin' o' the tartan plaidie.

4 And when Cope cam' to Aberdeen,
   The English fleet was lying ready
   To carry them ower the Firth o' Forth
   To catch the lad wi' the tartan plaidie.

5 At Prestonpans they formed the clans
   To fecht for the lad that heired his daddy,
   Our noble prince led on the van,
   And showed the men his tartan plaidie.

6 Then Sir John Cope addressed his men,
   Saying 'Gin you will be stern and steady,
   It's thirty thousand pounds I'll gie
   To catch the lad wi' the tartan plaidie.'

7 Then Charlie he addressed his men,
   Saying 'Gin you will be stern and steady
   I'll get for you, your country free,
   If you fecht wi' me, and keep the plaidie.'

8 Then they drew up five hundred men
   Five hundred men, baith stoot and steady,
   Like wind and rain they garred them flee,
   At ilka daud o' the tartan plaidie.

9 The Duke of Perth stood on the right,
   The bold Munro and brave Glengarry,
   From the Isle o' Sky[e] cam' brave Lochiel,
   McLaren bold, and bold Incharrie.

10 A painted room and silken bed
    Would hardly serve a German lairdie,
    But a better prince than ony o' them a'
    He lay on the heather in his tartan plaidie.

GD 126A. Duncan noted of the song: 'George F. Duncan, written in 1885 partly from father and mother, partly from another source he cannot recall.' Elsewhere Duncan wrote: 'It was learnt by father and mother from James Cruickshank, senior, Brownhill, about the middle of the nineteenth century.' He also noted the song in 1905 from his sister, Mrs Gillespie, who sang it in a nearly identical form. [I/M].

Editorial Note Tonic lowered from D to C; the text lyric does not include the repeat.

fecht – fight;   *stoot* – stout;   *daud* – shake

118. Tifty's Annie

GEORGE F. DUNCAN

At Mill o' Tif - ty there lived a man, In the neigh-bour-hood o' Fy - vie, He had a on - ly daugh - ter fair Was cal - lèd bon - nie An - nie.

1 At Mill o' Tifty there lived a man,
   In the neighbourhood o' Fyvie,
   He had a only daughter fair
   Was callèd bonnie Annie.

2 Her bloom was like the springing flower
   That hails the early morning
   With innocence and graceful mien
   Her beauteous face adorning.

3 Lord Fyvie had a trumpeter
   Whose name was Andrew Lammie,
   He had the airt to gain the heart
   O Tiftie's bonnie Annie.

4 Proper he was, baith young and tall,
   His like was not in Fyvie;
   Nor was there one that could compare
   Wi this same Andrew Lammie.

5 Lord Fyvie he rode by the door
   Where lived Tifty's Annie;
   His trumpeter rode him before,
   Even this same Andrew Lammie.

6 Her mother called her to the door,
   Said, 'Come here to me my Annie;
   Did you ever see a prettier man
   Than the trumpeter of Fyvie?'

7 Nothing she said but sighing sore,
   Alas for bonnie Annie!
   She durst not own her heart was won
   By the trumpeter o Fyvie.

8 At nicht when a' gaes to their bed,
   A' sleeps fu soun but Annie;
   Love so oppressed her tender breast
   And love will waste her body.

201

9 Love comes in at my bedside
   And love lies down beside me,
   Love so oppressed my tender breast
   And love will waste my body.

10 The first time I was with my love
   In the bonny woods o Fyvie,
   His manly form and speech so soft
   Soon gained the heart o Annie.

11 He called me mistress, I said no,
   I'm Mill o Tifty's Annie;
   With apples sweet he did me treat
   And kisses soft and many.

12 'Tis up and down in Tifty's glen
   Where the burn rins clear and bonnie,
   I've often gaen to meet my love,
   My bonnie Andrew Lammie.

13 But now alas! her father heard
   That the trumpeter o Fyvie
   Had had the airt to gain the heart
   O' Mill o' Tifty's Annie.

14 Her father soon a letter wrote
   And sent it on to Fyvie,
   To say his daughter was bewitched
   By his servant Andrew Lammie.

15 Then up the stair his trumpeter
   He called soon and shortly,
   'Pray tell to me what's this you've done
   To Tifty's bonnie Annie.'

16 'Woe be to Mill o Tifty's pride
   For it has ruined many;
   They'll not have't said that she should wed
   The trumpeter o Fyvie.

17 'In wicked airt I had nae pairt
   Nor in it am I canny,
   True love alone the heart has won
   O Tiftie's bonnie Annie.

18 'Where will I find a boy so kind
   That'll carry a letter canny,
   And will him on to Tifty's town,
   And gie it to my Annie?

19 'Tifty he has daughters three
   Who all are wondrous bonny;
   But ye'll ken her owre aboon the rest,
   Gie it to bonnie Annie.'

20 'It's up an down in Tifty's den
   Where the burn rins clear and bonny,
   There wilt thou come and I'll attend,
   My love I long to see thee.

21 'Thou must come to the brig o Shigh,
   I'll come and meet thee,
   And there we will renew our love
   Before I gang and leave thee.

22 'My love, I go to Edinburgh town
   And for a while maun leave thee.'
   She sighed fu sore and said no more
   But, 'I wish that I were wi ye.

23 'I'll be true and constant too
   To thee my Andrew Lammie
   But my bridal bed it will be made
   In the green church yard o Fyvie.'

24 'The time is gone and now comes on,
   My dear, that I must leave ye,
   If longer here I should appear,
   Mill o' Tifty he wid see me.'

25 'I'll buy to you a bridal gown,
   My love I'll buy it bonnie.'
   'But I'll be dead ere ye come back
   To see your bonny Annie.'

26 'If ye'll be true and constant too,
   As I am Andrew Lammie
   I will thee wed when I come back
   To view the lands o Fyvie.'

27 'I now for ever bid adieu
   To thee my Andrew Lammie;
   Or ye come back I will be laid
   In the green churchyard o Fyvie.'

28 He hied him to the castle tower,
   To the house top o Fyvie,
   He blew his trumpet loud and shrill,
   Twas heard at Mill o' Tifty.

29 Her father locked the door at nicht,
   Laid up the keys fu canny;
   And when he heard the trumpet sound,
   Said, 'Your coo is lowing Annie.'

30 'My father dear, I pray forbear
   And reproach not your Annie,
   For I'd rather hear that coo low
   Than all the kye in Fyvie.

The Trumpeter at Fyvie Castle

31 'I widna for my braw new gown
　　Nor a' your gifts sae many,
　　That it were known in Fyvie's lands
　　Sae cruel ye are to Annie.

32 'But if ye strike me I'll cry out
　　And gentlemen will hear me,
　　Lord Fyvie he'll be riding by
　　And he'll come in and see me.'

33 At that same time the lord came in,
　　And said, 'What ails thee Annie?'
　　'It's a' for love that I maun die,
　　For bonny Andrew Lammie.'

34 'Pray Mill o Tifty gie consent
　　An let your daughter marry.'
　　'It will be wi some higher match
　　Than the trumpeter o' Fyvie.'

35 'If she'd been come of as high kind
　　As she's advanced in beauty
　　I would take her unto myself
　　An make her my own lady.'

36 'Fyvie's lands are far and wide
　　An they're a' wondrous bonny,
　　But I widna leave my ain true love
　　For a' the lands o Fyvie.'

37 Her father struck her wondrous sore
　　As also did her mother,
　　Her sisters also did her scorn,
　　But woe be to her brother.

38 Her brother struck her wondrous sore
　　With cruel strokes and many;
　　He broke her back on the hall door
　　For loving Andrew Lammie.

39 'Alas my father and mother dear,
　　So cruel you are to Annie,
　　My heart was broken first by love,
　　My brother broke my body.

40 'O mother dear now make my bed,
　　An lay my face to Fyvie,
　　Thus will I lie and thus will die,
　　For my dear Andrew Lammie.

41 'Ye neighbours hear baith far an near,
　　An' pity Tifty's Annie,
　　Who dies for loving one poor lad,
　　My bonny Andrew Lammie.

42 'No kind of vice e'er stained my life,
　　Nor hurt my virgin honour,
　　My youthful heart was won by love,
　　But death will me exoner.'

43 Her mother then she made her bed
　　And laid her face to Fyvie,
　　Her tender heart it soon did break,
　　An she ne'er saw Andrew Lammie.

44 Lord Fyvie he did wring his hands,
　　'Alas for Tifty's Annie,
　　The fairest flower cut down by love,
　　That ever sprang in Fyvie.

45 'Woe be to Mill o Tifty's pride,
   He might have let them marry
   I would have gien them land an gear,
   Within the lands o Fyvie.'

46 Her father deeply now laments
   The loss o his dear Annie,
   And wishes he had gien consent
   To wed wi Andrew Lammie.

47 When Andrew hame from Edinburgh came
   Wi muckle grief an sorrow,
   'My true love died for me today,
   I'll die for her tomorrow.

48 'Now I will run to Tifty's den,
   Where the burn rins clear and bonny,
   With tears I'll view the brig o Shigh,
   Where I parted wi my Annie.'

GD 1018B. Child 233 *Tifty's Annie*. Duncan noted that this version is from the 'MS. of George F. Duncan (1885) from father and mother'. Greig wrote of the ballad in the *Buchan Observer*, 17 March 1908: 'No ballad is better known than "Mill o' Tifty's Annie." The scene – a ruined mill, lies about a mile and a quarter N.E. of Fyvie Castle. The heroine was Agnes Smith, who died in 1673, and the hero, Andrew Lammie, the Laird of Fyvie's Trumpeter.' [M].
Editorial Note Tonic lowered from C to A; text lyric has 'a lovely' in place of 'a only' (1.3), and 'Her name was' in place of 'Was callèd' (1.4). 'Trumpeter' (7.4) is a correction from manuscript.

airt – art; *durst* – dare; *hied* – went; *exoner* – exonerate

119. Ye Gowden Vanitie

GEORGE F. DUNCAN

1   There was a gallant ship and a gallant ship was she
    Eek-eedle-ee and the Lowlands low,
    And she was called 'Ye Gowden Vanitie'
    As she sailed to the Lowlands low.
    She hadna sailed a league a league but only three
    Eek-eedle-ee and the Lowlands low
    Till she fell in wi' a French gallee
    As she sailed to the Lowlands low.

204

2   Then up spak' the captain and up spoke he
    'Oh, wha'll sink for me yon blessed French gallee?'
    Then up spak' the cabin boy and up spak he,
    'What will ye gie to me gin I sink the French gallee?'

3   Then up spak' the captain and up spak he
    'I'll gie ye lands and hooses in the North countrie.'
    'Then roll me up ticht in a black bull's skin,
    And throw me owerboord, though sink I or swim.'

4   They've rolled him up ticht in a black bull's skin,
    And thrown him owerboord, though sink he or swim.
    Then a-down, and a-down, and a-down sunk he,
    And he swam up to the French gallee.

5   Now some were playing cards and some were playing dice
    Then out he took an instrument, bored holes in a trice.
    Then some they ran wi' cloaks, and some they ran wi' caps,
    But they tried a' in vain to stop the saut draps.

6   Then aroon', and aroon', and aroon', went she,
    And she went down to the bottom of the sea.
    Then aroon' and aroon' and aroon' swam he
    Till he cam' up to 'Ye Gowden Vanitie'.

7   'Throw me oot a rope and haul me up on board
    And prove unto me as good as your word.'
    'We winna throw a rope nor haul you up on board,
    Nor prove unto you as good as our word.'

8   Then up spak' the cabin boy and up spak' he,
    'Hang me but I'll sink you as I sank the French gallee.'
    They threw him doon a rope and hauled him up on board
    And proved unto him far better than their word.

GD 37A. Child 286 *The Sweet Trinity* (*The Golden Vanity*). The words and music were written out by George F. Duncan and sent to James B. Duncan with a letter dated 2 May 1908. In the letter he commented: 'I am not sure where I got it from, but I have a notion that I have heard mother sing it.' In a letter of 21 July 1908, he added: 'I have also another form of the song in an old song-book, and it was from it I took the form "Ye Gowden Vanity". I was aware that the form "Ye" was not really old, but being in the book I thought it might be the commonly received form'. Greig wrote in the *Buchan Observer*, 1 March 1910: 'This ballad . . . is very widely known and sung, and appears in many collections, set to a variety of tunes. In the earliest printed copy extant the Owner and Master of the ship is the famous Sir Walter Raleigh. It is quite possible, however, that there was an earlier ballad with the same or a similar burden.' [I, inflected 4th].

Performance Note Since the 'y' of 'ye' is simply an old spelling of 'th' the word could be pronounced as 'the'.

Editorial Note Tonic lowered from G to D.

gowden – golden

Margaret Gillespie

1841–1913

Mrs Margaret Gillespie

Margaret Duncan was born on 21 December 1841 in New Deer parish to William Duncan and Elizabeth Duncan (née Birnie).[1] In November 1867, at Weetingshill in New Deer parish, she married James Gillespie, a journeyman slater who was then living in Turriff.[2] The couple had four children: William, b. 1868, Mary Jane, b. 1869, Leslie, b. 1871 and James, b. 1874.[3] Her husband died in 1899.[4]

A sister of James Bruce Duncan and of George F. Duncan (see also his biography), she had a very extensive repertoire, and a total of four hundred and sixty-six songs are given from her in the published collection. Her sources were very varied.[5]

At the time of the 1891 census she was living at 71 Garscube Road in the Milton area of Glasgow. Her occupation is given as 'sewing machinist'. Also present at the house were her son Leslie, and a boarder called James Matthew Brown, an insurance agent, aged forty-three, who came from Old Deer.[6] The 1901 census lists her as keeping a boarding house at 222 West Regent Street,[7] and James Matthew Brown was still lodging with her at this time.

A variety of methods was used to obtain Mrs Gillespie's songs. Duncan sent her lists of songs to help jog her memory and James Matthew Brown wrote down most of the words that appear in a 674-page manuscript book, referred to as 'Gillespie'. Duncan sometimes visited her in Glasgow, and Mrs Gillespie sometimes visited her brother at Lynturk, and Duncan noted her tunes on these occasions.

The opening of a letter from Margaret Gillespie to James Bruce Duncan

The opening page of a letter from Mrs Gillespie to Duncan, probably sent soon after 7 May 1907, is reproduced above. In it, she mentions James Brown ('Mr B') and discusses song versions that occur in 'Gillespie' between pages 531 and 569: 1365 'Aul' Widow Greylocks' A, 1054 'The Rigs o' Rye' C, 1658 'Simon Brodie', 584 'Hooly and Fairly' A, 1184 'Ye Girls of Equal Station' A, and 867 'The Braes o' Abernethy' B.

In 1909, Mrs Gillespie went to live in South Africa where her sons, William and Leslie, were resident. Her granddaughter, Ursula Gillespie, described her as 'a very outstanding person and very hard-working – everything she did was done as well as it could be done!' She was also known in the family for being a 'splendid dancer' and 'used to play the piano by ear'. About her singing, Ursula said: 'Grandma had a very nice voice, not high nor low. The songs she sang at her sewing-machine were ditties such as "Who's dat knockin' at the door".'[8] Mrs Gillespie died in 1913 in South Africa.[9]

NOTES

1 OPR 1841/225/3.
2 Marriage record 1867/225/18.
3 Birth records 1868/225/19, 1869/247/116, 1871/154/25, 1874/247/39. Mary Jane and James were both born in Turriff.
4 See article on Mrs Margaret Gillespie by Elaine Petrie, *Greig–Duncan*, vol. 8, p. 562.
5 See Petrie, pp. 559–64.
6 Census record 1891/644/8/014/015.
7 Census record 1901/644/9/042/013.
8 Letter from Ursula Gillespie to Emily Lyle, 13 March 1981, held in the School of Scottish Studies Archives, department of Celtic and Scottish Studies, University of Edinburgh.
9 *Greig–Duncan*, vol. 8, p. 596.

120. Johnnie's Grey Breeks

MARGARET GILLESPIE

When I was lit-tle Jea-ni-kie, I was a wan-ton tow-dy, O, The lads loved me baith far and near, But I loved neen but John-nie, O. My John-nie was a bon-nie lad Was ser-van' to my dad-die, O, He had se-ven mark an' grey breeks, An a' his boord an bed-die, O.

1 When I was little Jeanikie,
   I was a wanton towdy, O,
   The lads loved me baith far and near,
   But I loved neen but Johnnie, O.
   My Johnnie was a bonnie lad
   Was servan' to my daddie, O,
   He had seven mark an' grey breeks,
   An a' his boord an beddie, O.

2 Johnny he gangs out an' in
   An dis his wark sae steady O
   An I did dry his gray breeks
   When a' wis in their beddie O.
   Now Johnny's gotten his Jeanikie
   An bairnies weel an happy O
   An they a' sup out o ae dish
   An Johnny claws the cappie O.

GD 1280. The music was noted by Duncan in 1905. The song had been learned by Margaret Gillespie from their mother and was also known as 'When I was little Jeanikie'. The words differ from GD 1279 'Johnnie's Gray Breeks' although the tune is similar to version D given by the Rev. John Calder. [Æ].

Editorial Note Tonic lowered from Bb to A; text lyric has 'An' for 'But' (1.4), 'Johnny' for 'My Johnnie' (1.5), 'He was servant' for 'Was servan" (1.6), and 'He'd' for 'He had' and 'marks' for 'mark' (1.7).

towdy – young unmarried woman; *boord an beddie* – food and lodging;
claws the cappie – scrapes the bowl

121. The Birken Tree

MARGARET GILLESPIE

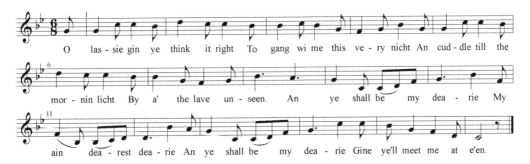

O las-sie gin ye think it right To gang wi me this ve-ry nicht An cud-dle till the
mor-nin licht By a' the lave un-seen. An ye shall be my dea-rie My
ain dea-rest dea-rie An ye shall be my dea-rie Gine ye'll meet me at e'en.

1 O lassie gin ye think it right
   To gang wi me this very nicht
   An cuddle till the mornin licht
   By a' the lave unseen.
   An ye shall be my dearie
   My ain dearest dearie
   An ye shall be my dearie
   Gine ye'll meet me at e'en.

2 I daurna from my mammie gee
   She locks the door an keeps the key
   At e'en an mornin scauling me
   An aye aboot the men.
   She says they're a deceivers
   Deceivers deceivers
   She says they're a deceive[r]s
   She widna trust to ane.

3 O never min yere mammie's yell
   I'se waurnt she's meet yere dad hersel
   An fan she scauls ye may her tell
   She's aften de'en the same.
   Sae lassie gie's yere haun on't
   Yere bonnie milk white haun [on't]
   Sae lassie gie's yere haun on't
   An scorn to lie yere leen.

4 O lad my haun I daurna gie
   But maybe I may steal the key
   An meet you at the birken tree
   That grows doun in the glen.
   Bit dinna lippen laddie
   I canna promise laddie
   O dinna lippen laddie
   For fear I dinna win.

5 Now he's gane to the birken tree
   In hopes his true love for to see
   An wha cam trippin o'er the lea
   Bit jist his bonnie Jean.
   She link'it doun beside him
   Beside him beside him
   She link'it doun beside him
   Upon the grass so green.

6 I'm overjoyed wi rapture noo
   Cried he and pree'd her cherry mou
   An Jeanie ne'er hid cause to rue
   That nicht upon the green.
   For she has got her Johnnie
   Her ain dear lovin Johnnie
   For she has got her Johnnie
   An Johnnie's got his Jean.

GD 802A. The music was noted in 1905 by Duncan. The song had been sung by their mother and by
   Johnnie Rennie of New Pitsligo, but it was also 'often sung by others'. There are three versions of
   the song in the collection. [Dor/M].

Editorial Note Tonic lowered from D to C; 'on't' is editorial (3.6); the tune used is that of 1130 'Glasgow
   Green' B from the same singer.

I'se waurnt – I'm sure; *lippen* – depend on it; *link'it* – sat arm in arm; *pree'd* – kissed

122. The Duke of Athole's Nurse

MARGARET GILLESPIE

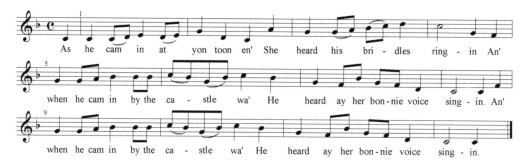

As he cam in at yon toon en' She heard his bri - dles ring - in An'
when he cam in by the ca - stle wa' He heard ay her bon - nie voice sing - in. An'
when he cam in by the ca - stle wa' He heard ay her bon - nie voice sing - in.

1 As he cam in at yon toon en'
   She heard his bridles ringin
   An' when he cam in by the castle wa'
   He heard ay her bonnie voice singin.
   An' when he cam in by the castle wa'
   He heard ay her bonnie voice singin.

2 I am the Duke o' Athole's nurse,
   And my post it is very well becoming,
   I wad gie a' my half-year's fee,
   For ae sicht o' my leman.

3 Ye say ye're the Duke of Athole's nurse
   And yere post it is very well becoming
   Keep weel keep well yere half-year's fee
   You'll get twa sights o your leman.

4 He lean'd him owre his saddle-bow
   An cannily kissed his dearie
   Said ye hae my heart but another his
                                    my han'
   What bettar can ye be o' me.

5 Gin I hae yere heart an another his
                                    yere haun
   These words hae fairly undone me
   But let us set a time an tryst to meet again
   Then in good friendship you'll twine me.

6 Ye'll do you down to yon tavern house
   An drink till it be dawing
   And as sure as I'm a woman true
   I'll come an clear your lawing.

7 Ye'll spare not the wine although it be fine
   Nor any drink though it be rarely

But ye'll aye drink to the bonnie
                                    lassie's health
That's to clear your lawing fairly.

8 Then he's deen him doun to yon
                                    tavern house
   And drank till the day was dawing
   An ilka gless he drank, he drank the
                                    lassie's health
   That wis coming to clear his lawing.

9 It's a wonder to me the squire he did say
   My bonnie lassie's sae delaying
   She promised as sure as she loved me
   She wid be here by the dawing.

10 He's teen him up to a shott window
   A little before the dawing
   And there he spied her brothers three
   Wi their swords a' well-drawn.

11 O where shall I rin or where shall I gang
   Or where shall I gang an hide me
   She that was to meet me in friendship
                                    this day
   Has sent her brothers to slay me.

12 He's gane to the landlady o the house
   To see gin she could save him
   She dressed him in her ain clothing
   An she set him to the baking.

13 She gae him a suit o her ain female claes
   An set him to the baking
   The birds never sang mair sweet on the bush
   Than the young squire sang at his baking.

210

14 As they came in at the ha door
      Sae loodly as they rappit
      An when they came upon the floor
      Sae loodly as they chappit.

15 O had ye a quarterer here last night
      Who drank till the day was dawing
      Come show us the room where the
                              quarterer lies in
      An wee'l shortly clear his lawing.

16 There was a quarterer here last night
      That drank till the day was dawing
      He called for a pint an he paid it e'er
                              he went
      You've got nothing to do with his lawing.

17 One o them being in a very merry mood
      To the young squire fell a-talking
      The wife took her foot an she gae him a kick
      Says hist ye bonnie Annie wi yere baking.

18 They sought the house up an they sought the house down
      An they spared nae the curtains for the riving
      An' ilka ane o' them as they passed by
      They kissed the bonnie lassie at her baking.

GD 160A. Child 212 *The Duke of Athole's Nurse*. The tune was noted by Duncan in 1905 and the words
      are from the Gillespie MS. The song was sung by their mother. [M].
Editorial Note Tonic lowered from D to C; text lyric has 'O I'm' for 'I am' (2.1), 'My post is' for 'And my
      post it is' (2.2), and 'But I' for 'I' (2.3); 5.5 and 9.5 were originally crotchets.

leman – lover; *cannily* – kindly; *twine* – part from; *do you down* – go down; *dawing* – dawning;
clear your lawing – pay your bill; *shott window* – small window with shutters;
chappit – knocked; *quarterer* – lodger; *hist ye* – make haste, hurry up; *riving* – tearing

123. To a Meeting One Evening, To a Meeting Went I

MARGARET GILLESPIE

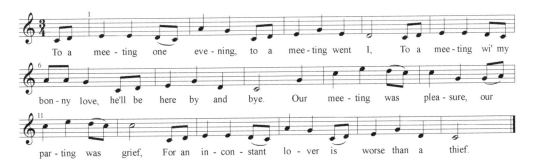

1   To a meeting one evening, to a meeting went I,
      To a meeting wi' my bonny love, he'll be here by and bye.
      Our meeting was pleasure, our parting was grief,
      For an inconstant lover is worse than a thief.

211

2   A thief he will rob you, take all that you have;
     But an unconstant lover, will bring you to your grave.
     The grave will consume you, bring your body to dust;
     There's not a man among a hundred, a woman should trust.

3   The cuckoo's a fine bird, she sings as she flies;
     She brings us good tidings, and she tells us no lies.
     She feeds on the small birds, to keep her voice clear;
     But she never sings cuckoo, till the summer is near.

GD 1157A. The music was noted by Duncan in September 1905. The song had been learned by
    Margaret Gillespie from their mother around 1855. [Pent].
Editorial Note Tonic lowered from D to C; text lyric has 'meet' for 'a meeting' (1.2), and 'unconstant' for
'inconstant' at (1.4).

124. Binorie

MARGARET GILLESPIE

There lived twa sis-ters in yon-der ha' Bi - no - rie O, an' Bi - no - rie, They
hid bit ae lad a - tween them twa, He's the bon-nie mil-ler lad o Bi-no-rie.

1   There lived twa sisters in yonder ha'
    Binorie O, an' Binorie,
    They hid bit ae lad atween them twa,
    He's the bonnie miller lad o Binorie.

2   It fell aince upon a day
    Binorie O an Binorie
    That the auldest ane to the youngest
               did say
    At the bonnie mull dams o Binorie.

3   O sister O sister will ye gang to
               the brooms,
    Binorie O an Binorie,
    An hear the little blackbirdie changing
               its tunes
    At the bonnie mull dams o Binorie.

4   O sister O sister will ye gang to the dams
    Binorie O an Binorie
    An see your father's fish boats safe to
               dry land
    An see the mullart lad o Binorie.

5   They hidna been half an hour at
               the brooms
    Binorie O an Binorie
    Till they thrice heard the blackbirdie
               changing its tunes
    At the bonnie mull dams o Binorie.

6   They hidna been an hour at the dams
    Binorie O an Binorie
    Till they saw their father's fish boats safe
               on dry land
    But they sawna the bonnie mullart laddie.

7   The youngest ane she stood on a stane
    Binorie O an Binorie
    The aulest ane dung the youngest in
    To the bonnie mull dams o Binorie.

8   She swam up an she swam down
    Binorie O an Binorie
    Till she swam back tull her sister again
    In the bonnie mull dams o Binorie.

9 O sister O sister will ye reach me
                         yere glove
Binorie O an Binorie
An I'll make you heir o my true love
The bonnie mullart lad o Binorie.

10 It wisna for that, that I dang ye in
Binorie O an Binorie
It's because ye are fair an I am din
An ye'll droon in the dams o Binorie.

11 Oot cam the aul' mullart's daughter to
                         the dams
Binorie O an Binorie
For water tae wash her father's hands
Fae the bonnie mull dams o Binorie.

12 O father O father go a-fishing your dams
Binorie O an Binorie
For there's either a mermaid or a milk
                       white swan
In the bonnie mull dams o Binorie.

13 They socht up an they socht down
Binorie O an Binorie
But they got naething but a droon'd womán
In the bonnie mull dams o Binorie.

14 Some o them kent her by her skin so fair
Binorie O an Binorie
But weel kent the millart by her bonnie
                       yellow hair
She's the millart's bonnie lass o Binorie.

15 Some o them kent her by her goon o silk
Binorie O an Binorie
But the millart laddie kent her by
                   her middle so jimp
'Twas his ain bonnie lass o Binorie.

16 Mony a ane was at her oot takin
Binorie O an Binorie
An mony ane mair at her green
                   grave makin
At the bonnie mull dams o Binorie.

GD 213A. Child 10 *The Twa Sisters*. The tune was noted by Duncan in 1905 as remembered by Margaret Gillespie, George F. Duncan and himself. The words are from the Gillespie MS. Duncan noted: 'This ballad was very early in print, the first published versions going back to the middle of the seventeenth century; and its popularity continued. . . . [Our] records from tradition indicate how popular the ballad was in the North-East, and how far it even yet remains.' The ballad continues to be popular amongst present-day folksingers in Scotland. [Æ/Dor].

Editorial Note The tune lyric has 'go' for 'gang' (4.1); the word 'to' (4.3) comes from the tune lyric – the text lyric has 'on'. Notes 1.2, 3.2 and 8.1 were each originally a dotted quaver followed by a semiquaver, and 2.1 was two quavers.

mullart/millert – miller;   *dung/dang* – pushed;   *changing* – varying;   *din* – dun;   *jimp* – slender

125. Mairins Gibberlin

MARGARET GILLESPIE

Once there was a plough - man, and he cam fae the Isle o' Man, He was as good a
plough - man as e-ver drew a fur on lan'. The coul - ter ran sae nim - 'ly, the
sock it would nae tak the lan', And aye he damned the hin - tins o' aul' Mair - ins
Gib - ber - lin. Sing roo and sing roo and sing ah roo the rad-dy tad-dy,
Wak fal de dye a doo, roon a - boot the bor - ders o' aul' Mair - ins Gib-ber - lin.

1   Once there was a ploughman, and he cam fae the Isle o' Man,
    He was as good a ploughman as ever drew a fur on lan'.
    The coulter ran sae nim'ly, the sock it would nae tak the lan',
    And aye he damned the hintins o' aul' Mairins Gibberlin.
    Sing roo and sing roo and sing ah roo the raddy taddy,
    Wak fal de dye a doo, roon aboot the borders o' aul' Mairins Gibberlin.

2   The next there was a weaver all o' the orange and the blue,
    He weave a web to Mairins that neen o' a' the lave could do.
    The shuttle ran sae nimbly, the yarn ran fae han' to han',
    He reeled it in the pern box o' aul' Mairins Gibberlin.

3   The next he was a watchmaker, and he cam fae the Isle o' Man
    He made a clock to Mairins, the hands thereof they wadna gang
    But he screwed up the pendulum, the strikkin piece he made to stan',
    And touched the regulator o' aul' Mairins Gibberlin.

4   The next he was a blacksmith, and set it up upon the stock,
    And Mairins she cried after him, 'Come back, pit tee the horn till it.'

GD 1434A. The tune for this bawdy song was noted by Duncan from Mrs Gillespie in 1905. Duncan stated at the end of the words: 'There is some wanting here [the second half of verse 4], but it is plenty of the kind. Mrs Gillespie had heard it sung all the more readily because its meaning lies not in direct badness, but in *doubles entendres*. It was sung among farm servants, and is a specimen of one type of their songs.' [Pent].

Performance Note The 'g' of Gibberlin is pronounced as in 'give' (*Greig–Duncan*, vol. 7, p. 524).

Editorial Note Duncan commented that the second half of the verse was sung to the same tune as the first half. He gave only the first two lines and the chorus in his music notation. The text lyric has been used for verse 1: the tune lyric has 'on' for 'in' in (1.2). 'Stock' (4.1) and 'horn' (4.2) could refer to the wind instrument played by shepherds.

fur – furrow; *sock* – ploughshare; *hintins* – furrow between the two ridges (in ploughing); *pern* – bobbin

126. The Duke o' Gordon's Three Daughters

MARGARET GILLESPIE

The Duke o' Gor - don had three bon - ny daugh - ters, E - li - za, Mar - get an Jean; And they wad - na stay in Cas - tle Gor - don, But went to bon - ny Ai - ber - deen.

1 The Duke o' Gordon had three
                        bonny daughters,
Eliza, Marget an Jean;
And they wadna stay in Castle Gordon,
But went to bonny Aiberdeen.

2 They hidna been in bonnie Aberdeen
A year but an a day
Lady Jean's faun in love wi Captain Ogilvie
An from him she winna stay.

3 Word came to the Duke o Gordon
In the chamber where he lay
That Lady Jean's faun in love wi Captain
                        Ogilvie
An from him she winna stay.

4 Go saddle to me the black horse
Yersel ride on the grey
And we'll reach bonnie Aberdeen
By the dawning o the day.

5 They were not a mile fae bonnie Aberdeen
A mile bit barely three
When the duke met his two daughters
To bear him company.

6 O where is your sister, maidens,
He unto them did say
Lady Jean's faun in love wi Captain Ogilvie
And from him she winna stay.

7 O pardon O pardon us father
O pardon us they did say
Lady Jean's faun in love wi Captain Ogilvie
An awa wi him she did gae.

8 When he came to bonnie Aberdeen
And stood upon the green,
And there he saw Captain Ogilvie,
A trainin o his men.

9 O woe be to you, Captain Ogilvie,
An ill death may ye dee
For takin to you my daughter
High hangèd ye shall be.

10 The duke he wrote a broad letter
And sent it to the king
Said Ye'll cause hang Captain Ogilvie
If ever ye hanged a man.

11 I will not hang Captain Ogilvie
For nae lord that I see
I'll cause him put off the lace and scarlet
And put on the single livery.

12 Word came to bonnie Captain Ogilvie
In his chamber where he lay
To put off the lace and scarlet
And don the single livery.

13 If this be for bonnie Jeanie Gordon,
A' this an mair wid I dree
If this be for bonnie Jeanie Gordon
It's thrice welcome to me.

14 Lady Jean had not been married,
Years but only three,
When she had twa babies at her fit
An anether on her knee.

15 O bit I'm weary wandering
O bit I think lang
It ill sets the Duke o Gordon's daughter
To follow a single man.

16 Woe to the hills and the mountains
Woe to the frost and snow
My shoes and stockings are all torn
Nae farther can I go.

17 But O gine I were at the bonnie hills
            o Foudland
For mony merry day I hae been
I wid get the road to Castle Gordon
Without either stockin's or sheen.

18 When she came to bonnie Castle Gordon
And stood upon the green
The porter lead out a loud huzza
Here comes our Lady Jean.

19 O you're welcome home, Jeanie Gordon
You and yere bairnies three,
Ye're welcome here Jeanie Gordon
Bit awa wi' your Ogelvie.

20 Now over the seas went the captain
As a soldier under command
A message soon followed after
To come an heir his brother's land.

21 Come hame, come hame Captain Ogelvie
And heir your brother's land
Come hame ye pretty Captain Ogelvie
An be Earl o Northumberland.

22 O what does this mean captain
Where are my brother's children three
They are all deed an buried
Northumberland is waiting for thee.

23 Then hoist up your sails said the captain
And let us be jo[y]ful an free
For I'll to Northumberland an heir
            my estates
And then my dear Jeanie I will see.

24 When he came to bonnie Castle Gordon
And stood upon the green
He was the prettiest young man
That ever they had seen.

25 Ye're welcome here Captain Ogelvie
Ye're thrice welcome to me
Ye're welcome here Captain Ogelvie
To your wife an bairnies three.

26 The last time I was a[t] your gates
Ye widna let me in
I am come for my wife and my children
Nae ither friendship I claim.

27 Come in my pretty Captain Ogelvie
Drink the red beer an the wine
And we'll count ye out gold an silver
Untill that the clock strikes nine.

28 I winna come in said the captain
I'll drink neither yere red beer nor wine
I want neither yere gold nor yere silver
I've enough in Northumberland.

29 Down the stairs came bonnie Jeanie
            Gordon
The tears were blindin her eye
Down came bonnie Jeanie Gordon
Wi her bairnies three.

30 Ye're welcome my bonnie Jeanie Gordon
You and my young family
We'll haste an go to Northumberland
An a countess you shall be.

GD 1099B. Child 237 *The Duke of Gordon's Daughter*. Duncan took down two tunes from his sister: (a) which is used here, came from their father and mother, and (b), which was learned by Margaret Gillespie from the singing of Miss Michael, New Deer. [Æ/Dor].

Editorial Note Tonic lowered from F to E; the text lyric has 'Margaret' for 'Marget' (1.2) and 'at bonnie' for 'in' (1.3).

single livery – uniform of a private;   *dree* – endure;   *think lang* – am pining;   *sets* – becomes;
   single man – soldier of the lowest rank, private

127. I Love My Love

MARGARET GILLESPIE

I love my love as I love my life, An' I love my own life dear - ly. My whole de-light's in her weel-faur'd face, An' I long to have her near me.

I love my love as I love my life,
An' I love my own life dearly.
My whole delight's in her weel-faur'd face,
An' I long to have her near me.

1   The first thing that I asked of her,
Where did her father dwell, O,
And the answer that she gae to me
Was, 'Between the cloods an' hell, O.'

2   The next thing that I asked at her
Was, if she wad tak a man,
And the answer that she gae to me
Was, 'Files noo an' than, O.'

3   The next thing that I asked at her,
If she wad mairry me,
And the answer that she gae to me,
'I think I'm better free, O.'

GD 964A. The tune was noted by Duncan at Lynturk Manse on 2 September 1909 and the words are from the Gillespie MS. Duncan noted that the song begins with the chorus and that the air is the same for the chorus and verses. There are three versions of this song in the collection. [I/Ly].

Performance Note Duncan stated: 'The chorus here seems out of harmony with the verses; it seems to express quite a different situation and spirit, and surely belongs to a different song.' However, similar verses with the same chorus are found in version B from Bell Robertson. Robertson's chorus to the last verse differs in its first two lines which run: 'But I love her yet, I love her yet, / I love her yet most dearly'. The singer may wish to sing the last refrain with these lines.

Editorial Note Tonic lowered from F to D.

files – sometimes

217

128. Heely and Fairly

MARGARET GILLESPIE

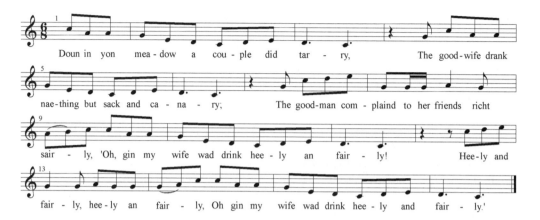

Doun in yon mea - dow a cou - ple did tar - ry, The good-wife drank nae-thing but sack and ca - na - ry; The good-man com - plaind to her friends richt sair - ly, 'Oh, gin my wife wad drink hee - ly an fair - ly! Hee-ly and fair - ly, hee-ly an fair - ly, Oh gin my wife wad drink hee - ly and fair - ly.'

1 Doun in yon meadow a couple did tarry,
   The goodwife drank naething but sack and canary;
   The goodman complaind to her friends richt sairly,
   'Oh, gin my wife wad drink heely an fairly!
   Heely and fairly, heely and fairly,
   Oh gin my wife wad drink heely and fairly.'

2 First she drunk Crummie an sine she drank Gerrie
   An sine she drank my bonnie grey marie
   That carrit me through a the dubs in the glaurie
   Oh gine my wifie wid drink hooly an fairly.

3 She drank her hose an she then drank her sheen O
   An n'oo she drunken her bonnie new goun O
   She drunken her sark that cover'd her rarely
   Oh gine my wifie wid drink hooly and fairly.

4 Wid she drink bit her ain things I widna much care O
   Bit she drink my claes that I canna weel spare O
   An when I'm wi my gossips it angers me sairly
   Oh gine my wifie wid drink hooly and fairly.

5 My braw Sunday's coat she his laid it in wad O
   An the best blue bonnet that e'rr was on my head O
   At kirk or at market I'm cover'd bit barely
   Oh gine my wifie wid drink hooly and fairly.

6 My bonnie white mittens I wore on my hands O
   Wi her ne'ebours wife she laid them in the pawn O
   My bane headed staff that I liket sae dearly
   Oh gine my wifie wid drink hooly and fairly.

7   I never was fond o wrangling or strife O
    Nor did I deny her the comforts o life O
    For when there's a war I'm aye for a parley
    Oh gine my wifie wid drink hooly an fairly.

8   When there's any money she maun keep the purse O
    If I seek bit a babee she'll scold an she'll curse O
    She lives like a queen while I'm scrimpit an sparely
    Oh gine my wifie wid drink hooly and fairly.

9   A pint wi her cummers I wid her allow O
    Bit when she sits down the jade she gets fu O
    An when she is fu she is unco camsterrie
    Oh gine my wifie wid drink hooly and fairly.

10 When she comes to the street she roars an she rants O
    Has nae fear o her ne'ebours nor minds the house wants O
    She sings up a foul sang like 'Up yer heart Charlie'
    Oh gine my wifie wid drink hooly an fairly.

11 When she comes hame she lays on the lads O
    The lasses she ca's them baith bitchs and jades O
    An myself she ca's an auld cuckle carlie
    Oh gine my wifie wid drink hooly and fairly.

GD 584A. The music was noted by Duncan on 7 April 1907. The song had been sung by their father and
    also by Mrs Imlah, Woodhead, Delgaty. [I/Ly].

Editorial Note Tonic lowered from D to C; text lyric has 'wine' for 'sack' (1.2), 'wifie' for 'wife' (1.4), and
    'heely' is spelled 'hooly' throughout.

sack – a kind of white wine;   *canary* – a light sweet wine from the Canary Islands;
    heely, hooly – moderately;   *dubs* – puddles;   *glaurie* – mud;   *gossips* – cronies;   *wad* – pawn;
    babee – bawbee, halfpenny;   *scrimpit* – in want;   *cummers* – female friends;
    camsterrie – quarrelsome;   *cuckle* – cuckold

129. Oh Daughter Dear, Wad Ye Hae the Lad?

MARGARET GILLESPIE

1   O daughter dear wid ye hae the lad
That has his livin by the plough
Eh na mither she said
A ploughman's wife his much to do.

2 O daughter dear wid ye hae the lad
That has his livin by the mill
Eh na mither she said
The smell o the dist wid de me ill.

3 O daughter dear wid ye hae the lad
That has his livin by the pen
Eh ay, mither, she said
I always liked young gentlemen.

GD 1332C. The music was noted by Duncan in 1905. The song had been learned by Margaret Gillespie from their mother. Greig wrote in the *Buchan Observer*, 26 October 1909: 'In rustic verse, when mother and daughter engage in dialogue, we are pretty certain to find that love and matrimony constitute the theme, and that the two characters are more or less at issue as regards opinions and proposals. As a rule the mother urges considerations of worldly prudence against the rashly romantic views of her daughter. In this song, however, we have a girl who is practical enough to be able to take care of herself.' [Dor, with inflected 7th].

Editorial Note Tonic lowered from C to A; 7.1 was originally two quavers (A and E); tune lyric has 'man' for 'lad' (2.1).

130. There Was a Gallant Soldier

MARGARET GILLESPIE

1   There was a gallant soldier walking on the shore;
There was a pretty fair maid walking him before.
Wi' my narry eeten nit not, narry eeten nair;
Wi' my darra reedle, darra reedle darra reedle dair O.

2　Fair may, O rare may, I fear ye go wi bairn.
　　Oh yes indeed an that I do a word I winna scorn.

3　Fair may O rare may, fa is yere bairn tull,
　　It's tull a gallant soldier jist like yersel.

4　O fair may, O rare may, far is your soldier gane.
　　He's awey to foreign countries to fight for his king.

5　O fair may O rare may, fat if he be slain.
　　The king will loose a man she said an I will loose a frien.

6　O fair may O rare may, O fat an I be he.
　　O yes indeed an' that ye are a word I winna lee.

GD 1472A. The music was noted by Duncan in 1905. The song had been learned by Margaret Gillespie from their mother. [I/M].

Editorial Note Tonic lowered from A to G; Duncan noted at the start of the chorus that it was sung at the 'same rate' as the 'very fast' section just indicated; the change of time-signature in bar 8 is editorial.

tull – to

131. Clean Pease Strae

MARGARET GILLESPIE

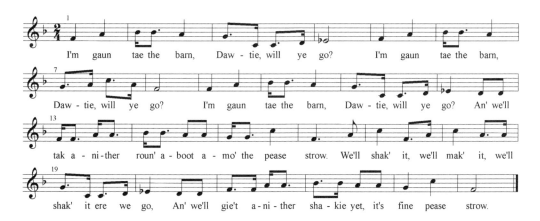

1　I'm gaun tae the barn, Dawtie, will ye go?
　　I'm gaun tae the barn, Dawtie, will ye go?
　　I'm gaun tae the barn, Dawtie, will ye go?
　　An' we'll tak anither roun' aboot amo' the pease strow.
　　We'll shak' it, we'll mak' it, we'll shak' it ere we go,
　　An' we'll gie't anither shakie yet, it's fine pease strow.

2   When John an' I were married, oor haddin' was but sma',
     My minnie, cankert carline, wad gie us nocht ava'.
     I spent my fee wi' canny care, as far as it wad gae,
     But weel a wyte, oor bridal bed was clean pease strae.
     Clean pease, lang pease, fine pease strae,
     An' we'll gie't anither shakie yet, it's fine pease strae.

3   Wi' workin' late an early, we've come to what ye see,
     For fortune thrave on ilka han', an eydent aye were we.
     The lowe o' love mak's labour licht, ye're sure to find it sae,
     When kin' you cuddle doon at e'en amo' the pease strae.
     Clean pease, etc.

4   The rose blows gay on cairnie brae as weel's in birken shaw
     An' love will live in cottage low as weel's in lofty ha'.
     So lassie, tak the lad ye like, whate'er your minnie say,
     Tho' ye should mak your bridal bed o' clean pease strae.
     Clean pease, etc.

GD 1278A. The song was noted by Duncan from Margaret Gillespie on 22 March 1909. She remembered the song being sung by her mother and by Betty Mitchell. Duncan commented that the song was made up of traditional material (verse 1 and chorus) with the remainder being from Robert Tannahill's song 'Lassie Tak the Lad Ye Like'. [M].

Performance Note The notes at 16.2, 17.3, 18.3 and 19.2 were bracketed in the original to indicate that they are omitted in choruses 2–4.

Editorial Note Tonic lowered from G to F; the dotted crotchet in bar 16 was originally a minim and the quaver following it was in a bar of its own.

haddin' – possessions;   *minnie* – mother;   *carline* – old woman;   *weel a wyte* – well I know;   *eydent* – industrious;   *lowe* – flame;   *cairnie* – stony;   *shaw* – thicket

132. Welcome My Bonnie Lad

MARGARET GILLESPIE

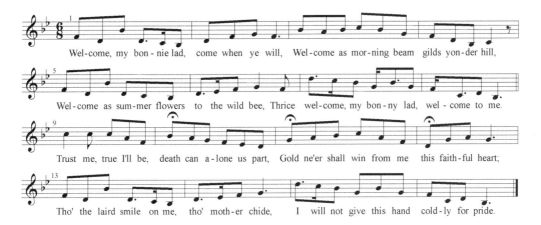

Wel-come, my bon-nie lad, come when ye will, Wel-come as mor-ning beam gilds yon-der hill,

Wel-come as sum-mer flowers to the wild bee, Thrice wel-come, my bon-ny lad, wel-come to me.

Trust me, true I'll be, death can a-lone us part, Gold ne'er shall win from me this faith-ful heart;

Tho' the laird smile on me, tho' moth-er chide, I will not give this hand cold-ly for pride.

1   Welcome, my bonny lad, come when ye will,
Welcome as morning beam gilds yonder hill,
Welcome as summer flowers to the wild bee,
Thrice welcome, my bonny lad, welcome to me.
Trust me, true I'll be, death can alone us part,
Gold ne'er shall win from me this faithful heart;
Tho' the laird smile on me, tho' mother chide,
I will not give this hand coldly for pride.

2   Oftimes my mither scolds till I grow sad
Scolds me for loving you my bonnie lad
Tak' the rich laird says she Donald is poor
And love will fly quickly when want's at the door.

3   What are riches and broad lands to me?
For if I wed, bonnie lad, you it will be
So welcome my bonnie lad come when you will
Welcome as morning beams gild yonder hill
Welcome as simmer flowers to the wild bee
Thrice welcome my bonnie lad ever to me.

GD 997. The song is undated in Duncan's manuscript. It was learned by Margaret Gillespie in Glasgow and was said to be old. Duncan noted: 'Both words and air, however, are evidently recent. It was doubtful whether the refrain given is correct – whether the second half of it is the music to be used there, and whether those words also are not part of a stanza.' [I].

Performance Note It is suggested that singers repeat bars 5–8 in verse 3 to accommodate the six lines.

Editorial Note Tonic lowered from C to Bb; lyric of verse 1 and chorus from 997a, other verses from 997b (but an additional verse which was equivalent to the chorus has been omitted); 'win' in 1.6 was 'wed' in the original, but the former was suggested by Duncan and is used here; the rhythm and barring in bars 3 and 4 have been slightly altered.

133. Jeanie Nettle

MARGARET GILLESPIE

Saw ye my wi-fie, Jea-nie Net-tle, Jea-nie Net-tle? Saw ye my wi-fie Rin-nin' fae the mar-ket?

1 Saw ye my wifie,
Jeanie Nettle, Jeanie Nettle?
Saw ye my wifie
Rinnin' fae the market?

2 A peck o' meal upon her back,
Upon her back, upon her back,
A peck o' meal upon her back,
A babby in a blanket.

GD 1725A. This dance song was noted by Duncan in 1906. Margaret Gillespie learned it from their mother and from a servant, Mary Cruickshank. [Pent].
Editorial Note Tonic lowered from F to C; note 1.6 originally a quaver.

134. The Sodger's Joy

MARGARET GILLESPIE

Bon - ny las - sie, will ye dance at my fo - y, O? Bon - ny las-sie, will ye dance at my
fo - y, O? Bon - ny las - sie, will ye dance at my fo - y, O? And
ye'll be the sod - ger's joy, O. No, I win-na dance at your fo - y, O, No,
I win-na dance at your fo - y, O, No, I win-na dance at your
fo - y, O, Though I should be the sod - ger's joy, O.

1 Bonny lassie, will ye dance at my fo-y, O?
Bonny lassie, will ye dance at my fo-y, O?
Bonny lassie, will ye dance at my fo-y, O?
And ye'll be the sodger's joy, O.

2 No, I winna dance at your fo-y, O,
No, I winna dance at your fo-y, O,
No, I winna dance at your fo-y, O,
Though I should be the sodger's joy, O.

GD 1743A. This dance song was collected by Duncan from his sister, Margaret Gillespie. She learned it from James Buchan 'who sang the whole,' and noted that 'the first verse was often heard'. Duncan indicated that the second part of the song could also be sung to the first strain [I].
Performance Note It is suggested that 'fo-y' is pronounced 'foy-ee'.
Editorial Note Tonic lowered from Bb to A; the rests at bars 8 and 16 are editorial (these were originally crotchets); quavers at 9.2–3, 11.2–3 and 13.2–3 are editorial (originally crotchets).

sodger – soldier; *foy* – farewell feast, party

135. Johnny Jiggamy

MARGARET GILLESPIE

I'm gaun to tak ye by the tae, fair maid o' Wig-ga-my, 'Faith,' says she, 'ye better nae, kin' John-ny Jig-ga-my.' 'But gin ye do it do it right, do me nae mair in-ju-ry, And by the tae ye may tak me, kin' John-ny Jig-ga-my.'

1 I'm gaun to tak ye by the tae, fair maid o' Wiggamy,
 'Faith,' says she, 'ye better nae, kin' Johnny Jiggamy.'
 'But gin ye do it do it right, do me nae mair injury,
 And by the tae ye may tak me, kin' Johnny Jiggamy.'

2 I'm gaun to tak ye by the heel, fair maid o' Wiggamy,
 'Gin ye dee that ye'll pit me feel, kin' Johnny Jiggamy.
 But gin ye do it do it right, do me nae mair injury,
 And by the heel ye may tak me, kin' Johnny Jiggamy.'

3 I'm gaun to tak ye by the knee, fair maid o' Wiggamy,
 'Gin ye do that we winna gree, kin' Johnny Jiggamy.
 But gin ye do it do it right, do me nae mair injury,
 And by the knee ye may tak me, kin' Johnny Jiggamy.'

4 I'm gaun to tak ye by the thie, fair maid o' Wiggamy,
 'Gin ye do that ye'll pit me mad, kin' Johnny Jiggamy.
 But gin ye do it do it right, do me nae mair injury,
 And by the thie ye may tak me, kin' Johnny Jiggamy.'

GD 1412A. The music was noted by Duncan on 21 October 1907. He wrote: 'The words, it seems, came from a woman called Katie Steven, in New Pitsligo; and they illustrate the gross note of the songs that were once current enough, even among women, it seems.' [M].

Editorial Note Tonic lowered from F to D; tune lyric (of verse 2) written in shorthand; note 4.3 originally a dotted quaver followed by a semiquaver, and the quavers at 12.3 and 12.4 originally a crotchet (these changes were made to accommodate the words). The word 'thie' (4.1 and 4.4) is editorial: Duncan left spaces at these points.

pit me feel – make me mad;   *thie* – thigh

136. Oor Little Pigs

MARGARET GILLESPIE

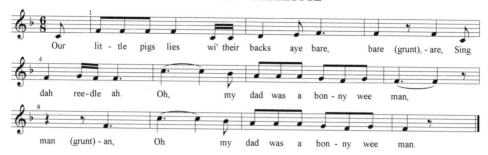

1 Our little pigs lies wi' their backs aye bare, bare (grunt), -are,
   Sing dah reedle ah.
   Oh, my dad was a bonny wee man, man [spoken shrilly] (grunt) -an,
   Oh my dad was a bonny wee man.

2 The little pigs lies wi' their tails half cocked, cocked (grunt), -ocked.

3 Oor old soo maks the finest o' pork, pork (grunt), -ork.

4 Oor old soo maks the finest o' bacon, bacon (grunt), -acon.

GD 1661. Duncan noted the music for this nursery song from Margaret Gillespie on 21 October 1907. She had learned it from Jamieson, a music teacher in New Pitsligo, and called it 'Lillibulero'. Duncan wrote: 'The rhythm is kept up where the rests are marked – at the first place by a grunt through the nose to imitate a pig; at the second, by the word "Man" spoken very shrilly (apparently to imitate a young pig), followed by a grunt as before, succeeded by the truncated word "–an".' [I]. Editorial Note Tonic lowered from A to F; text lyric used for verse 1.

137. The Hen's March

MARGARET GILLESPIE

1 Tick, tick, tick, tick, tick tick-a-lairy;
   Tick-a-lairy; tick-a-lairy;
   Ticky, ticky, ticky, ticky, ticky, ticky, tick;
   And the aul' hen cries oot, 'Tick-a-lairy.'

GD 1664. The song was noted by Duncan on 21 October 1907. Margaret Gillespie had heard it in childhood and Duncan recalled that there were more words describing all the actions of the hens. The tune is often heard played on the fiddle under the title 'The Hen's March O'er the Midden'. [Pent].

Ann Lyall

1869–1945

Ann Lyall and her husband, David

A letter from Mrs Lyall to Duncan

Mrs Ann Lyall (née Roy) was born on 18 July 1869 at Lawfolds in the parish of Rayne. Her parents were Grigor Roy, a farm servant, and Elspet Roy (née Florence).[1] The 1881 census places her at the home of the Ledingham family at Lawfolds where she was working as a nurse, and in 1891 she was working as a servant to the minister, George Wisely, at Skene.[2] In 1895 at the age of twenty-six, Ann married David Lyall, a master shoemaker, aged fifty-four, at Durno in the Chapel of Garioch.[3] The couple had five children. All the family were musical, and Mrs Lyall played the harmonium and was a soprano with a 'very sweet voice'.[4] She was an exceptionally vigorous, intelligent and enterprising woman. She wrote straight away to Duncan when she saw a report of his lecture in Alford in the *Aberdeen Free Press* on Monday 5 November, sending him a batch of fragments she recalled from the singing of her mother, and telling him that she had the tunes for these (see letter above). When Duncan visited her at Mosscroft, Lyne of Skene, on 4 June and 7 November 1907, she was able to give him forty

227

tunes, and Duncan returned for further recording sessions with her on 17 April, 11 August and 26 November 1908, 2 and 14 February and 23 October 1911, and 10 November 1913.[5]

Mrs Lyall followed Greig's column in the *Buchan Observer* and sent him a version of 'The Jolly Beggar' which Greig acknowledged in a warm and appreciative letter of 17 July 1908.[6] Mrs Lyall made energetic efforts to obtain fuller texts than she knew herself, and she both collected from singers and made enquiries about songs in the *People's Journal*.[7] She received a visit from Carpenter in 1930 and the materials he collected from her include a sound recording of the 'Battle of Harlaw'.[8] She died on 25 January 1945 at Moss Croft, Lyne of Skene.[9]

NOTES

1 Birth record 1869/236/28.
2 Census records 1881/236/1/11 and 1891/238/4/1.
3 Marriage record 1895/179/3.
4 See article on Mrs Lyall by Anne Neilson in *Greig–Duncan*, vol. 8, pp. 566–7.
5 *Greig–Duncan*, vol. 8, pp. 519–21, 523.
6 The letter is given in *Greig–Duncan*, vol. 8, p. 490.
7 See *Greig–Duncan*, vol. 8, pp. 567, 597.
8 The recording is AFC 1972/001, Cylinder 120. See further *The James Madison Carpenter Collection Online Catalogue* http://www.hrionline.ac.uk/carpenter
9 Death record 1945/238/2.

138. Hog an Tarry

ANN LYALL

Hog an tarry, baloo bonny,
Hog an tarry, hishy ba;
Hog an tarry, baloo bonny,
Hog an tarry, hishy ba.

GD 1555. Collected by Duncan from Mrs Lyall on 7 November 1907. The song was learned from her mother and was used as a cradle song. Another verse that was not fully remembered included the words: 'He's a sailin' on the sea'. [Æ/Dor].
Editorial Note Tonic lowered from E to C.

hog an tarry – lull to sleep

139. Jessie of Old Rayne

ANN LYALL

Fare weel my friends an com-rades all I now must go a-way May for-tune smile u-pon you all An' cheer you night an' day An' weel I min' I leave be-hind Sweet Jes-sie of Old Rain.

1 Fare weel my friends an comrades all
   I now must go away
   May fortune smile upon you all
   An' cheer you night an' day
   An' weel I min' I leave behind
   Sweet Jessie of Old Rain.

2 To leave you all it greives my heart
   It makes me sigh again
   When I do mind I leave behind
   Sweet Jessie of Old Rain
   O weel I min' I leave behind
   Sweet Jessie of Old Rain.

3 The last time that I Jessie saw
   'Twas near the Kirk o' Rayne
   We parted when the sun went doon
   In hopes to meet again
   An' weel I min' I leave behind
   Sweet Jessie of Old Rain.

4 But oh that time has not arrived
   An' I am on the main.
   An' sailin wi' a heart deprived
   O' Jessie o' Old Rayne.
   O weel I mind I leave behind
   Sweet Jessie of Old Rain.

5 Fareweel Culsalmond, Rayne, an' Oyne
   Likewise to Fyvie too
   Where I hae spent my youthfu' days
   But they're a' ended noo
   An' weel I min' I leave behind
   Sweet Jessie of Old Rain.

6 Fareweel to Newton's bonnie woods
   Where lovers aftimes meet
   Where aften I an' Jessie's been
   Where time does flee sae fleet
   O weel I min' I leave behind
   Sweet Jessie of Old Rain.

7 So fare-ye-weel my dearest dear
   For ever an' for aye
   The fervent love I bear for you
   Shall never quite decay
   An' weel I min' I leave behind
   Sweet Jessie of Old Rain.

GD 1523A. The song was collected by Duncan on 26 November 1908. Mrs Lyall learned the air from her mother and the words from her mother's sister, Mrs Gerrard, who had learned them 'from a mistress at Mill o' Barns' forty years earlier. There are only two versions of this song in the collection, the other being from Robert Alexander. [I/M].

Editorial Note Tonic lowered from D to Bb. Tune lyric has 'Rayne an' Een' for 'Rayne, an' Oyne' (5.1), and 'But weel' for 'An' weel' (5.5).

140. The Coasts of Barbary

ANN LYALL

1   Keep a good look out ahead, our jolly captain said,
    Blow high, blow low, and so sailed we.
    'We see nothing out ahead,' our jolly crew they cried,
    Cruising down along the coasts of Barbary.

2   Keep a good look-out ahead, our jolly captain cried,
    We saw a lofty frigate sailing yonder on our lee.

3   'Oh hail her, oh hail her,' our jolly captain cried.
    'Are you a man-o'-war or a privateer?' said he.

4   'I am neither man-o'-war or a privateer,' said he,
    'But I am a saucy pirate a-seeking for my fee.'

5   First the Queen of Russia shot the pirate's masts away,
    And next the Prince of Wales sank her deep into the sea.

6   The ship it was a coffin and the grave it was the sea,
    The ship it was a coffin and the grave was in the deep.

GD 38. This pirate song was collected by Duncan on 7 November 1907. The song is also called 'Blow High Blow Low' in the collection. Ann Lyall got the song from her husband who learned it in the Mearns. [I].

Editorial Note Tonic lowered from C to A. Some editorial additions have been made where there were gaps in the text. 2.2 had a space followed by 'saw a ship sailing yonder on our lee', and this line has been completed, and lines 3.2 and 4.1–2 added, from versions in Bronson (especially 3 and 10) of Child 285 *The George Aloe and the Sweepstake*.

141. The Minister's Wedder

ANN LYALL

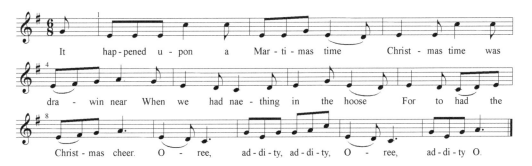

It hap-pened u-pon a Mar-ti-mas time Christ-mas time was dra-win near When we had nae-thing in the hoose For to had the Christ-mas cheer. O-ree, ad-di-ty, ad-di-ty, O-ree, ad-di-ty O.

1   It happened upon a Martimas time
Christmas time was drawin near
When we had naething in the hoose
For to had the Christmas cheer.
O ree, addity, addity, O ree, addity O.

2   The minister he has a good fat wedder
As ever was fed on corn an' hay
I will tak some crums in my pocket
For to wile her on the way.

3   A little wee boy sat in the hoose
Warmin himsel afore the fire
'An' ye wad gie me a bit o' the wedder
I'll gether you sticks to mak a fire.'

4   The little wee boy went to the wood
An' aye sae merrily as he sang
My father stealt the minister's wedder
I wadna tell that to ony man.

5   The minister himsel' being in the wood
Just leaning himsel' against an oak
Says Gin ye wad sing that on the kirk
                       on Sunday
I'll gie ye a croon an' a braw new coat.

6   The morn it being Christmas Sunday
As Christmas comes but once a year
The people flockèd to the church
As people flockin' to a fair.

7   The little wee boy's intae the kirk
An' aye sae merrily as he sang
The minister was in bed wi my mither
I wadna tell that to ony man.

8   Gin ye had seen the little wee boy
Sae merrily he cairrit on the joke
Rinnin cryin' after the parson
Come gee's ma croon an' my braw new coat.

GD 309A. The song was noted by Duncan on 4 June 1907 and had been learned by Mrs Lyall from her
maternal grandfather. There are four versions of this song in the *Greig–Duncan* collection. [Dor, –2].
Editorial Note Tonic lowered from C to A; alternative note 'e' in anacrusis. Tune lyric has 'Gin ye had
bit seen the little wee boy' (4.1), and the text lyric refrain runs 'O ree addie O ree addie O'. Verse 7
is editorial: 7.2 and 7.4 are repeats of 4.2 and 4.4, and the other lines are based on version D and on
a text from *Tocher*, vol. 1 (no. 4, 1971–2), p. 119.

had – keep; *wedder* – sheep

142. Did Ye Not Promise to Marry Me?

ANN LYALL

Did ye not pro-mise to mar-ry me Doon by yon bon-ny wa-ter side? Did ye not pro-mise to mar-ry me An' to make me your bride?

1   Did ye not promise to marry me
     Doon by yon bonny water side?
     Did ye not promise to marry me
     An' to make me your bride?

2   'When a' the girls go to the wood
     To hear the blackbird sing,
     But I poor girl maun sit at home,
     And rock my cradle and spin.'

3   'Gin ever I promised to mairry you,
     It's been in some very merry mood,
     For I've vowed a vow, an' I will keep it true,
     I'll wed none that's easily wooed.'

GD 978A. Duncan noted this song on 4 June 1907. Mrs Lyall learned it from her mother and Duncan wrote: 'Mrs Lyall's mother learnt this from her own mother, who in turn learnt it from her mother. That goes back about a hundred and twenty years. The family came from Auchterless.' The other versions of this song in the collection are from Miss Lizzie Crighton and Miss Jemima Milne. [I].
Editorial Note Tonic lowered from A to F.

Elizabeth Greig

*c.*1846–1924

Mrs Elizabeth Greig (née Norrie) was born *c.*1846 in New Deer, and died on 14 April 1924 at Midmar, aged seventy-eight. Her parents were Andrew Norrie, a meal miller, and Margaret Norrie (née Stuart).[1] Elizabeth's husband, James, a shoemaker, was born in Rathen in Aberdeenshire, and the pair married in 1865 at Mill of Elrick, Old Deer, where Elizabeth was working as a domestic servant.[2] The 1881 census lists the couple at 'Crofty' in Cluny parish along with six children: Margaret, Elizabeth, Mary, James, Andrew and Elspet. In 1891 the couple were at the same address and also present was another daughter, Barbara, who was born in the parish of Cluny.[3] Elizabeth's husband, James, died in 1902.

Mrs Greig's daughter Margaret, who was herself a singer and had a musical training, was the wife of William Harper, schoolmaster, Cluny. Duncan gave a folk-song lecture at Cluny, which is about six miles east of Lynturk, on 23 January 1907, and she wrote to him a week later to tell him about her mother's repertoire.

> My mother has a lot of good ballads never seen in print and if she still remembers the words I can take down the notes the first time I go to see her in Aberdeen. There was a pretty one she used to sing about a 'proud young porter' [1023 Lord Brechin A]. . . . I remember the tune perfectly well if mother could remember the words.[4]

She commented in another letter on 7 February that her mother's people had 'sweet voices and quick ears' but had no musical training.[5] Margaret Harper noted tunes from her mother's sisters, Mrs Robertson and Mrs Kelman, as well as from her mother, and mentions that many of the family songs came from their mother, Mrs Norrie, who in turn had learned songs from *her* mother, Mrs Stuart, née Jean Scott, Strichen.[6] Mrs Norrie was said to have known 'ever so many old ballads'.[7]

Elizabeth Greig recalled the communal nature of the singing that took place in her youth:

> They met at somebody's house one evening, the women taking their knitting, all sat round in a circle while some one of the company sang a ballad, the whole assembly joining in or repeating the last line of each verse in order to give the singer time to get breath for his next verse. Then some others contributed, and all the while a large pot boiled on the fire, cooking kail or turnips which were ladled out on to a beremeal scone before the guests departed![8]

Margaret Harper wrote to Duncan from her mother's home in Aberdeen on 7 August 1907, saying:

> 'I had your letter all right this morning and enclose another lot to see if you have any thing to ask about them as long as I am here. If you have not please never mind

acknowledging as I am not nearly done with them yet. Mother remembers new ones nearly every day.'[9]

One of the sheets she sent to Duncan is shown below. It includes tunes for 'Fat'll Mak' a Bonnie Lassie Blythe an' Glad' (146 in this volume) and GD 1668 'There was a Tree' A (cf. the version from Alexander Robb, no. 58 in this volume).

Margaret Harper's transcription of two of her mother's songs

NOTES

1 Death record 1924/222/A/5.
2 Marriage record 1865/237/B/9.
3 Census records 1881/181/3/5 and 1891/181/3/5.
4 998/7/1/1.
5 998/7/1/3.
6 See *Greig–Duncan*, vol. 8, p. 518, and the article by Emily Lyle on Mrs Harper and Mrs Greig in *Greig–Duncan*, vol. 8, p. 565.
7 998/7/1/3.
8 *Greig–Duncan*, vol. 8, p. 565.
9 998/7/1/34.

143. The Banks o' Clyde

ELIZABETH GREIG

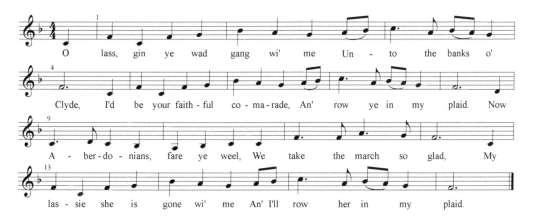

1   O lass, gin ye wad gang wi' me
    Unto the banks o' Clyde,
    I'd be your faithful comarade,
    An' row ye in my plaid.
    Now Aberdonians, fare ye weel,
    We take the march so glad,
    My lassie she is gone wi' me
    An' I'll row her in my plaid.

2   The Ninety-Second Highlanders,
    They lie in Aberdeen,
    Wi' stars upon their breastplate
    And buckles on their sheen.

GD 1520A. The song was noted by Mrs Harper from her mother, Elizabeth Greig, in August 1907.
[I/M].
Editorial Note Tonic lowered from A to F.

144. The Beggar Man

ELIZABETH GREIG

1   A beggar man cam' owre the lea,
    And mony a fine tale he taul' me,
    He was askin help for charitee,
    'Could you lodge a beggar man?'
    Ladlee a tow row ree.

2   The nicht bein' dark, an somewhat wat,
    Doun by the fireside the aul' man sat;
    He cuist the mealpock aff his back,
    An' sae loudly he lilted an' sang.

3   The lassie sat ayont the fire,
    An' aye she sang to his desire;
    An' aye she sang to his desire,
    'Would you lodge a leal puir man?'

4   'I'll bend my back an' bow my knee,
    An' tie a black patch owre my ee,
    An' for a beggar they'll tak me,
    An' awa' wi' you I'll gang.'

5   'Rise gudeman an' wauken your bairn,
    The cheese is to mak' an' the claes to
                                    iron,
    An' tell her to come speedily ben,
    For I'm sure she has lain owre lang.'

6   Up i' the mornin' the auld man rase,
    He missed the beggar an' his auld claes;
    He missed the beggar an' his auld claes,
    'I hope there's nane o' oor gude
                                    gear gane.'

7   He ran to the cupboard he ran to the kist,
    There was naething awa' that he could miss,
    'Since a'thing's right then Praise be blest!
    We lodged a leal puir man.'

8   Then he gaed to the bed where his
                                    dochter lay,
    The sheets were cauld an' she was away,
    The sheets were cauld an' she was away,
    Away wi' the beggar man.

9   When ten months were past an' a
                                    twelvemonth gane
    The same beggar carle came again,
    An' was askin' help for charitee
    'Could you lodge a beggar man?'

10 'I never lodged a beggar man but ane,
    I never had a dochter nane but ane,
    An' awa' wi' a beggar she has gane,
    An' I dinna ken when nor where.'

11 'Yonder's your dochter comin' owre the lea,
    An' mony a fine tale she'll tell thee,
    She has got a bairn on ilka knee,
    An' anither on the road comin' hame.'

GD 275C. Child 279 *Appendix The Gaberlunyie-Man*. The song was noted by Mrs Harper from her mother, Elizabeth Greig, in February 1907 and sent to Duncan. There are twenty-seven versions of this ballad in the collection. [I].

Performance Note Singers may prefer to use 'Laddie' in place of 'Ladlee' in the refrain.

Editorial Note Tonic lowered from G to F.

wat – wet; *cuist* – cast; *mealpock* – bag for collecting meal; *leal* – faithful; *Praise* – God

145. The Weaver Lad

ELIZABETH GREIG

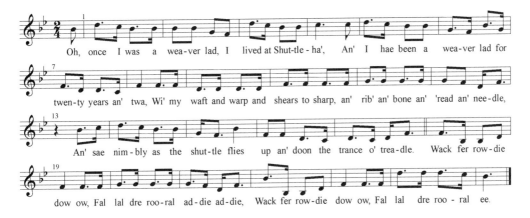

Oh, once I was a wea-ver lad, I lived at Shut-tle-ha', An' I hae been a wea-ver lad for twen-ty years an' twa, Wi' my waft and warp and shears to sharp, an' rib' an' bone an' 'read an' nee-dle, An' sae nim-bly as the shut-tle flies up an' doon the trance o' trea-dle. Wack fer row-die dow ow, Fal lal dre roo-ral ad-die ad-die, Wack fer row-die dow ow, Fal lal dre roo-ral ee.

1. Oh, once I was a weaver lad, I lived at Shuttleha',
   An' I hae been a weaver lad for twenty years an' twa,
   Wi' my waft and warp and shears to sharp, an' rib an' bone an' 'read an' needle,
   An' sae nimbly as the shuttle flies up an' doon the trance o' treadle.
   Wack fer rowdie dow ow, Fal lal dre rooral addie addie,
   Wack fer rowdie dow ow, Fal lal dre rooral ee.

2. We'll maybe live to see the time when things'll tak' a come,
   When we'll get notes to buy braw coats and breeks to hap oor bum,
   Fouth a' ale fae cock and pail and reamin' in a luggit bicker,
   Besides a dish o' gweed fat brose an' iron girds to haud them siccar.

GD 477. The song was noted from Elizabeth Greig by her daughter, Mrs Harper, in August 1907 and sent to Duncan. There are a number of songs about weaving in the Scots song tradition, but this one is unusual in that it includes a lot of technical language. It was written by David Shaw under the title 'Tammy Traddlefeet' and published by Andrew L. Fenton in *Forfar Poets* (Forfar, 1879), pp. 61–2 (*Greig–Duncan*, vol. 3, p. 650). The pieces of weaving equipment mentioned in line 1.3 are referred to in Shaw's poem as 'rubbin' bane, my reed an' haddles', and in line 1.4, he has 'tramp' for 'trance'. [Pent].

Editorial Note Tonic lowered from C to Bb; text lyric has 'in' for 'at' (1.1), and 'owdie' for 'rowdie' and 'al' for 'lal' (1.5 and 1.6).

waft – weft; *shears* – scissors; *hap* – cover; *cock* – cog, bowl; *reamin'* – frothing;
luggit bicker – beaker with handles; *girds* – hoops; *siccar* – secure

146. Fat'll Mak' a Bonnie Lassie Blythe an' Glad

ELIZABETH GREIG

Fat-'ll make a bon-nie las-sie blythe an' glad,
Fat-'ll mak' a bon-nie las-sie blythe an' glad? A lang win-ter's nicht an' her ain dear-est lad, That-'ll mak' a bon-nie las-sie blythe an' glad.

1   Fat'll make a bonnie lassie blythe an' glad,
     Fat'll mak' a bonnie lassie blythe an' glad?
     A lang winter's nicht an' her ain dearest lad,
     That'll mak' a bonnie lassie blythe an' glad.

2   Fat'll mak' a bonnie lassie weary sune,
     Fat'll mak' a bonnie lassie weary sune?
     A lang winter's nicht an' an ill spinnin' wheel,
     That would mak' a bonnie lassie weary sune.

GD 932A. The song was sent to Duncan by Elizabeth Greig's daughter, Mrs Harper, who wrote: 'Noted by me from my mother's singing August 1907.' There are three versions of this song in the collection. [Pent].

Archibald Knowles

1838–1924

Archibald Knowles

The opening of 'Braw Black Jug'

Archibald Knowles was born on 23 November 1838 in the parish of Fetteresso in Kincardine-shire to Alexander Knowles and Susan Knowles (née Smart).[1] At the time of the 1841 census the family – including two further sons – were living at Baldcraigs Farm in the same parish.[2] In 1863, Archibald, who was then working as a saw miller in Aberdeen, married Mary Thomson, a domestic servant, aged twenty-four, who was born in Grange.[3] By 1891, he was living in St Nicholas parish in Aberdeen along with his family and is recorded as being an unemployed joiner.[4] The 1901 census places the family at 54 Baker Street, Aberdeen, in the parish of St Machar. Knowles was then working as a house carpenter. The children listed in the census were William, aged twenty-six, a granite mason; Adam, aged twenty-two, a plumber; John, aged nineteen, and Mary, aged seventeen.[5] Archibald Knowles had twelve children in all, and the Knowles musical tradition has persisted in subsequent generations of the family.[6]

Knowles contributed sixteen songs to the collection. He responded to the appeal that Duncan made in November 1906 by sending 1266 'Charlie Napier Gordon' B and writing: 'If this be the stuff you want I have more songs than pennys'. Duncan noted down tunes from Knowles, 57 Esslemont Avenue, Aberdeen, on 19 December 1906,[7] beginning with this one. Knowles wrote out the words himself either before or after this visit as follows: 607 'The Wedding' B, 1533 'Farewell to Fintray' A, 406 'The Band o' Shearers' B, 48 'Johnnie and the Landlady' C, 9 'The Greenland Fishery' C, 78 'Arthur McBride' B, 1702 'Jock o' Arnha'', 590 'The Braw Black Jug' A, 1436 'The Miller and the Maid' B, 1130 'Glasgow Green' C, 130 'The Highland Maid' F, and 855 'Here's a Health to Lord Ronald MacDonald'. Titles only are given for 'Jock o' Rhynie' (cf. 348) and 'The Fox and the Goose' (cf. 499 'Father Fox'). The words of 'Braw Black Jug' written out in his own hand and sent to Duncan are given on the previous page. Duncan made revisions in the text and crossed the words out once he had transcribed them in shorthand.

A good deal of information is available on the sources of Knowles's songs, which were very varied. 'The Greenland Fishery', for example, was heard from whale fishers in Aberdeen in his boyhood. Knowles's father worked as a fireman in a shipyard for a time which may explain this sea connection.[8] 'Arthur McBride' was learned c.1846 from a brother, and 'Charlie Napier Gordon' was also learned at this time. 'Glasgow Green' was said to have been learned in Fintray, Aberdeenshire, in 1850 and another song learned there was 'Farewell to Fintray'. 'The Band o' Shearers' was learned in Skene c.1851 from an old Highlandman, and 'The Braw Black Jug' was learned at Kinaldie about 1855 from a young man from Banff. 'Johnnie and the Landlady' was learned about 1859 in Rothiemay from a piper and 'Here's a Health to Lord Ronald MacDonald' was learned about 1856 or 1859 in the same place. 'The Miller and the Maid' was learned in Skene and Knowles notes that it was 'heard in bothies everywhere'. He remembered the fragment, 'Jock o' Arnha'', from his father's singing.

Archibald Knowles died on 7 October 1924 in Aberdeen, aged eighty-five.[9]

NOTES

1 Information from Mr James Archibald Knowles, Toronto, a great-great-grandson of Archibald Knowles. I am most grateful to Mr Knowles for his kind help. I would also like to thank Elizabeth Knowles, Letham, Fife, and Mrs Dorothy Reid (née Knowles), Aberdeen, for their help with my enquiries.

2 Information from 1841 census from Mrs Dorothy Reid.

3 Marriage record 1863/159/19: the marriage took place in Keith.

4 Census record 1891/168/1/007/031.

5 Census record 1901/168/2/008/A/23.

6 Information from Mr James Archibald Knowles.

7 *Greig–Duncan*, vol. 8, p. 518.

8 Death record, 1924/168/3/400.

9 See note 8.

147. Farewell to Fintray

ARCHIBALD KNOWLES

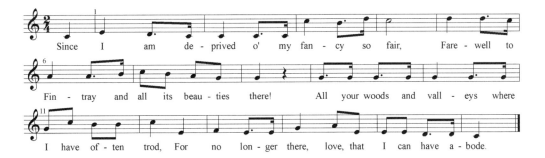

Since I am de - prived o' my fan - cy so fair, Fare - well to
Fin - tray and all its beau - ties there! All your woods and vall - eys where
I have of - ten trod, For no lon - ger there, love, that I can have a - bode.

1   Since I am deprived o' my fancy so fair,
    Farewell to Fintray and all its beauties there!
    All your woods and valleys where I have often trod,
    For no longer there, love, that I can have abode.

2   Pox upon poverty and all for want of cash
    Causes me and mony a bonny lad gang wintin his lass
    For the teemness of my pockets causes muckle greif and woe
    Sae farewell my bony lass for I'm obliged to go.

3   Farewell to father and farewell to mother
    Sisters and brothers adue all together.
    Friends and relations I bid ye all adue
    For this is the last night that I will be with you.

GD 1533A. Duncan noted the tune in December 1906. It was learned in Fintray *c*.1851, and Mr Knowles
    recalled that it was sung by the oldest people there at that time. Duncan wrote: 'Mr Knowles . . .
    said that in Fintray the song was said to have been written by a member of the Fintray proprietor's
    family of a former day, who had to leave.' There are four versions of this song in the collection. [I].
Performance Note 'Trod' (1.3) should rhyme with 'abode'.
Editorial Note Tonic lowered from D to C; text lyric has 'rare' in place of 'there!' (1.2) and 'trode' in
    place of 'trod' (1.3).

pox upon – curses on;   *wintin* – wanting;   *teemness* – emptiness

148. Cheapside

ARCHIBALD KNOWLES

As I went out one mor-ning in May, Doon by Cheap-side I chan-cèd to stray, 'Twas there I met a bon-ny bon-ny lass, And she trea-ted me to kis-ses sweet. I was up to the rigs, done to the gay, O' the sly lit-tle gir-lies o' Lon-don town.

1   As I went out one morning in May,
    Doon by Cheapside I chancèd to stray,
    'Twas there I met a bonny bonny lass,
    And she treated me to kisses sweet.
    I was up to the rigs, done to the gay,
    O' the sly little girlies o' London town.

2   She took me to a house of fame
    And she asked what was my name
    And then for supper she did call
    And she thought she would make me
                                pay for all
    But I was up to the rigs done to the gay
    Oh the sly little girleys of London town.

GD 299A. Duncan noted the tune in December 1906. There are four versions of this song in the *Greig–Duncan* collection under the general title 'The Rigs of London'. [I].

Editorial Note Tonic lowered from G to F; text lyric has 'And there' in place of ' 'Twas there' (1.3). Duncan suggested that 'done' in the refrain meant 'down'.

149. The Braw Black Jug

ARCHIBALD KNOWLES

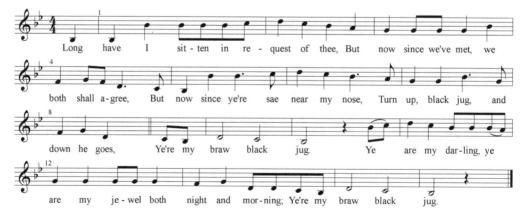

Long have I sit-ten in re-quest of thee, But now since we've met, we both shall a-gree, But now since ye're sae near my nose, Turn up, black jug, and down he goes, Ye're my braw black jug. Ye are my dar-ling, ye are my je-wel both night and mor-ning; Ye're my braw black jug.

1   Long have I sitten in request of thee,
But now since we've met, we both shall agree,
But now since ye're sae near my nose,
Turn up, black jug, and down he goes,
Ye're my braw black jug.
Ye are my darling, ye are my jewel both night and morning;
Ye're my braw black jug.

2   But oft times ye make me pawn my clothes
And oft times ye make my friends my foes
But now since ye are sae near my nose
Turn up black jug and down it goes.

3   And if my wife should me despise
Oh I would give her two blue eyes
But if she loves me as I love thee
Oh what a loveing couple as we would be.

4   And when that I am dead and gone
I will have it engraven on my grave stone
I will have it engraven on my grave stone
Grim death though me from my black jug have torn.

GD 590A. Duncan noted the tune in December 1906. Knowles had learned it at Kinaldie about 1855 from a young man from Banff. There are two versions of the song in the *Greig–Duncan* collection. [I/Ly].

Editorial Note Tonic lowered from D to Bb; text lyric has 'And now' for 'But now' and 'ye are' for 'ye're' (1.3), 'down it goes' for 'down he goes' (1.4), and 'And ye are my darling both the night and the morning' (1.6).

150. Whale Fishing Song

ARCHIBALD KNOWLES

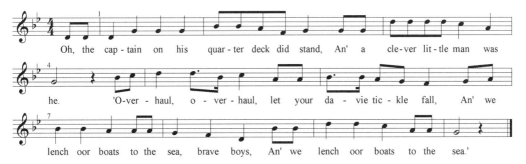

1   Oh, the captain on his quarter deck did stand,
An' a clever little man was he.
'Over-haul, over-haul, let your davie tickle fall,
An' we lench oor boats to the sea, brave boys,
An' we lench oor boats to the sea.'

2 Oh we struck that whale and away she went
   With a flourish in her tail
   But oh alas we lost one man
   And we did not kill that whale brave boys
   And we did not kill that whale.

Whalers in Peterhead Bay

GD 9C. This song is also known as 'The Greenland Fishery' or 'The Greenland Whale Fishery'. Duncan noted the tune in December 1906. He stated: 'Mr. Knowles heard this among the whale fishers in Aberdeen, in his boyhood, when the last ships were being prepared for the Franklin expedition. There were two other verses.' A note in *Greig–Duncan* indicates the context in which Knowles learned the song: 'Ships searching for traces of the expedition sailed from Aberdeen between 1850 and 1857, the last being the Fox which brought definite news of Sir John Franklin's death' (vol. 1, p. 498). [Æ/Dor].

Editorial Note Tonic lowered from A to G; text lyric has 'The captain' for 'Oh, the captain' (1.1), 'david tackle' for 'davie tickle' (1.3), 'we will launch' for 'we lench' (1.4), and 'we'll launch' for 'we lench' (1.5). Duncan glosses 'davie tickle' as 'davit tackle': a davit is a small crane.

Time-line of Singers

The following table lists the singers included in this edition in chronological order according to their date of birth. A question mark is used where the date of birth or death is unknown. (G) or (D) indicates contact with Greig or Duncan.

1820	1830	1840	1850	1860	1870	1880	1890	1900	1910	1920	1930	1940	1950	1960

George Garioch c.1824–1917 (D)
James Mackie 1830–1920 (G)
Robert Alexander 1835–1917 (D)
William Watson 1836–1919 (G)
Archibald Knowles 1838–1924 (D)
Mary Cruickshank c.1840–1911 (G)
Margaret Gillespie 1841–1913 (D)
John Mowat 1841–1916 (G)
Ann Sangster 1843–1920 (G)
Elizabeth Greig c.1846–1924 (D&G)
John McAllan c.1847–1927 (G)
John Quirrie 1848–1913 (G)
William Wallace 1849–1925 (D)
Eliza Clark c.1849–1934 (G)
Robert Chree 1852–1915 (D)
James Angus 1852–1929 (G)
Isaac Troup 1853–1938 (D)
Mary Dunbar 1855–1932 (G)
Alexander Mackay 1857–? (D)
George F. Duncan 1860–1927 (D)
Helen Rettie 1860–1941 (G)
Alexander Robb 1863–1940 (G)
Sam Davidson 1864–1951 (G)
James W. Spence 1867–1928 (G)
Georgina Reid 1868–1958 (G)
Ann Lyall 1869–1945 (D)
Kirsty Morrice c.1879–1913 (G)
Miss Henderson – (G)

List of Articles in the *Buchan Observer*

Gavin Greig's articles on 'Folk-Song of the North-East' appeared weekly in the *Buchan Observer* between 3 December 1907 and 6 June 1911, with the exception of 5 January 1909, 8 June 1909, 14 February 1911 and 11 April 1911. They were printed in book form in two volumes as *Folk-Song of the North-East* (Peter Scrogie: Peterhead, 1909, 1914) and have been reprinted in facsimile in *Folk-Song in Buchan and Folk-Song of the North-East by Gavin Greig*, foreword by Kenneth S. Goldstein and Arthur Argo (Hatboro, Pennsylvania: Folklore Associates, 1963).

1	3 December 1907	31	30 June 1908	61	2 February 1909
2	10 December 1907	32	7 July 1908	62	9 February 1909
3	17 December 1907	33	14 July 1908	63	16 February 1909
4	24 December 1907	34	21 July 1908	64	23 February 1909
5	31 December 1907	35	28 July 1908	65	2 March 1909
6	7 January 1908	36	4 August 1908	66	9 March 1909
7	14 January 1908	37	11 August 1908	67	16 March 1909
8	21 January 1908	38	18 August 1908	68	23 March 1909
9	28 January 1908	39	25 August 1908	69	30 March 1909
10	4 February 1908	40	1 September 1908	70	6 April 1909
11	11 February 1908	41	8 September 1908	71	13 April 1909
12	18 February 1908	42	15 September 1908	72	20 April 1909
13	25 February 1908	43	22 September 1908	73	27 April 1909
14	3 March 1908	44	29 September 1908	74	4 April 1909
15	10 March 1908	45	6 October 1908	75	11 May 1909
16	17 March 1908	46	13 October 1908	76	18 May 1909
17	24 March 1908	47	20 October 1908	77	25 May 1909
18	31 March 1908	48	27 October 1908	78	1 June 1909
19	7 April 1908	49	3 November 1908	79	15 June 1909
20	14 April 1908	50	10 November 1908	80	22 June 1909
21	21 April 1908	51	17 November 1908	81	29 June 1909
22	28 April 1908	52	24 November 1908	82	6 July 1909
23	5 May 1908	53	1 December 1908	83	13 July 1909
24	12 May 1908	54	8 December 1908	84	20 July 1909
25	19 May 1908	55	15 December 1908	85	27 July 1909
26	26 May 1908	56	22 December 1908	86	3 August 1909
27	2 June 1908	57	29 December 1908	87	10 August 1909
28	9 June 1908	58	12 January 1909	88	17 August 1909
29	16 June 1908	59	19 January 1909	89	24 August 1909
30	23 June 1908	60	26 January 1909	90	31 August 1909

91	7 September 1909	121	5 April 1910	151	1 November 1910
92	14 September 1909	122	12 April 1910	152	8 November 1910
93	21 September 1909	123	19 April 1910	153	15 November 1910
94	28 September 1909	124	26 April 1910	154	22 November 1910
95	5 October 1909	125	3 May 1910	155	29 November 1910
96	12 October 1909	126	10 May 1910	156	6 December 1910
97	19 October 1909	127	17 May 1910	157	13 December 1910
98	26 October 1909	128	24 May 1910	158	20 December 1910
99	2 November 1909	129	31 May 1910	159	27 December 1910
100	9 November 1909	130	7 June 1910	160	3 January 1911
101	16 November 1909	131	14 June 1910	161	10 January 1911
102	23 November 1909	132	21 June 1910	162	17 January 1911
103	30 November 1909	133	28 June 1910	163	24 January 1911
104	7 December 1909	134	5 July 1910	164	31 January 1911
105	14 December 1909	135	12 July 1910	165	7 February 1911
106	21 December 1909	136	19 July 1910	166	21 February 1911
107	28 December 1909	137	26 July 1910	167	28 February 1911
108	4 January 1910	138	2 August 1910	168	7 March 1911
109	11 January 1910	139	9 August 1910	169	14 March 1911
110	18 January 1910	140	16 August 1910	170	21 March 1911
111	25 January 1910	141	23 August 1910	171	28 March 1911
112	1 February 1910	142	30 August 1910	172	4 April 1911
113	8 February 1910	143	6 September 1910	173	18 April 1911
114	15 February 1910	144	13 September 1910	174	25 April 1911
115	22 February 1910	145	20 September 1910	175	2 May 1911
116	1 March 1910	146	27 September 1910	176	9 May 1911
117	8 March 1910	147	4 October 1910	177	16 May 1911
118	15 March 1910	148	11 October 1910	178	23 May 1911
119	22 March 1910	149	18 October 1910	179	30 May 1911
120	29 March 1910	150	25 October 1910	180	6 June 1911

Select Bibliography

Bishop, Julia C. 1998 ' "Dr Carpenter from the Harvard College in America": An Introduction to James Madison Carpenter and his Collection', *Folk Music Journal*, vol. 7, no. 4, pp. 402–20.

Bishop, Julia C. et al. 2003 *The James Madison Carpenter Collection Online Catalogue* http://www.hrionline.ac.uk/carpenter (hosted by the University of Sheffield).

Bronson, Bertrand H. 1959–72 *The Traditional Tunes of the Child Ballads*, 4 vols. Princeton, New Jersey: Princeton University Press.

Child, Francis James 1882–98 *The English and Scottish Popular Ballads*, 5 vols. Boston: Houghton, Mifflin and Co.

Christie, William 1876–81 *Traditional Ballad Airs*, 2 vols. Edinburgh: Edmonston and Douglas, and David Douglas.

DSL 2007 Online *Dictionary of the Scots Language*, www.dsl.ac.uk

Greig, Gavin 1963 *Folk-Song in Buchan and Folk-Song of the North-East* by Gavin Greig (with a foreword by Kenneth S. Goldstein and Arthur Argo). Hatboro, Pennsylvania: Folklore Associates.

Greig–Duncan 1981–2002 *The Greig–Duncan Folk Song Collection*, 8 vols. Vol. 1, ed. Patrick Shuldham-Shaw and Emily B. Lyle (contains Nautical Songs, Military Songs, Historical Songs, and Songs in Which Characters Adopt the Dress of the Opposite Sex), 1981; vol. 2, ed. Patrick Shuldham-Shaw and Emily B. Lyle (contains Narrative Songs), 1983; vol. 3, ed. Patrick Shuldham-Shaw, Emily B. Lyle and Peter A. Hall (contains Songs of the Countryside and Songs of Home and Social Life), 1987; vol. 4, ed. Patrick Shuldham-Shaw and Andrew R. Hunter, general editor: Emily B. Lyle (contains Songs about Particular People, Night Visiting Songs, Songs of Courtship), 1990; vol. 5, ed. Patrick Shuldham-Shaw and Adam McNaughtan, general editor: Emily B. Lyle (contains Songs of Love and Marriage: Part 1), 1995; vol. 6, ed. Patrick Shuldham-Shaw and Elaine Petrie, general editor: Emily B. Lyle (contains Songs of Love and Marriage: Part 2), 1995; vol. 7, ed. Patrick Shuldham-Shaw and Sheila Douglas, general editor: Emily B. Lyle (contains Songs of Love and Marriage: Part 3), 1997; vol. 8, ed. Patrick Shuldham-Shaw, Emily B. Lyle and Katherine Campbell (contains Songs of Parting; Children's Songs, Nonsense Songs, Dance Songs and Rhymes; and Miscellaneous Songs, also general indexes and commentaries on the whole collection), 2002.

Volumes 1–4 published by Aberdeen University Press for the University of Aberdeen in association with the School of Scottish Studies, University of Edinburgh; volumes 5–8 published by Mercat Press for the University of Aberdeen in association with the School of Scottish Studies, University of Edinburgh.

Keith, Alexander (ed.) 1925 *Last Leaves of Traditional Ballads and Ballad Airs*. Aberdeen: The Buchan Field Club.

Lyle, Emily 2007 *Fairies and Folk: Approaches to the Scottish Ballad Tradition* (B.A.S.E.: Ballads and Songs – Engagements, vol. 1). Trier: WVT Wissenschaftlicher Verlag Trier.

Munro, Ailie 1996 *The Democratic Muse: Folk Music Revival in Scotland*. Aberdeen: Scottish Cultural Press (2nd edition).

Olson, Ian A. 2007 'Bothy Ballads and Songs', in John Beech et al. (eds), *Scottish Life and Society: Oral Literature and Performance Culture* (A Compendium of Scottish Ethnology, vol. 10), pp. 322–59. Edinburgh: John Donald in association with the European Ethnological Research Centre.

Ord, John 1930 *The Bothy Songs and Ballads of Aberdeen, Banff and Moray, Angus and the Mearns*. Paisley: A. Gardner.

Robinson, Mairi (ed.) 1985 *The Concise Scots Dictionary*. Aberdeen: Aberdeen University Press.

Shuldham-Shaw, P. N. and E. B. Lyle (eds) 1974 '"Folk-Song in the North-East": J. B. Duncan's Lecture to the Aberdeen Wagner Society, 1908', *Scottish Studies*, vol. 18, pp. 1–37.

List of CD Tracks

The CD contains songs from fourteen of the singers in the edition, performed by Katherine Campbell, with fiddle accompaniment by James Alexander. The CD was recorded by James Hunter at ARC Recording Studio, Mintlaw. Please note that, in a number of instances, the tonic differs from that given in the edition. All the tunes in the edition can be found in electronic format at www.celtscot.ed.ac.uk/greig-duncan

Track Number	Song Title	Contributor	Song Number
1	Clean Pease Strae	Margaret Gillespie	131
2	Cameloun	James W. Spence	84
3	The Rovin' Sailor	James Mackie	23
4	The Thiggin' Song	Isaac Troup	95
5	The Banks of Clyde	Elizabeth Greig	143
6	Kilbogie Toon	Robert Chree	100
7	Young Emma	Georgina Reid	73
8	Daffin Doon	Alexander Robb	56
9	The Term Time	Sam Davidson	86
10	Ye Gowden Vanitie	George F. Duncan	119
11	The Exciseman in a Coal Pit	Robert Alexander	93
12	The Plooman Laddie	William Watson	36
13	The Souters' Feast	John Mowat	29
14	Whale Fishing Song	Archibald Knowles	150

Subject Index

D
fo
th
it

Index of Song Titles and First Lines

Song titles are in capitals.